Defeating Depression

Defeating Depression

The Calm and Sense Way
to Find Happiness and Satisfaction

Leo J. Battenhausen, MA, MSW, LCSW, LCADC

New Horizon Press
Far Hills, NJ

This book is not associated or affiliated with Calm and Sense, LLC of Scotch Plains, New Jersey. The phrase "Calm and Sense" is used here by agreement between the author and Calm and Sense, LLC.

Battenhausen, Leo J.
Defeating Depression: The Calm and Sense Way to Find Happiness and Satisfaction
Cover design: Robert Aulicino
Interior design: Susan M. Sanderson

Library of Congress Control Number: 2010906907

ISBN 13: 978-0-88282-324-9
New Horizon Press

Manufactured in the U.S.A.

2015 2014 2013 2012 2011 / 1 2 3 4 5

Dedication

This book is graciously and genuinely dedicated to that most wonderful, magical, special, outstanding, surprising, amazing, unique, incredible and totally awesome YOU!

In the following pages I offer nothing more than simple facts, plain arguments, and common sense; and have no other Preliminaries to settle with the reader, than that he will divest himself of prejudice and prepossession, and suffer his reason and his feelings to determine for themselves; that he will put ON, or rather that he will not put OFF the true character of a man, and generously enlarge his views beyond the present day.

Thomas Paine, *Common Sense*

Author's Note

This book is based on the author's research, personal experiences and clients' real life experiences. In order to protect privacy, the names and some of the circumstances of the clients (and their families) who graciously allowed me to share their stories have been changed. I thank them for their generosity and their courage. The symptoms and therapeutic approaches remain as they occurred.

For purposes of simplifying usage, the pronouns his/her and s/he are sometimes used interchangeably.

The information contained herein is not meant to be a substitute for professional evaluation and therapy with mental health professionals.

Contents

Introduction 1

Part One **What Is Calm and Sense?** 7

Chapter 1 Calm, Defined 9

Chapter 2 Sense, Defined 17

Chapter 3 Calm and Sense in Action 21

Chapter 4 When Calm Calls, How Do You Respond? 27

Part Two **How to Live a Life of Calm** 39

Chapter 5 Your Life Is Yours 41

Chapter 6 Your Social, Emotional and Professional Portfolio 49

Chapter 7 You Are Not a Slave to Your Past 59

Chapter 8 Social Maturity 69

Chapter 9 Emotional Maturity 73

Chapter 10 Identity 77

Chapter 11 Time Keeps On Ticking 85

Chapter 12 Where Are You? Where Are You Going? 89

Chapter 13 Believe in Yourself 101

Chapter 14 Live in the Moment 105

Chapter 15 Surviving 111

Chapter 16 Worry and Fear 123

Chapter 17 Finding Courage 135
Chapter 18 Making Your Own Happiness 139

Part Three Calm and Sense in Love and Relationships 157
Chapter 19 You Must First Love Yourself 159
Chapter 20 You Cannot Change Anyone but Yourself 165
Chapter 21 We All Need a Purpose 173
Chapter 22 Having a Healthy Romantic Relationship 181
Chapter 23 Trust Me: I Love You Just the Way You Are 189
Chapter 24 Some Tips for Women 193
Chapter 25 And Some Tips for Men 205

Part Four Some Calm and Sense Tips 209
Chapter 26 Family Matters 211
Chapter 27 You Can Pick Your Friends 215
Chapter 28 Career and Finances 219
Chapter 29 In Closing 223

Appendix: Calm and Sense Acronyms 229
Acknowledgments 231
Editor's Note 235
Endnotes 239

Introduction

Imagine a life free from unpleasant and disturbing feelings of sadness, loneliness, despair, worry, anger, blame, resentment, jealousy and fear. Imagine having unlimited confidence and the ability and power to feel good about your life *regardless of the circumstances you face.* What if I told you that there *is* such a way of living and that you already have the ability to make it happen? It's true! And you have the keys to that success in your hands right now.

You have picked up this book either because your life is not as Calm as you would like it to be or because something in your life is not making Sense to you. You are looking for both Calm and Sense in your life and you deserve it. We all do!

Regardless of age, gender, stage of life, economic status, race, religion, daily circumstances, profession, family composition, etc., there are many things in life today that can cause feelings of unrest, anxiety, insecurity, frustration, sadness, fear, immobility, lack of confidence, stress, not fitting in...The list goes on and on.

Imagine what your life would be like if you could remain Calm and make Sense of all the adverse and unpleasant situations and people you encounter. Can you picture it?

I have worked with countless individuals from all walks of life who have come into my office seeking help with these or other issues in their lives that are interfering with their abilities to enjoy life. They believe that they cannot overcome their issues on their own.

It is my belief that everyone who comes into therapy is "stuck" somewhere on the journey that is his or her life. They have tried several things to get "unstuck," but it didn't work. Now they seek help. Did you know that seeking help is a sign of *strength*, not of weakness?

Very early in my career, I often struggled with how I could be most helpful in my role as therapist in people's lives. After all, what greater responsibility is there than to be relied on to truly help others—especially in a time of crisis—and what greater honor is there than to be trusted by a stranger to do so? I spent hours thinking about all I'd been taught and all I'd read throughout my undergraduate, graduate and ongoing studies, trying to put it all together in concise and practical answers to the questions "What am I going to do to help people get past their pain and feel better?" and "How will I help them get 'unstuck'?"

The solution was simple. Instead of relying solely on the "book smarts" and theories I had learned in college and graduate school to lead my working style and to help guide my clients, I started using more and more Calm and Sense in my approach and—more importantly—I started teaching this approach to my clients. The results were amazing! Of course, Freud, Jung, Rogers, Ellis, Glassner and all the greats of psychology are certainly important to learn and understand, but the true "how to" when it comes to *helping* others comes only from genuine care for others and the use of Calm and Sense. Truthfully, the best "teachers" I have ever had and continue to have are my clients. They never cease to surprise, amaze and educate me.

One of the things I have learned from my clients, regardless of what specific "issue" they present to me in their first sessions, is that they are *all* struggling with some aspect of their lives that is somehow, some way, causing them to experience some degree of depression.

Nobody wants to be depressed. Granted, sometimes feeling a little depressed—to the point where we just can't get that looming task done (whatever it may be, from vacuuming the house to cooking a meal to just plain getting up and facing the day)—is a gift in disguise. Why? It signals us that we need to take some time off; that we need to put aside what's weighing heavily on our minds and recharge ourselves. Sometimes, indulging that feeling for a short time (a few hours, maybe a day) and giving ourselves permission to "just be" for a bit so that we can rest and refocus is a good thing. But only if we get back up and start moving forward again.

On the other end of the spectrum, feeling depressed all the time is a signal that we need to seek professional advice.

Oftentimes, we find ourselves somewhere in the middle, feeling stuck and wanting relief but not really knowing how to get it.

There are so many things—some unavoidable, some preventable—that can cause us to feel depressed. No matter what the circumstances or causes are, feelings of depression are common, unpleasant (to say the least) and disrupting. Feeling depressed gets in the way of accomplishing what we want and need to do. It impedes our ability to feel healthy, both physically and emotionally. It makes the people around us uncomfortable in a variety of ways. No one wants to feel this way. Calm and Sense tells us that *it is all manageable*; life can be brighter, happier and more wonderful if we learn to use Calm and Sense in all we think and do.

Sometimes all it takes to escape a feeling of depression is to turn off the news instead of continuing to be bombarded with information about the frightening state of the economy, the wildlife being destroyed by the tremendous oil eruption in the ocean, the child who was abducted on his way to school, the woman and her coworkers who were murdered by the woman's estranged husband (who had a restraining order against him) and all of the other unhappy news that seems to be on television, on radio or in the newspapers. Sometimes all it takes is finding something to laugh about. Sometimes it takes a good night's sleep or a healthy meal. Other times it requires reexamining (with a physician or pharmacist) the medications we are taking to see if they may be causing us to feel depressed. Sometimes it takes comforting words from a close friend, clergyperson or family member. And sometimes it takes a lot more than any of these things.

The reality of depression is this: Today, depression afflicts nineteen million Americans and millions more worldwide.[1] According to a World Health Organization report on mental illness, major depression is the leading cause of disability in the United States and other developed countries. Depression will be the second largest killer after heart disease by 2020 and studies show depression is a contributory factor to fatal coronary disease.[2] Fifty years ago, the average age for the onset of depression was twenty-nine; today, it is fourteen and a half.[3] Additionally, a study published in *Psychiatric Services* in April 2004 reported that the amount of preschoolers who are clinically depressed has reached at least 4 percent or more than one million. This age category is the fastest growing group for which antidepressant medication is being prescribed.[4] However, while pharmaceutical companies continue creating more "new and improved" antidepressants, the seeming "epidemic" of depression continues to rise.

Unfortunately, many people who are depressed don't feel comfortable seeking help, so they continue to struggle and suffer alone. Mental Health America (formerly the National Mental Health Association) found that 41 percent of depressed women are too embarrassed to seek help.[5] A study by the same organization found that 22 percent of people believe depression is a personal weakness.[6] It is *not*.

Calm and Sense and Depression

What is happening to the world's state of satisfaction and happiness? Why are so many men, women and, now, children so sad and depressed? As I said earlier, there are many things that can lead to feelings of depression and dissatisfaction: things like work, finances, family relationships, romantic relationships, friendships, *lack* of relationships, activities, social situations, health, etc. The mere thought of being depressed is depressing and being reminded that we are depressed is probably even more so.

Just as there is a variety of things that can cause us to feel depressed, there are different degrees of experiencing depression. Some people feel depressed about a particular thing for a few moments; some feel overwhelmed with many things and feel depressed for a few days; some are stuck in cycles of clinical depression they just can't seem to get out of; some have chemical imbalances that cause them to feel depressed without any other contributing causes; some fall elsewhere along the continuum.

It's unfortunate that the English language has only one word to describe *all* of those varied circumstances. The important question here, though, is: What can you do if you find yourself feeling depressed?

One of the keys to understanding feelings of depression begins with the identification and understanding of what the underlying cause or causes *are* as well as what they *are not*. Once the basis for that understanding is in place, we are better equipped to solve the problem ourselves and are well on our way to doing so.

Calm and Sense will guide you toward understanding common problem areas—things that can lead to feelings of depression or keep you trapped (or "stuck") in a cycle of loneliness, despair, discontent, sadness and depression—so you can begin to identify them in your own life and defeat them before you feel like they are defeating you. Calm and Sense also gives you the tools to face whatever life throws your way and keep you emotionally protected from the undesirable feelings, attitudes, reactions and falsities that cause most of us to feel powerless. The truth is that Calm and Sense empowers you to take control of your life and feelings, not just for today, but forever!

Through twenty years of experience working with hundreds of adults, families, adolescents and children, the essential secrets to living a life that embraces Calm and makes Sense—for *everyone*—have become clear to me and in this book I share them with you. You see, while it's true that no one is born with Calm and Sense and it is not some genetic trait that only a lucky few possess, it is also true that we *all* have the ability to learn Calm and Sense. The good news is that through reading this book you can learn it too!

Calm and Sense works like no other approach to treating depression. Why? Because it is honest, simple, realistic, practical, genuine and puts *you* in charge of your own destiny, no matter who you are, where you have been or what is in your past.

In a world that is rarely Calm and hardly makes Sense, using Calm and Sense can and will help you out of unhappiness and guide you toward a future you only dreamed was possible! It is my hope that this book will provide you the insight and encouragement to live a fulfilling and happy life.

Part One

What Is Calm and Sense?

"Believe in yourself! Have faith in your abilities! Without a humble but reasonable confidence in your own powers, you cannot be successful or happy."

Norman Vincent Peale
Minister, radio and television broadcaster and author

In this section we'll explore the concepts of Calm and Sense. You will learn about the basic components of Calm, gain some insight into how life crises challenge our ability to stay in a place of Calm and learn how you can attain and maintain a state of Calm even through what may seem like overwhelming or impossible circumstances.

We'll also explore the concept of Sense—a necessary component of Calm—and how Sense helps us intellectually and logically put things into perspective.

Throughout this book I share the stories of some of my clients with you to help illustrate how the components of Calm and Sense work in our lives and how our choices affect our outcomes. In these stories you will find things to which you can relate and situations you may have encountered in your own life in one form or another. You may find something that matches an experience or feeling in your life exactly; you may find something that resembles an experience or feeling you had. You may even recognize some of yourself or someone you know in the descriptions of these clients.

We all experience life in different ways, but we all have the same basic needs to be loved, feel safe and be happy. Calm and Sense will help you recognize where you can make changes in your own life to help you defeat your feelings of depression, find happiness and satisfaction, bring you closer to living the life you envision for yourself and give you the tools you need to do it.

Chapter 1

Calm, Defined

Calm is the ability to stay focused and at peace with yourself regardless of what happens around you or to you. We often encounter circumstances (the flat tire that happened on the way to the concert you've been waiting six months to attend), events (a car that drives through a puddle and saturates you) or people (a nagging boss who is impossible to please) that disrupt our sense of peace and happiness. When you have Calm, that disruption quickly finds its place. You can discern whether or not to allow yourself to spend time being upset about it, take action to rectify it, challenge how you perceive it or just let it go. Having Calm does not mean that you do not feel the disruption or that you don't have a gut reaction of anger or frustration. Calm allows you to have the negative experience and move quickly—and, eventually, immediately—to a place of putting it in perspective and moving forward without absorbing the negativity of it and allowing it to make you feel badly about yourself.

Calm provides us with a sense of Emotional Invincibility in which we are in control of our emotions and don't hand control of them over to other people or circumstances. With Emotional Invincibility, we know that when someone does something that angers us, we can still respond in a productive and positive way instead of allowing the other person's behavior to drag us down into mirroring his behavior. For example, we know that when someone insults us, we don't have to respond by insulting her back. When someone yells at us, we don't have to respond by yelling back. We can take the *information* the person provided (not the tone or emotion) and choose to either ignore it or use it as part of our constant evaluation of "Am I the person I really want to be?"

To have Emotional Invincibility is to have an unwavering, unchangeable respect for ourselves that is not in jeopardy of diminishing when someone says something negative about us. Self-doubt, jealousy, dishonesty and false perceptions do not impede our sense of well-being and worth. When we have Calm in our lives, we know that we can experience circumstances, events and people in a positive way and not dread encounters or fear they will take away from who we are.

When we have Calm, we have three essential life skills that help us stay focused and repel the negativity that comes into our lives from the outside world and from other people's "stuff"—the things that interfere with our appreciation of self and the lives we are entitled to live should we choose to do so. Those three essential life skills are the ability to love, appreciate and accept ourselves for who we are. When we have Calm, not only do we have those strengths, we also truly understand that those three gifts can come *only from ourselves*. Looking elsewhere, to other people, places or things to bring us Calm and to give us a positive sense of self makes as much sense as expecting someone else to make a living for us. In both cases we are responsible for the work and we reap the benefits. This concept ties in to much of what we'll talk about in this book and you will find that we return to it often.

When we are living in Calm, we also acquire the ability to use what I call Reasonable Reasoning, which is a component of Sense and inextricably tied to Calm. (We'll talk more about Sense and its relationship to Calm in chapter 2.) Reasonable Reasoning empowers us to see our own lives and the world around us in a way that allows us to function and feel positive and that keeps us from seeing the proverbial glass as being half empty all the time or blaming circumstances, people, society, jobs, spouses, etc., for all the problems in our lives. We understand that no matter what life throws our way, we will survive it and rebalance our emotions. We know that the outside influences do not define us, because we are content with who we are. Reasonable Reasoning helps us take responsibility for our circumstances and makes it possible for us to look at the things we, ourselves, are doing that may need to be changed or fixed, instead of looking for others to blame or for others to fix them for us. It allows us to take a good, honest look at what *we* are doing that causes us so much negativity, blaming, unhappiness and misery in our lives. With Calm, we can reason reasonably and guide ourselves in a direction toward *solutions*, not blame!

Every day we are challenged by events, people and situations that are extremely frustrating and anger producing. The secret to Calm lies in our ability to choose to use the power and instincts we have within us to react in productive and positive ways instead of overreacting to these challenges and disturbances in life or allowing them to negatively influence our love, appreciation or acceptance of ourselves.

I told you that you can begin living a Calm life right now and that Calm depends on your ability to react to everyday unpleasant situations in a positive way. Here are two tools I often teach my clients to help them make *immediate* progress on their ways to Calm. You can begin to use them now too.

The Ten Year Rule

The Ten Year Rule is a very simple tool that helps determine how much energy you should invest in an encountered challenge or disturbance. It works like this: When you experience an unpleasant event or situation, ask yourself, "Will this matter much to me ten years from now?" If the answer is yes, then the situation definitely requires some energy and thought as to how to react to it accordingly. If the answer is no, then why give it so much energy, frustration or the power to ruin your day? With this perspective, you can choose not to invest (and waste) your energy but embrace Calm instead.

The Five Minute Rule

I also teach my clients the Five Minute Rule. Sometimes we find ourselves over-involved in trying to change other people in order to help them. The Five Minute Rule works like this: If you notice something you feel needs changing in a friend, relative or coworker, etc., ask yourself, "Will this change take more than five minutes to fix?" Things like a crumb on his shirt, a collar turned inside out or smeared lipstick can be quickly corrected in five minutes or fewer. Things like being overweight, loud, insulting or arrogant could take years to correct and how much good would it do (for them or for you) to try to change things in that moment?

Knowing when it's beneficial to become involved and when it's not is a major component of Calm. You have the power of choice. Another major component of Calm is understanding your own limitations and respecting others' boundaries as well as you do your own. Using these tools will help you begin to reserve your power, make positive, healthy choices, reduce the negative effects outside circumstances have on your daily life and may even help improve your relationships with those around you.

Consider how many times you have said or heard someone say things like, "I've told him a million times that he needs to stop drinking so much!" or "How many times do I have to tell her that she doesn't squeeze the toothpaste out the right way?" While these are two extremely different examples, both are potentially toxic subjects in a relationship. (Sadly, I have seen people divorce over the "toothpaste conflict.") Will there be an eventual "last time" that we tell someone to make this change and he or she finally listens? Probably not. There are some things in life we either choose to learn to live with when we care about someone or we choose to leave the situation. Outside of personal relationships, we also encounter situations where we can choose to accept things as they are or walk away from them. Living a Calm lifestyle and reasoning reasonably allows you to make these choices confidently and comfortably.

Our lives follow a path that is based on the choices we make, whether they are conscious and deliberate or unconscious and by default. Yes, circumstances that are out of our control arise and affect the course of our lives. Even then, we can choose how we react to them. Calm is a lifestyle we can intentionally choose to live and in choosing Calm we also choose to make positive, healthy decisions about how we handle negative experiences and circumstances. Calm is a permanent state of mind that does not come and go. When we fully embrace Calm, it becomes who we are. We radiate it, we live by its principles, we encourage it and we demonstrate it in all we do. In fact, we dwell happily and comfortably in Calm, because it allows us to believe in who we are and does not allow any negative intrusion (like judgmental or accusatory comments or negative circumstances) from others or outside forces to bring us down. When you're happy with who you are, none of those things matter. Calm is a protective space where we flourish, create and grow!

Let me share with you the story of Hank, one of my clients. Hank first came to me when he was twenty years old. His main problem was depression. Hank was an only child, born in New York to parents who immigrated to the United States from Asia. Hank's father was well-educated and worked for a large pharmaceutical company; his mother was a registered nurse. Hank's father was also an alcoholic, which was the reason that he eventually lost his high-paying position. When I first met Hank, his father had been out of work for three years and was spending his days consuming too much alcohol, while Hank's mother worked hard to keep the family afloat.

Hank had all the classic symptoms of depression: anxiety, sleeplessness, poor concentration, lack of interest in outside activities and feelings of hopelessness. Hank was also extremely angry. He was openly angry toward his father, but he was also angry at the world. While it was good that Hank was able to direct his anger toward the cause of his anger (his father), Hank also internalized that anger and it seeped out and affected every aspect of his life.

Hank was very interested in cars and racing. After completing high school, Hank went to a technical school to learn automobile mechanics. Although he completed the program, the only job he could get was at a commercial tire and lube shop doing tire and oil changes. He felt this was hardly a mechanic position—especially after spending two years and twenty thousand dollars on his education. Hank developed more anger and blamed the school.

Later, after months of perceived insults from "everyone at the shop," Hank hit a coworker in the head with a hammer and, consequently, lost his job at the tire and lube shop. He entered community college. It wasn't long before Hank stopped attending classes. He continued, however, to leave his house every day, telling his mother he was going to class. This time, according to Hank, the people in college were not accepting of him. His anger continued to increase, now with the addition of another school and peers to blame.

Why did Hank believe that people weren't accepting of him at school? Let me begin by describing Hank's general mood and demeanor. Hank did not smile. His answers were short and curt; his body language was tight and indicative of being a guarded person. He, quite frankly, came across as frightening, mean and unapproachable. On top of that, Hank was doing nothing to invite people in. (We'll talk more about this in chapter 6.) It is not difficult to understand why people would shut him out or why Hank believed people were not accepting of him.

The work ethic is very strong in Asian culture. Expectations of success from the family are quite normal. How much pressure Hank's family put on him to succeed was not clear. In fact, Hank often spoke of his mother as being "saintly" and the "only one who cares" for him. Nevertheless, Hank perceived pressure to succeed from his family—especially because he was a male child. When he experienced difficulty in doing so, he believed the family thought less of him. Whether they did or not is not known for certain. However, Hank did put tremendous pressure on himself.

With the negative feedback Hank received from people at school (because of his demeanor), the belief that his family saw him as a failure (based on his work history and his family's cultural work ethic) and the fact that he wasn't accepting of himself (a concept we'll address more fully beginning in chapter 2), Hank believed everyone and everything was against him and success just wasn't possible no matter what he did.

It was at this point in his life that I met Hank, an angry young man with severe depression, an alcoholic father and a very loving mother. Hank had not as yet succeeded in his work or educational endeavors, because, according to him, everyone had been against him and didn't see things his way.

Hank was not living in Calm and was continuously getting in his own way. He was a perfect candidate for Calm and Sense. Let's discuss how, after some time and intense lessons, he achieved this.

Hank's anger was fueled by the fact that his experience of life did not match what he *believed* life was *supposed* to be. Like many of us, he got caught up in a fantasy—the unrealistic expectation of what the world owes us and how we think things should be. For Hank, this disillusionment stemmed from his belief that having an alcoholic father prevented him from experiencing the typical family situation that many people (including Hank) believe they are supposed to have. Does anyone in the world truly grow up in a perfect situation?

Once we begin to enter adulthood, our reasoning skills should become more, well, reasonable. Calm and Sense says that as we mature we become more tolerant of situations and people we have no control over and we learn how to experience them in a way that is not detrimental to our sense of self-worth. We begin to understand that our parents are not superheroes, that no one is perfect, and that the world does not exist or function for us alone. We get to the point of Reasonable Reasoning. However, in many cases, as in Hank's, we do *not* get to that point. We continue thinking like a child, believing that what we want should be what we get. This is a setup for emotional failure and frustration. These unrealistic expectations begin to limit our ability to adapt, to grow and to appreciate and love ourselves. *The inability to love ourselves is the greatest contributor to personal disaster and emotional unrest!*

Love, appreciation and acceptance of ourselves are key components to living a Calm lifestyle. Without them, we cannot maintain a life of Calm.

Hank's family situation was not what he perceived it should be, so he began to internalize false beliefs. This eroded his sense of worth. As a result, he saw himself as lacking, less than others and missing something he believed everyone else had in their own lives. He could no longer see the positive or any potential in himself. Of course, this type of thinking is not reasonable. It is harmful to our sense of Calm. You can see how Hank's distorted thinking was causing him to become more depressed, angrier and less confident in himself.

When we allow our distorted thinking to disrupt our sense of Calm all the time, we begin to see situations as "proof" that we somehow deserve our misfortunes. We expect failure when we try new things, meet new people or go beyond our "comfort zone" in life. Then, when failure comes, we erroneously convince ourselves that we were right to expect to fail. We tell ourselves, "See? I can never win, do the right thing or take any chances!" These are self-defeating beliefs that we tell ourselves over and over again. When we repeatedly tell ourselves anything, we begin to believe it. We make it who we are. The good news is that this also works for positive beliefs! Repeating positive, self-affirming beliefs will also become habitual and can free us from the negative perceptions we have of ourselves.

Humans have an innate need to seek comfort over discomfort. For many of us, in an effort to feel "okay" with our misfortunes, the goal becomes finding justification for our failures and our faulty belief that we can only fail. We do this to avoid having to do what we perceive would be painful, difficult or even impossible: stepping out of our comfort zones, letting down our guards and believing that we can be successful. We seek validation that our negative self-thoughts and self-images are accurate, instead of reasonably looking at our own behavior and its role in creating or maintaining an unpleasant situation.

Life has its fair share of disappointments, but there are also victories. Hank expected to fail. His disillusionment and expectation of failure led him to fail. Then he continuously used that failure to justify his disbelief in himself. This added more credibility and strength to his faulty beliefs and, even more dangerously, further lessened his ability to do something to help himself improve his life. If we can't believe in ourselves, can we reasonably expect others to believe in us? No! But we do. Hank didn't believe in himself (more on this in chapter 13) and was angry that others didn't believe in him. This was Hank's first issue to undo.

Chapter 2

Sense, Defined

We cannot talk about living a life of Calm without also talking about Sense. Calm and Sense are inter-dynamic—they rely on each other to help us reach our emotional, social, professional, financial and personal peaks of performance. While Calm pertains to the heart and soul of a person—our *feelings*—Sense pertains to our intellectual ability, logic and thought processes—our *minds*. Sense is the energy source or "fuel" we need to have Calm. Whereas Calm is emotion-based and brings feelings of wellness and completeness, Sense helps us to intellectually and logically see and accept who we are, understand the world we live in and stay based in reality when it comes to distinguishing fact from fiction, truth from falsehood and "if" thinking from "how" thinking (read more about this in chapter 15).

Sense is the belief, understanding and acceptance that no one, no thing and no place can make us happier than we can make ourselves. Sense requires that we truly, once and for all abandon the false belief that there is "someone or something out there" that's going to come along and make all of our pain and suffering go away or bring us the life and happiness we want. When we take the responsibility to give ourselves what we truly need to improve our lives and levels of self-acceptance, then we are making Sense!

Sense is the process of re-thinking and re-learning how we perceive ourselves, eliminating all negative self-beatings in which we habitually engage and replacing all the old, false beliefs that tell us we can't get what we want in life until a certain thing happens. These false beliefs might include things like, "If I don't make a certain amount of money a year, I can never be happy!" or "I'm too shy to ever meet and date anyone!" or even "I am not (pretty, thin, strong, rich, outgoing, smart, popular, etc.) enough." Enough is enough! It's time to start making Sense.

Sense tells us to cease the negative self-talk and to believe in what we *can* do. It tells us that our pasts will not and cannot dictate what today or tomorrow will bring but that we can and must learn from where we have been so we do not have to be prisoners of our pasts. The negative thinking so many of us participate in has become second nature to us. Does it make sense that it is easier to condemn ourselves than congratulate ourselves? No! This makes no Sense and keeps us from Calm.

The process of beginning to "make Sense" may seem a little awkward. Why? Because it requires us to make the effort to remind ourselves that we are intrinsically good people and deserve love, value and respect. It also requires us to be aware of the self-talk we engage in. We must consciously replace our negative self-talk with positive thoughts about who we are. To begin gaining Sense, we must actually begin to tell ourselves positive things. Whatever we tell ourselves enough times, be it negative or positive, we will believe and become. So, when you hear those ugly stories you tell yourself about how "bad/unworthy/useless" you are, stop immediately! Replace those thoughts with positive thoughts about who you are.

If talking to yourself seems silly, think about the negative "tapes" you have playing in your head. Do they serve you any good purpose or are they sillier than talking to yourself? Remember: The more we tell ourselves something, the more we believe it! If you're going to make the effort to speak to yourself, it makes more sense to expend the energy filling your mind with comforting, kind, warm and forgiving statements rather than punishing, mean, cruel and false ones. Now *that* makes Sense!

The more you practice positive self-talk, the less you have to be conscious of doing it. Just like the "negative tapes" automatically filled your head with what you couldn't do, so will positive thoughts become your automatic response to a challenge after just a short amount of practice.

One of the first questions I ask new clients is, "What are your positive attributes?" Think about your answer to that question for a moment. Have you ever been on a job interview and been asked that question? Chances are you have and chances are you reacted to it the way most of my new clients do: You felt uncomfortable. You panicked and felt like you had to struggle hard to answer it. Why don't we know what our strengths are? Why is it difficult to speak positively of ourselves?

On the other hand, many of my clients (how about you as well?) can rattle off quite a number of their own perceived weaknesses or faults without much effort. This is *not* Calm and Sense thinking. Calm and Sense thinking always produces the opposite effect: our strengths are as easily known and identifiable as our areas of need.

So, how does this happen?

Imagine for a moment there are two entities in your mind: "Positive Pat" and "Negative Nick" (you decide their genders). Your thoughts feed these two entities who are constantly battling for power over your state of Calm. Pat eats only your positive thoughts, while Nick thrives on the negative cuisine. Every time you throw a piece of negative steak at Nick, he gets bigger and stronger. Nick's fangs grow longer and longer; claws, sharper and sharper.

Meanwhile, in most cases, poor Pat is underfed, emaciated and too weak to fight back. Pat needs to eat positive protein. Positive comments and self-talk will fatten Pat up and eventually, when fed frequently, Pat will outgrow Nick and win control over your sense of Calm. Simply stated, Calm and Sense says we need to feed our minds a negative-free, fortified diet of positive beliefs, self-statements and affirmations. You *are* what you eat—negative and positive. The choice—the *responsibility*—is yours. Pat is starving for some nutrition! Feel free to feed Pat plenty of positive *all the time* and put Nick on a starvation diet.

Positive thinking is nothing new. In fact, it's been around for ages. Buddha (563-483 BCE) understood and believed in the value of positive thinking. He said, "Do not be a harsh judge of yourself. Without kindness toward ourselves, we cannot love the world." English novelist George Eliot, a popular writer of the Victorian era, said, "There is nothing will kill a man so soon as having nobody to find fault with but himself." And Axel Munthe, a Swedish physician and psychiatrist of the late 1800s and early 1900s, said, "A man can stand a lot as long as he can stand himself. He can live without hope, without friends, without books, even without music, as long as he can listen to his own thoughts."

We must begin to think we are able, deserving and worthy of all we truly desire in this world and put a stop to any thoughts or ideas that try to limit or defeat our attempts to lead lives of happiness, self-acceptance, worthiness, love and Calm. Calm requires Sense to provide us with the logic that pulls us forward instead of being stuck or moving backward.

Chapter 3

Calm and Sense in Action

Let's return to Hank's story. Hank had finished his certification as an auto mechanic and thought any garage, auto shop or car dealership should have been begging him to work for them. After all, he was now a certified mechanic. What he wasn't seeing was how his anger and unrealistic expectations of the world were coming across to others around him. He was closed off, entitled and bitter and his attitude reflected it. That is not Calm! Calm is confident, open and curious about and around others, not arrogant, guarded and suspicious. To attain success, you must believe in your abilities, yourself and your worth. You must be confident. There is a world of difference between confidence and arrogance. Hank was not using Calm and could not understand why he was not getting job offers after he "wasted two years and lots of money" at an auto mechanic school. He applied, waited and sometimes got interviews but never any job offers.

Hank believed he was "screwed" by his father, his trade school and now, also, the auto industry. Hank's anger just kept intensifying and he was becoming more and more convinced that he had no control over his circumstances. In his thinking, he was destined to fail no matter what he did. His self-pity became even more apparent when he was not yet able or willing to examine himself and the effects his own thoughts and behaviors had in shaping his disappointing situation.

In his mind, because he felt he was cheated out of what he perceived to be a normal childhood, he believed the world certainly must owe him something in return. Hank wasn't able to understand that he wasn't willing to give himself the gifts he expected to receive from everyone else: love, appreciation and acceptance—the three main ingredients of Calm.

It is frightening for some of us to think of letting go of our "old selves" and the defense mechanisms we have been using to survive for so long. Some of us are truly fearful of success so we sabotage our own efforts to succeed. Have you ever heard the expression, "The devil we know is safer than the devil we don't"? So it goes with some people's fear of success. We have difficulty creating the life of which we dream, because it is foreign to us. Some people can actually become so attached to their bad or negative self-perceptions that the thought of leaving them behind seems either frightening or impossible to do!

We all function day-to-day with certain defense or coping mechanisms—survival skills—that we have learned throughout our lives. Some of them are good; some are not. Those that are not good prevent us from being able to succeed. Take, for example, a situation where a friend or family member makes a negative, thoughtless or nasty comment to you. A positive, healthy defense mechanism is to walk away from the remark and let it go, because you know that it is not really you the person is attacking. A negative, unhealthy coping mechanism is to use the comment to validate any self-doubt you may have and erroneously take on the belief that "He or she must be right! I suck!" Check again: who is this person criticizing you? Why are you giving the person this power over your sense of self-esteem? Allowing the negative comment to creep into your self-talk leads you to tell yourself that person must be right, which then leads you to believe, "I am no good." This is clearly counterproductive to your success.

Sound a bit crazy? Think about this: Hank grew up with an alcoholic parent and in a home where there was no predictability, no emotional safety and no chance just to "be a kid." The efforts of the family mostly went to covering up, filling in for and focusing all energies on the alcoholic parent. Hank learned to protect himself from disappointment and emotional hurt by lowering his expectations, shutting off his emotions and internalizing his feelings. These were the coping mechanisms that became part of who he was because of his home life experience. Hank was never encouraged to try new things and make mistakes in order to learn from them, so he had no incentive to grow and believe in himself. Instead, he became angry, guarded and locked in a fantasy that someday "I will be rewarded for the pain I endured in losing my childhood."

As children, we adapt to the environments in which we grow up. Through experience, we learn how certain situations affect our feelings of safety and comfort. Children are amazing! They adapt easily to the circumstances in which they find themselves. It is during this childhood adaptation period that our minds become "wired" with coping skills and beliefs—even a particular view of the world—that allow us to survive, to function successfully and to live as emotionally comfortably as possible in whatever our circumstances are. This "wiring" becomes our version of "normal"; it becomes who we are and how we believe the world really works.

If we are raised in a home with chaos, unpredictability, danger and turmoil, to survive we learn not to hope, expect or try, because we know from experience that we will only be disappointed if we do. We live on the edge, never feeling comfortable, relaxed or Calm. We are always on guard, waiting for the next catastrophe to occur. Oddly, as uncomfortable as it is, that state of unrest becomes our comfort zone. The way we wire ourselves leads us to become hypervigilant. We expect turmoil, family fighting or danger in the home, because that is what we know. We do not feel safe just "being" or just "going with the flow." We have learned from experience that when we let our guard down, bad things happen that put us in distress, cause fear and disturb our sense of Calm and equilibrium. We believe we must be ready for the next catastrophe before it gets us and we find comfort in that readiness. Then, regardless of the actual circumstances—chaotic and unstable or not—we live in a constant state of defense, feeling somewhat safe surrounded by our survival skills but, in actuality, living far away from Calm!

These coping skills are very helpful, even necessary, to us as children. They become part of who we are. They are a benefit to us. Unfortunately, we carry that wiring into adulthood with us. Once we become adults and begin to live life outside of that childhood environment, some of those same skills and behaviors that kept us safe and allowed us to reach adulthood begin to cause us harm.

As children, we learn that when we let our emotional guard down we are struck with a scary, unexpected situation in the household. For example, Mom crashed the car driving drunk, lost her license, lost her job and now there's no money. So we learn, as a survival skill, never to relax or expect happiness, because if we do, something will always happen to disappoint us again and again, threatening our well-being and making us feel as if we are different from all the other kids we know. We believe, "They don't go through this!"

Knowing that we carry this type of thinking, this childhood wiring, into adulthood, Calm is not automatically present in our adult lives. We're wired to expect to be hurt, let down and disappointed. How can we overcome these factors? How can we live a life of Calm if we are wired in this way?

As adults no longer living directly in the circumstances of our childhoods (but certainly still affected by them), we need to "rewire" our thinking so we can get past the ingrained fears (of something always going wrong) and doubts (in ourselves) that produced the survival skills and coping mechanisms that worked so well for us as children. While they protected us and kept us feeling safe from being devastated and vulnerable in the past, many of them no longer serve us positively and, as we've seen in Hank's case, are detrimental to our finding happiness and success as adults. Until we learn Calm and Sense thinking, we are continuously trying to stay in our pre-wired version of "safe," which leaves us doubting our abilities and fearing success.

In our search for Calm, we must reassess our current coping mechanisms, fears and self-perceptions. Do they serve any good purpose now? Were they positive assets only in our pasts, protecting us while we were children and had no other conception of how to stay safe at home or with others when catastrophe struck? We must know our old "stuff" to determine if it is helping us or hindering us now. If it is keeping us back, we must send it back! We will talk more about the true value our pasts hold for us in chapter 7.

We'll return to Hank's story in a bit. Right now I'd like to go back to the three essential life skills that help us repel the things that interfere with our ability to think positively about and to believe in ourselves: our ability to love, appreciate and accept ourselves for who we are.

Mark Twain said, "A man cannot be comfortable without his own approval." Eleanor Roosevelt said, "No one can make you feel inferior without your consent." These similar pronouncements underscore the idea that our ability to love, appreciate and accept ourselves begins with a conscious choice to do so. Despite this, many people choose to be their own worst enemies, viciously judging and attacking themselves in the deep recesses of their own minds. The belief that there is someone or something out there that is going to one day bring us bountiful bundles of joy and happiness is a fantasy. We have to find that bounty within our own self-perception and integrity.

For those of you fortunate enough to be raised in a home where your parents practiced Calm in their lives and encouraged you, as a child, to foster it in your own life, you were fortunate to hit the ground running. How wonderful! However, the majority of my clients—and, I suspect, many other people—have not had that luxury in life and need a little bit of coaching and encouragement to begin the process of attaining Calm. May I again add how wonderful for you! Why? Because there is no better feeling than Emotional Invincibility. The freedom that comes with it begins when you *choose to take the power of your emotions back*. Your emotions and your feelings belong to *you* and *only you*. No one can make you feel anything you do not choose to feel!

Now let's return to discussing Hank's problems. Hank was not Calm. No matter what situation he found himself in, he was always on the defensive. He was always looking for someone or something on which to blame his misfortunes, rather than looking at himself or, more specifically, his own behaviors. If Hank had been truly accepting of himself, loved himself and appreciated himself, he would have been much better prepared to face the unfortunate circumstances that occurred in his life. Why? Because he would have had the natural ability to reason reasonably. The Reasonable Reasoning component of Calm allows us not to personalize unfortunate circumstances or negativity from others. In other words, when we stop looking outside of ourselves for the reasons we are so unhappy and instead look for inner understanding of what we want, need, feel, etc., we regain power and place it where it belongs—within ourselves!

If Hank had had the ability to reason instead of needing to place blame, he could have thought more along the lines of, "Wow! I really do love cars and have learned a lot about fixing them, but maybe I'm better equipped for another line of work. At least I can always fix my own car." He would have been better able to move forward feeling positive about himself and his choices, instead of retreating to a place of anger and negativity. Since Hank wasn't able to reason this way, his faulty belief system continuously told him, "The world owes you for your suffering, Hank!" As a result, Hank viewed his choice to enter the field of auto mechanics as a mistake and justified it by blaming his father for preventing him from having a "normal" childhood. Remember: *You owe yourself much more than the world owes you.* There is a lot of power in that statement and if you truly absorb that philosophy, you are well on your way to having an abundance of Calm in your life.

You may be wondering, "This sounds good, but *how* do I start loving, appreciating and accepting myself? I want Calm, but this sounds like a lot of work and like it could take a long time to achieve." Not true! Beginning to grasp and live in Calm is not work: it's simply *living the way you are meant to live*. It takes much more effort and work to live a life of misery than it does to live a life of Calm!

Spending our lives comparing ourselves to others and using our own feelings and senses of self-worth as personal emotional punching bags hurts. *That* is work—and purposeless work at that! It inhibits our emotional, social, personal, professional and financial growth. Remember, we need to "rewire" our thinking. The transformation from hurt and misery to Calm and Sense is a joyous endeavor. Aristotle said, "Pleasure in the task puts perfection in the work." I think that when you believe in your efforts, the task does the work. We'll talk more about believing in ourselves in chapter 13.

Think about this for a few moments: Has any of your previous negative self-talk or disbelief in yourself allowed you to get anywhere you were trying to get? Probably not. *Disbelief in yourself is the cornerstone of disappointment.* Emotional self-abuse does not bring you to Calm, nor is there a certain person, place, amount of money or career that will bring you to Calm. Those gifts come naturally when you have truly grounded yourself in Calm.

It's important to understand that a key component in the process toward living in Calm is to dispel any fear of hard work or pain you imagine may come as a result of the process. You are assembling your emotional suit of armor. Nothing and no one can hurt you now!

Chapter 4

When Calm Calls, How Do You Respond?

We all strive for peace in our lives. Our natural inclination or instinct tells us that we want to stay in balance. When something happens in our lives that disrupts the balance or challenges our current way of living or thinking, our instinct is to bring things back to normal as quickly and painlessly as possible. For those of us living in Calm, peace and balance are found in accepting daily challenges and looking at crises as opportunities for positive change. The rest of us cling tightly to our lives as they are, as imperfect and as far away as they may be from our visions of what we want them to be. We hold on to the faulty belief that peace exists only in our comfort zones, in living life "just the way things are." We fear change.

All people feel the need for tranquility in their lives. We all experience that constant pull toward balance, whether we're aware of it or not. We live our daily lives making decisions and doing things that help keep our lives in balance. Some of the things we do are small and don't even register in our consciousness, like taking a different route to work when you see traffic on the interstate as you drive over the bypass. Some of the things are larger and are part of a thought process that leads to a conscious decision, like choosing not to go to a family event, because you don't want to get dragged into the middle of the latest family drama.

Sometimes the call for peace is quiet and gentle and sometimes, like when a life-changing event or crisis occurs, it is loud and abrupt. For most of us (those of us not yet living in Calm), we hear that thundering call as if it were a demand. We panic. And since no one likes to be told what to do, we react to that call with resentment, negativity and fear. We start to think, *How am I going to get back to normal?* Instead of thinking about *what* went wrong and how we can use this as an opportunity to make positive changes and move forward, we get caught up in a cycle of wondering, *What did I do wrong?* We focus on what must be wrong with *us* that caused this thing to happen or what we could have or should have done to prevent the event that disrupted equilibrium from happening in the first place. We get lost focusing on the negative, on the things we can't change or change back to the way they were. This type of thinking most times results in some form of destructive behavior and pushes us further from Calm in our lives.

Agnes, a client whom I counseled for some time, and her boyfriend, Marty, had been together close to ten years when Marty broke off their relationship. She was thirty-three; he was thirty-two. During the course of their relationship there was talk of marriage, a family, a house and a long life together. Agnes never believed there was anything wrong with them as a couple.

Marty had lived with his mother and immediate family his whole life and was still doing so after my work with Agnes, who had also lived with her parents her whole life. Despite their talk of marriage throughout the nine and a half years they "dated," there was no move toward a cohabitational living arrangement or toward a formal engagement. Every couple has their reasons for what they do and none of us has the right to make judgments on that. However, after nearly ten years of being in a relationship together and with both parties having professional occupations and making a decent living collectively, this is a bit extreme in the context of having discussed marriage, a family, a house and a long life together. Still, Agnes never saw the breakup coming.

I had been working with Agnes for a year prior to her breakup from Marty. She had come to see me for anxiety-related issues that she was able to learn to manage with counseling. During that time, she never expressed concern over her relationship with Marty and we were still working together when the breakup occurred. I had the opportunity to work with Agnes throughout the breakup and I was able to see how she responded to the call for peace in her life after the termination of the relationship. For Agnes, this was no quiet or gentle tug; it was a thundering demand.

Initially, when the breakup occurred, Agnes ignored the obvious: that Marty had made a decision to end the relationship and it was over. She focused completely on trying to rationalize why Marty did not want to be in a relationship with her anymore. She processed each and every possibility she could think of, from her weight to her not wanting to go "out for drinks and have fun anymore," as potential causes for the demise of the relationship. Her focus stayed fixated on the possibility of Marty regretting his decision and asking for her back. She was unable to accept her new reality and move forward, because she kept pulling the problem back in, spinning her wheels in a big muddy mess of trying to guess what Marty was thinking and what he thought she had done wrong. Agnes wanted to undo what had been done. She looked for things that Marty might have found unacceptable in her so she could change herself. She believed changing herself would make Marty realize he'd made a mistake and resume the relationship and Agnes could get back to her version of normal.

Agnes had been battling obesity the entire time I had been working with her. When we first met she was almost one hundred pounds overweight. She never followed through on planned diets and often missed meetings with her weight loss group. Her membership at the gym was money thrown out the window, because she never went. She knew *she* was not happy with her weight, but because Marty had never told her that her weight was a problem for him and because she was content in her long-term relationship, Agnes never had motivation to change. She based her acceptance of herself not on her own feelings but on Marty's input (or lack thereof).

The four months following the breakup of Agnes and Marty resulted in the quickest weight loss I have ever seen. Agnes shed eighty pounds and continued losing weight. She was certain that once she was thin again Marty would see her and come running back with arms wide open, regretting that "big mistake" he'd made. Agnes also started talking about going out more. After all, there is more to life than a box of cookies and a movie on a Friday night, isn't there?

While Agnes's efforts to address her weight (and therefore, also, her overall health) and her plans to start getting out and being social were positive steps forward, her reason for making these changes was not as positive. She was doing these things to prove to Marty that she was still that fun-loving girl he had met ten years earlier. She wasn't doing these things for herself but for Marty and for the relationship that she still wasn't acknowledging was over. She was still spinning her wheels, reacting to the demand and not living in Calm.

To me, the most interesting aspect of Agnes's "makeover" was that she showed no emotion throughout the whole breakup and the four months following. Most people, when "let go" from a relationship (or reacting to any kind of major disturbance in their status quo), experience and express a series of emotions: they are hurt, then angry, then scared. At some point after those feelings, there is acceptance that it is over and they move on. Agnes, on the other hand, never shed a tear, never raised her voice and never accepted that it was truly over. Instead, she did all the things she thought were needed to win Marty back. She continued to perceive the situation as a problem to be solved instead of an opportunity for positive change. She kept pulling the problem back in and propelling herself further away from Calm.

I'll return to Agnes's situation shortly. I want to talk a bit more about how we respond to the call for Calm. When situations that threaten our sense of stability or well-being (such as a breakup after a long-term relationship) arise in our lives, our natural tendency is to shift gears into panic overdrive: "I have to fix this! Oh, my gosh! What can I do? Why did this happen to me? Why did she/he/life do this to me?" We look to regain quickly a sense of equilibrium. The change brought upon us frightens us and we scramble to respond to the "demand" for peace in our lives. This response in itself is not all bad. It provokes us and motivates us to take action and make changes. That's good. It's necessary. However, allowing this demand to cause us to perceive that there is something wrong with us or that there is something unacceptable about ourselves is detrimental to our ability to respond in healthy, positive ways. We become unable to feel what we need to feel, accept the situation for what it truly is and move on.

Calm and Sense living encourages us to feel the loss or change, experience the emotions we need to have, examine the facts of the loss, change or disappointment, learn from these things and then strategize a plan of restructuring our lives or welcoming a new experience, whatever that may be.

With all this in mind, I am going to share with you a sure way to benefit *100 percent of the time* when life presents you with a change or a sneaky switcheroo throws you off course. When life changes without your consent, *do not* act on the "demand" for peace to be restored immediately. Instead, *listen to the invitation for change in your life, act on it and peace will follow!*

"But," you may ask, "when I get blindsided by a crisis and I can't tell which end is up, how do I hear that demand as an invitation? How do I do anything but panic?" The answer begins with *choice*. Choice, as I mentioned in chapter 1, is essential! You have the power of choice. Additionally, now you have access to another essential survival tool—one that you have always had but, let's say, misplaced. That survival tool is your *perception* and your ability to perceive things in a positive way. When faced with what feels like an earth-shattering catastrophe or one that's not so catastrophic but still surprising and life-changing, you can choose to perceive the situation as manageable and as an opportunity instead of as an insurmountable disaster or something that can't be handled. With that positive choice, you are also choosing to move forward toward peace and Calm.

Agnes's problem was that she perceived her world was ending and she made the choice to scramble about to regain equilibrium in her life in an effort to stop her world from ending. The truth of the matter was her world had ended long before she knew about it and the moment she found out about it was long after she could do anything at all to save it.

Calm and Sense thinking would have allowed Agnes to perceive the breakup with Marty as an opportunity for positive change and to make the choice to take advantage of that opportunity. More importantly, had Agnes had Calm in her life sooner, she would not have allowed more than nine years of a relationship to stagnate without her discerning something was wrong. You see, Agnes wanted desperately to marry Marty. He, on the other hand, was not forthcoming with Agnes and never told her he wouldn't marry her. He also never fully said he would. It wasn't until Agnes began to push the issue that Marty started backing away from the relationship. Throughout their relationship, Agnes never checked what Marty was really thinking. She never talked to him about his lack of fully committing to her. She took his general talk about their future as a guarantee of the future she wanted. She never looked at her reality—the fact that they were together for many years with no plans to move in together or to become officially engaged—and continued to live with her faulty perception of Marty's intentions.

While it may seem odd to some of us that Agnes didn't see a problem with their long relationship having no forward movement and while most of us would like to believe that we never would have let things go that far, it never occurred to Agnes that there was something wrong. Why? Because Agnes brought her childhood wiring and faulty perceptions into her adult relationships. Agnes was the eldest of three sisters who grew up in a home where her father was domineering, all-powerful and a "know-it-all." He commanded obedience and respect with outrageous restrictions on his wife and three daughters. No decisions were made and nothing was ever allowed without "Dad's approval." Agnes was wired with the belief that "Whatever the man says, goes." She also had the false perception that she had no control over her life. Can you see how Agnes's wiring worked against her? She never even thought about her own right to make choices and decisions. This left her waiting diligently until Marty was ready to make any moves toward marriage and left her believing that was how things were supposed to be! It was all she knew how to do, because that was how she protected herself and her feelings as a child. It never occurred to her that Marty wouldn't propose or that they wouldn't move in together. And it certainly never occurred to her that he would end the relationship.

Initially Marty told Agnes he needed "space"—an undefined amount of time to be apart from her. This is *never* a good sign in any relationship! Taking a short, defined period of time (a few hours, a day or two, a defined period of time based on some real deadline or event) to mull things over, initiate some personal growth or deal with some specific issue while still being committed to the relationship is a healthy thing for both the individual and the relationship. However, taking some lengthy, undefined period of time (many days, weeks) outside of the relationship should raise a huge red flag.

Because her wiring and personal goals led Agnes to believe this "space" would help her maintain equilibrium in her life, she agreed to Marty's request and gave him the "space" he needed to "work on himself" (another red flag here). Again, if someone ever tells you he or she needs to "work on" him or herself, get specifics. What is he or she working on? How is he or she going to work on it? Why can't it involve you? We all encounter opportunities to grow and improve throughout our lives and being in a healthy relationship shouldn't preclude us from growing and changing. If the work can't be done within the relationship and shared between the two people involved, there is something amiss in the relationship.

What further complicated Agnes's ability to answer the "demand" for calm in her life was that for nine and a half years she and Marty shared a relationship of assumptions. When she envisioned her future, Agnes saw herself together with Marty forever. She assumed her weight was not a problem and that Marty loved her and would eventually marry her. Since I never met or spoke with Marty, I cannot say for sure what his vision of the future was; however, his actions make it clear that it was different from Agnes's. With regard to relationships, actor Henry Winkler in the old television sitcom *Happy Days* clearly understood the concept of Calm and Sense when he said, "Assumptions are the termites of relationships."

The foundation of Agnes and Marty's relationship was slowly eaten away by those pesky termites of assumption. Agnes and Marty had two different visions of the future and Agnes lived her life assuming her vision was *their* vision. Neither Agnes nor Marty questioned the other as to why they were still living (separate from each other) with their parents after more than nine years, why no formal engagement had occurred, if Agnes's not going out more often was a problem to Marty, etc. The bottom finally fell out of the relationship when the beams of their love had become emotional sawdust. With an actual house, the homeowner needs to check for termites every once in a while before real, sometimes irreparable damage is done. Similarly, relationships require frequent "inspections" between both parties to avoid damage or to make the necessary repairs before it's too late.

Had Agnes and Marty been doing routine "inspections" throughout their relationship, perhaps it would have been saved or ended sooner and without the emotional devastation. The fact that neither of them spoke up throughout their time together leads one to ask, "Why?" Only Agnes and Marty know the answer to that. However, we do know that when Agnes began to press the issue of an engagement, Marty began to back away from the relationship. In a perfect world, one would expect a partner who had no intention of marrying the other to say what he or she truly felt. Marty did not. Perhaps he was not ready for marriage; perhaps he was not happy with Agnes's weight; perhaps he just did not want to marry Agnes. We really don't know. And while the truth in this case may never be known, we do know that in *every* case, honesty and open, respectful communication are critical to building and maintaining healthy, lasting relationships. We have all heard this stated a million times; nevertheless, it is the truth.

As for Agnes and Marty, a month after their "reunion" it was obvious that the "space" hadn't been enough. Marty said he needed to get out of the relationship but was "not closing the door completely." Instead of realizing the relationship was over, Agnes held on tightly to those last few words. She lost weight, socialized more often and continued to hope, wish and plan.

And then...she learned about Jolene.

Jolene was Marty's new girlfriend. Sadly, this news wasn't enough to signal Agnes that her relationship with Marty was over. Instead, she continued on a crash course of emotional destruction, trying to convince herself that Marty needed to "get that partying out of his system" and then he would "regret his decision" and come running back.

It was at this point I felt I had to get a little tough with Agnes. I needed to tear her away from the faulty beliefs that were keeping her from moving forward. I needed to do what was necessary to help motivate her to accept the invitation to peace in her life in order to gain Calm. I needed to give her information that would help her realize that not only was she putting all her energy into chasing a train that had already left the station, but also that the train she was chasing hadn't even been going her way to begin with. It had become imperative to help her truly learn that she had the choice to perceive her situation differently and more advantageously. For too long Agnes had been holding on to an impossible dream as far as Marty was concerned. Fortunately, that was about to end and Agnes was about to make a major breakthrough in self-acceptance and self-appreciation with a true love of herself for who she was!

Let me share with you another secret to living the life you envision for yourself—the same secret I shared with Agnes that helped her take the next important step: *Your life is happening right now! This is not a dress rehearsal; it is showtime. Live life now.* We have only a certain amount of time on Earth. While we sit around and wait for some specific person or thing—for life to happen—we miss out on the actual moments of life and the opportunities that are passing us by.

I use this frequently when my clients resist the invitation to Calm in their lives. Agnes was certainly determined to fix her relationship with Marty and, with conviction, she lost a lot of weight, made changes in her social life and was not going to let anyone or anything stop her from getting her man back—not even Jolene!

When I pointed out to Agnes the strength she demonstrated in this quest to undo the "done" and just how remarkable she was in taking action when a call to action was urgent (remember, she procrastinated her weight loss diet for months), it gave her proof that she did in fact have power over her life and her life was happening *now.* She realized that it was her faulty belief that she had lost power over her relationship that pushed her into panic overdrive. Now she was convinced that she was not in a "dress rehearsal" anymore. This *was* life! This realization was a major step forward for Agnes. However, what Agnes still did not understand was that although we all have power over ourselves, we never have power over other people or their thoughts.

Agnes had plenty of power, drive and determination, but she was using it for all the wrong reasons! Instead of using it to make positive changes for herself, she was using it to do things she hoped would make Marty change his decision. Instead of looking forward, she was still trying to change the past. Many of us, at some time or another, get caught up in trying to plan our futures with mistakes of the past. That does not bring us to Calm!

Just hearing that we hold the power over ourselves and our emotions and having that concept validated by her own actions allowed Agnes to begin accepting it. It allowed Agnes to start to change her perception of herself and her life. It began a massive feeling of liberation for her—as it does for many of us when we have that realization. Agnes agreed that she had "never looked at it like that." Remember, Agnes's wiring did not allow her *any* power growing up. "Dad" had it all. For Agnes, the realization that life is happening now was the jump-start she needed to change her perception, which then allowed her to make positive choices and move forward. Agnes's emotional suit of armor got shinier every day. She was also still losing weight and looking healthy and great.

As time went on, Agnes and I spent more time exploring her perceptions and what may have been keeping her from believing in herself, making positive choices and taking charge of her life sooner. We talked at length about what signs were present but not clear that kept her in a "dead-end situation." (Agnes used those words after she made the choice to regain power in her life.) She admitted that her self-esteem was never as good as she would have liked it to be and that she believed she'd feel better one day, once she and Marty "were married with a home and children." She was depending on Marty to provide her with a sense of fulfillment, success and even self-worth, not understanding that those things can come only from within ourselves. It became obvious that Agnes had all her life expectations based on her relationship with Marty—and the power over them wasn't even in her own hands! (In chapter 6 we'll talk more about how to keep ourselves free from "losing everything" in a single incident or the loss of a relationship.) This is why she was so devastated when Marty broke off their relationship. For Agnes, it was true that all she was living for was gone.

In chapter 1 we discussed the three essential life skills (the ability to love, appreciate and accept ourselves for who we are) and how looking to other people, places or things to bring us tranquility and provide a positive sense of self is counterproductive to living a life of Calm. Agnes was now well on her way to learning how these concepts play a role in how we respond when Calm calls. And, as Agnes did, you may be beginning to see how a positive belief in yourself and the innate power you hold over your own life and emotions can bring Calm to your life. The fact is that none of us is guaranteed anything from anyone in this world. As disappointing as that may seem and as much as we don't want to accept that, it's true. We trust our family, friends and lovers to be honest with us, believe in us and support us emotionally. We take them at their words and rely on their promises. But things can change and often do. When we live outside of Calm and allow our happiness and our feelings of success and self-worth to be completely dependent on the actions of others, we set ourselves up for disappointment. (We'll talk more about this in chapter 18.) When we live in Calm, we never let ourselves down—even if others do! We are prepared to encounter and address any changes in our life situations, learn from them and move past them. We are able to respond in positive ways when Calm calls.

In relationships, we cannot find and feel Calm if there is an undertone of suspicion or doubt as to what a partner is thinking or feeling. Can you recall a time when your partner was silent and you knew he or she had something on his or her mind? When you ask, "What's the matter?" and the response is "Nothing," do you get anxious? Frustrated? Frightened? All of the above? Many of us do. We sense something is amiss and we want to know what is wrong, but our loved ones won't budge.

Consider Hank's and Agnes's situations. Hank assumed his family had certain expectations of him; he sensed there was pressure to be the "successful son," but he had no proof of this. Agnes assumed things were going in the direction she was hoping they would; she sensed all was well with her relationship with Marty for many years, but all was not. Calm and Sense thinking tells us that we must address our perceptions and expectations of others when we don't know for sure what they are thinking. We cannot assume. When we feel something is making us uncomfortable, when a lack of information makes us feel suspicious or doubtful, we have the right *and* the responsibility to ask questions about it. Calm and Sense referees the battle between the unsaid versus what is.

Many of us live our lives in uncertainty, frequently accumulating fictitious stressors: false beliefs that others don't like us and doubts in our abilities and our meaning or value to others. Calm and Sense tells us that in order to know how others perceive us, we simply need to ask them. Some of us avoid asking these questions, because we are afraid of the answers. Calm and Sense allows us not to fear the response. We know if the answer is one that gives us information about something someone sees as a negative about us, we can decide whether it's something worth considering and then take advantage of the opportunity for positive change. The unasked question is a lost opportunity, no matter what the answer.

For example, maybe you think your boss is sure you are goofing off all day at work, surfing the Internet or taking care of personal business on company time. Maybe you are, but if you are not and you believe your hard work is going unnoticed or unappreciated, there is nothing wrong or inappropriate with scheduling a meeting with your boss to ask how he or she thinks you are doing on the job. This demonstrates your initiative, self-confidence, self-esteem and proactive work ethic! It will also leave you feeling a positive sense of self-worth and accomplishment and provide a feast for Positive Pat. It may also result in a promotion down the line, because you stand out to your boss. Most importantly, though, it dispels any uncertainty you may have been experiencing. Calm and Sense says to clear the emotional air.

Another example is that maybe you think a relative doesn't like you for some reason or another and you feel uncomfortable when you see him or her, but neither of you ever addresses it. Calm and Sense empowers us to eliminate uncertainty. For example, you could say, "Hey, Uncle Harry, did you know that every time we get together I get the feeling that you are avoiding me? Am I just paranoid or did I do something to offend you?" This approach uses a little humor but gets your uncertainty out there and puts the ball in Uncle Harry's court. Maybe you did say or do something he didn't like. If he is not using Calm and Sense, he won't address it, but you will. You will be compelled to, because Calm and Sense does not let the unknown dictate your sense of self-worth, nor will it allow your self-image to erode over speculation. (By the way, if Uncle Harry does have a complaint, you will come across as a strong, confident problem solver next to the isolated, grudge-holding avoider.)

In relationships, as we'll discuss more in detail in chapter 22, the silent treatment is sometimes a manipulative move used to get the other partner to do or say something he or she wouldn't have otherwise done or said. Sometimes it is a passive-aggressive action in which one partner wants the other to know he or she is angry about something but either does not want to give up the power by expressing what the problem is or wants the partner to feel guilty and struggle, wondering what he or she did wrong. This is ineffective communication! It serves no good purpose in any relationship. Calm and Sense living consists of being forthcoming with our feelings in regard to others, not resorting to guessing games. Being in love requires awareness of each other's needs and feelings, but does not require mind reading.

If Hank and Agnes had Calm in their lives sooner, both would have addressed their uncertainties, clarified their assumptions and been able to correct their faulty beliefs. They would have been prepared to respond to the call for Calm in positive, productive ways.

PART TWO

How to Live a Life of Calm

"He who cannot change the very fabric of his thought will never be able to change reality, and will never, therefore, make any progress."

Anwar Sadat
Third president of Egypt,
recipient of the Nobel Peace Prize

Sometimes life goes along on an even keel. There are sunny days and slightly cloudy days, but generally the weather is good. Sometimes life has bumps and ditches and feels like a roller coaster. There are cloudbursts, sun showers, heavy rains with thunder and lightning, heat waves, snow storms and the occasional out-of-nowhere hailstorm. And sometimes life feels like it's whipping like a tornado around us, threatening to rip us from our foundations forever. The things that happen around us and to us are external to ourselves—like the weather. When the weather turns bad, we know well enough to go inside where it's safe and dry to get out of the storm. Why then, when life presents us with challenges, do so many of us focus on the "storms outside" and what *could* happen to us instead of turning away, going "inside" and breathing a sigh of relief for the safety, protection and provisions we have already? The things around us should not threaten our inner wellness. We are protected when we take care of our needs, fears, activities, etc. So why do so many people choose to panic, stress and become depressed or anxious rather than look *inside of themselves* for Calm?

This section will explore the many ways we can better equip ourselves to brave any storms we come across and focus on what truly makes Sense in living a life of Calm. We will look at some old thought patterns that may be anchoring us to our pasts and preventing us from discovering new seas or terrains in life. We will also explore why some of us choose never to venture outside our comfort zones, avoiding taking steps toward the things we truly desire for fear of failing to obtain them.

We will also be introduced to letting go finally and once and for all of destructive, negative beliefs and thought patterns that continue to feed our inability to live Calmly and make Sense of ourselves and the world around us! For it is these things that cause us to continue looking outward, away from ourselves, our souls and our *being* for strength, happiness and fulfillment instead of looking inward and learning about the wonderful abilities we truly have and that are waiting to flourish. It is these things that prevent us from knowing that all we need to be able to step outside and take the risks and chances necessary to achieve the things we want for ourselves comes from within us.

Chapter 5

Your Life Is Yours

Consider this statement from Alex Haley, an African-American writer: "You have to deal with the fact that your life is your life." As you absorb this absolute fact, imagine the breakthrough you are about to experience. Your life *is* your life! It was given to you by someone or something and entrusted to you for eternal care, protection, satisfaction, enjoyment and fulfillment and to use to help yourself and others.

Your life is *yours*. It belongs to you. That means you are the only person who knows what it's really like to live your life. It means that if your life is unhappy, it's you who feels unhappy; if your life is prosperous, it's you who benefits; if your life is traumatic, it's you who experiences the consequences of that trauma. That also means it is *you* who is responsible for making the choices and taking the actions that affect how you experience your life—and how you feel about yourself. We don't get to switch lives with someone else, trade in for an upgrade or sit around watching time pass and waiting for "real life" to finally begin. This is it. There are probably very few who are living the exact lives they imagined they'd be living today. With this in mind, Calm and Sense reminds us: If you don't like your life (be it all the time, some of the time or just rarely), it is *you* who has the responsibility to change it. Living a life of Calm gives you all the tools you need to live the life you want.

It is our responsibility, as individuals, to keep ourselves as emotionally challenged, satisfied, healthy and stable as we possibly can. We are also responsible to know who we are and why we are the people we are. Calm and Sense would say that to know oneself is to love oneself. Perhaps you have heard this before and are saying, "I don't know how to love myself! That's been my problem all along!" Calm and Sense teaches us that if we don't love ourselves, we haven't yet tried to do so. The inner peace and happiness we desire so much is only accessible when we are ready to take a long, honest inventory of the reasons we have kept ourselves from accepting and loving who we are. We must make changes, take risks and challenge those barriers that keep us from embracing the wonderful people we are. Calm and Sense accepts no excuses for the inability to love ourselves after we have made a commitment to do so.

In chapter 3 I discussed the way in which we wired ourselves as children. We instinctually devised ways and means to protect ourselves when life did not run smoothly or predictably and when we were faced with traumatizing, frightening or unfamiliar situations. Reality reminds us that life is *never* smooth and predictable for long. Something invariably comes up and throws us off course—the death of a loved one, a serious illness, a divorce, infidelity, the loss of a job, etc. The list goes on.

I'm not referring here to the "normal" mishaps or life disturbances that occur in children's lives—things such as a parent forgetting to pay a traffic ticket or getting caught driving with an expired inspection sticker and having to deal with the consequences; missing a best friend's birthday party because of illness; failing a test; rushing out of the house and finding the bus has already left; witnessing parents arguing about the garbage not being put out. While these things do interrupt the flow of a day and can cause stress, these "normal" incidents can actually help children accept the inevitability of change in life and teach them to "go with the flow." They are not the kinds of things that impel children to create major coping strategies.

The situations that do cause children to wire themselves for protection include those that come about from growing up in a traumatic environment that includes things like living with a parent who struggles with addiction; being the recipient of or witnessing a sibling or parent being the recipient of physical, emotional or verbal abuse; being exposed to criminal activity or dealing with the consequences of having a parent who is involved in criminal activity; poverty, mental illness and homelessness. When children encounter these situations and their consequences, they often also experience them in addition to the absence of at least one stable parent or parental figure in their lives. (How does a person parent appropriately if he or she is drunk or high, in jail, emotionally unstable, abusive or otherwise negligent with regard to parental duty?)

It is in these types of family or home environments that children become frightened and insecure and feel unloved, unsafe and unworthy of self-love. Personal survival becomes key. Children develop survival skills and defense mechanisms and use them to gain a sense of safety and "normalcy"; however, these tactics are merely ways to avoid the reality and horror of what is truly occurring in the home.

When asked, most of us would say that the single most important thing a child needs when he or she is growing up is *love*. But the fact is that a child needs to feel *safe* more than anything else! Think about this: a child grows up in one of the "traumatic" environments mentioned earlier, not feeling loved and not feeling safe. This feels awful emotionally and it's obvious to the child that something is missing. As well, children are very hedonistic beings—they want things right away. There is no such thing as waiting or being patient. As children, they can't identify exactly what it is that they need, but they know they need to feel better *now*. They need life to be "normal" again as soon as possible. Their survival instincts kick in. What is the result? The majority of children react *not* by loving themselves more (quite the contrary) but by setting up defense mechanisms that help them feel safe. The deeper, more pressing need is for safety.

It's little wonder that we, as children, learn quickly to protect ourselves when our parents are unable to fully protect us. Because it's happened to us before, we know something else is going to happen, sooner or later, to derail our senses of stability. As children, during the time that we learned to anticipate this "next frightening and threatening nightmare" to come around and disrupt balance in life, we also prepared for it by expecting the worst and by expecting disappointment. We know failure; we know promises are sometimes not kept; we know we must not do or say this or that, because it will upset someone and then we will pay for it. We survive as best as we can, but in doing so, we unknowingly sacrifice our self-worth, self-esteem and ability to trust others as well as ourselves. We do this with no understanding of how to "undo" it later in life when we mature and the immediate needs or dangers we experienced as children are no longer a threat to our adult well-being. In a sense, we are functioning in adult bodies but with the coping skills and reasoning strategies of children, with under-developed abilities to judge and fully understand our emotions. It is in this condition that I meet most of my clients. It is in this condition that many of us walk around today. And it is this "condition" that impedes our ability to love ourselves for who we are and to value and enjoy the lives we have.

People tend to seek therapy when they are stuck somewhere—be it in a situation, in a relationship or with an emotion or feeling—and they cannot continue living the way they have been any longer without some type of emotional assistance, guidance or relief. The Calm in their lives is absent and they believe that they are missing out on something. In some cases they've also come to realize that whatever resources, coping mechanisms or survival tactics they have used in the past are just not working anymore. It is in this Calm-less condition that many people turn to drugs or alcohol, begin experiencing "panic attacks" or unexplained medical issues, suffer from depression, go on shopping sprees beyond their means, cheat on their spouses or directly withdraw from the responsibilities of life. We put up our own barriers to achieving and maintaining emotional and physical health.

Let me point out here that having Calm is priceless and essential to avoiding many of the problems that are, these days, all too often quickly categorized and labeled with some of the "designer diagnoses" that seem to pop up regularly in the world of popular psychology. By these, I mean diagnoses like seasonal affective disorder (better known as "SAD"), generalized anxiety disorder, ADD, panic attacks, depression, social phobia, ADHD, agoraphobia, sex addiction, bipolar disorder and obsessive-compulsive disorder: diagnoses that are frequently used as catchall labels for a set of uncomfortable, life-hampering symptoms (e.g., can't sleep, can't concentrate, have nightmares, have physical pain, etc.). While most of these diagnoses do exist and there are many people who do struggle with these mental and emotional disorders caused by chemical imbalances or genetics, there are also many more people who are told they have these disorders when, in fact, what's really going on is they are experiencing a lack of Calm in their lives and are not able to grasp mature, healthy self-concepts and self-esteem. These diagnoses, when based only on symptoms and not on a true in-depth assessment, are an easy way out and allow us to avoid digging deeper, looking at the causes, examining what our lives look like on a daily basis and asking ourselves, "Who am I? What have I experienced? What's been happening in my life?" They distract us from finding out what's really at the root of our unhappiness.

The treatment of these designer diagnoses typically includes the simple "popping" of the latest pill to make it "all better." We all lead busy, overscheduled, stressful lives and we all want to feel good about ourselves and our lives. The lure of a "quick fix," which can be attained by first attaching a recognizable (and socially acceptable) label to a set of symptoms and then taking a prescription medication, is enticing, but it's like using only novocaine to treat a dental cavity. Again, while these medications can be (and often are) very helpful to those suffering with mental and emotional disorders, they do nothing for the rest of us but allow us to relinquish our responsibilities to ourselves and to addressing what's truly causing our unhappiness.

If we think back to twenty years ago, children were not suffering from ADHD, ADD, Asperger's syndrome or depression as much as they seem to be today. Adults were not diagnosed with depression, sex addiction, anxiety disorder, SAD, agoraphobia and the like with the frequency with which they are today. Remember, more than nineteen million Americans are suffering from depression and depression is a contributory factor to fatal coronary disease. What has changed? What is going wrong? Our society is losing its sense of Calm—its Calm and Sense! We are handing our lives over to labels and quick fixes.

Calm and Sense does not dispute the fact that people do, in fact, have depression, anxiety, bipolar disorder and various other emotional disorders. However, Calm and Sense tells us that the *will* to get better is most times better than a *pill* to get better!

Remember: Your life is *yours* and *you* are responsible for doing all you can to enjoy it and live it well. This is not to say that taking medication is unnecessary or bad. It does, however, remind us that oftentimes the underlying cause of our unhappiness is something we do have power over and responsibility for working on. It also gives us the tools to do so—the tools to address and solve the issues that pharmaceutical companies (who survive only when you buy into their advertisements and purchase their products) want us to believe can easily and only be solved by using their medicines. And while taking these products may make us feel relief, they alone do not and cannot bring forth the self-appreciation and love we can find only within ourselves when we embrace Calm and truly take control of our lives! These benefits come from the medicine cabinet of self-forgiveness, self-esteem, self-determination and courage to be who and what we aspire to be and from letting no person, place, belief or thing stop us. Too many people are taking medications and putting chemicals (which often cause "unwanted side effects") into their bodies to resolve symptoms that are actually "curable" once Calm and Sense is achieved.

Calm and Sense is in the business of helping people help themselves not only to solve their problems but also to learn how to welcome problems without fear, frustration or worry. Pharmaceutical companies are in the business of selling medicine, not solving your problems.

Even when we are able to take an honest look at our lives and begin to discover what may be causing our unhappiness, some of us run into trouble when making the changes we need. Now, I'd like to discuss how fear plays a role in our lives and in our acceptance of ourselves. (We'll talk more in depth about fear in chapter 16.)

Many of us are afraid to make changes—especially when we are faced with life-disrupting events. We are also afraid to try new things. We are afraid of rejection. We are afraid of many things. Calm and Sense encourages us to replace these (and any other fears we may have) with curiosity. It encourages us to examine our fears by asking ourselves questions like "Why do I feel that way? What do I have to lose? What is it in me that holds me back? What am I so scared about?" When we begin to answer these questions, we get to know ourselves and why we are the people we are. We can then make choices that help us move forward with our lives and make changes that allow us to grow, succeed and accept and love ourselves regardless of circumstances.

We all know that life isn't always going to run smoothly. We also know that fear isn't always bad. A healthy, controlled amount of fear helps us to prepare, to "put our ducks in a row" and to be ready "just in case." It also guides us to ask ourselves the right questions about what is going on and why we are stuck. It's when we allow fear to consume us, to restrict us, to leave us in a paralyzed state of continual worry that it becomes the enemy. The reality is that "stuff happens" and we do have to protect ourselves and be prepared.

Fearing not being able to pay your bills should lead you to ask yourself, "What can I do to create a financial buffer in case my income situation changes?" It shouldn't consume you to the point where you cannot go to work or cannot work when you are there. That's not Calm and Sense thinking. Fearing failing a test should inspire you to ask yourself, "How can I better prepare for this test?" It shouldn't create so much anxiety that when you sit down to take the test (if you haven't called in "sick" because of fear) you can't remember anything you've studied. Calm and Sense thinking allows us to put our fears in perspective and use them to our advantage. Remember, your life is yours. Do not hand it over to your fears!

Wired as we are because of our childhood experiences and living with fears that control our ability to act, we often isolate ourselves. We think, *No one understands me* or *I don't want to burden them*. Sometimes we are ashamed of our situations or of who we are and we don't want others to know what we are going through. Sometimes we're just so used to being unable to trust anyone else that we don't even consider asking for help. Feeling isolated and overwhelmed leads us to relinquish our lives in another way. Life seems too much to handle, so we just give up. We give up on caring about our lives and we give up on loving ourselves.

Hiding behind defense mechanisms and isolating ourselves won't bring success, it won't help us get to know and understand ourselves and it won't help us learn to love ourselves. That is not Calm and it does not make Sense. It won't bring peace, happiness, a sense of safety or feelings of love. Calm and Sense reminds us that we cannot do it all ourselves and encourages us to make use of our outside resources to help us through life's traumas. (We'll talk more about this in chapter 6.)

It is vital to understand that a healthy sense and appreciation of *self* is the foundation of personal growth and success in life. Even if we have grown up in less than perfect situations or environments that placed us in perpetual fear or harm's way, we *have* survived and will continue to do so. It serves us no good purpose in later life to believe falsely that we are restricted or unable to challenge things that frighten us or cause our inner senses of calm to be disrupted. In fact, it is our duty to face the fears that have held us back and to cease blaming fear, embarrassment, other people or our pasts for our being "stuck." Remember: Your life is yours!

Chapter 6

Your Social, Emotional and Professional Portfolio

The *American Heritage Dictionary* defines *bankruptcy* as "lacking quality or resources." Social, emotional and professional (SEP) bankruptcy exists when you don't have sufficient social, emotional or professional resources to take care of yourself appropriately; in other words, when your life lacks quality or resources. Unfortunately, many of us don't take notice that our SEP portfolio is deficient until we are in the midst of a crisis.

Calm and Sense advises that when striving to avoid social, emotional or professional bankruptcy (and to maintain a healthy, positive, Calm and Sense life), we should develop and maintain a healthy SEP portfolio by maximizing our profits with the least amount of overall risk. The best way to do that is by spreading our assets over a variety of wise investments.

Your SEP portfolio is an investment in *yourself*! This means that your SEP portfolio should contain things that help you attain positive relationships with friends, lovers, family and coworkers, a greater understanding of and respect for yourself and success in whatever it is you are moved or called to do for a living. That is the goal of your SEP portfolio, so all that you choose to invest in should in one way or another be in support of that goal. Now, how would Calm and Sense advise you to invest wisely? Let's take a look.

Like any good investor, you should know about the companies and products in which you plan to invest. For example, if you are an animal lover, you most likely would want to avoid investing in a company that uses animals for testing purposes or in a product that was tested on animals. Before investing, Calm and Sense advises that you learn a bit about the investment: find out if it matches your values, needs and goals. If environmental preservation and protection are important to you, investing in a green-powered industry might be the perfect fit for you. Your Calm and Sense investment might also include volunteering time at an animal shelter or starting a task force at work to find greener ways to save money for the company and spare the environment unnecessary waste.

To invest wisely and to be able to decide which of the investments you have looked into—or are considering looking into—are right for you, you must take some time and really get to know yourself well. Figure out what's important to you, what you like, what excites you and what challenges you. Are you a risk taker? Are you able to be patient for long-term, high-return results versus the possibility of losing your investment completely? Or do you like "guaranteed" results that may not bring you big gain but will produce some form of profit and do it sooner rather than later? Most of us fall somewhere in the middle of these options. Calm and Sense says that once we know ourselves, we can make SEP investments that work well for us. For example, if you are a cautious investor and you *know* you love to read, joining a book club would definitely be a good, "safe" investment. If you are more of a risk taker, you may feel comfortable going with something you *think* you might like. Perhaps you always wanted to play guitar but never took lessons or pursued that interest. If you are a moderate-risk taker, you could borrow a guitar and invest in a few trial lessons to see if you like it or not. If you are a high-risk taker, you might choose to go out and buy that really awesome guitar and commit to the full series of lessons. Get the picture? In any case, the decision you make on how to invest and what to invest in is based on what you know about yourself and the investment. Going at it this way, no matter how the investment works out, at the very least it teaches you something valuable about yourself in the process.

Now that you know how to choose your investments, let's talk a little about what your SEP portfolio really is. Your social, emotional and professional portfolio consists of friendships, activities, hobbies, interests, professional skills, qualities, family, education, self-care, passions, health, social skills, spirituality and romantic relationships (and more). All of these things make up the person you are. With that in mind, it becomes clear that the goal we should all have for our SEP portfolios is to invest in as much as we can—spread ourselves out as much as we can manage. Join a gym, volunteer at a charity of your choice, take a class, start a walking group, visit family more often, write a book, try a new style of clothing, join a wine-tasting club. *Do things for yourself*—invest in yourself! There is nothing in life more worthwhile in which to invest.

It may sound as though Calm and Sense recommends to invest in too much and attempt to "do everything" and "be everything." This can leave you feeling overwhelmed. Here's the key: Contributions to your SEP portfolio are not unchangeable, nor should they be. None of them has to be a lifetime commitment. Calm and Sense advises that you diversify your SEP portfolio investments, because the more diversely you invest, the more new opportunities you find in which to invest. For example, you join a club of some sort. At one of the meetings, you meet a new person who tells you about another "investment" that sounds interesting to you. Then you become involved with a new challenge and perhaps meet another person who is looking for someone to fill a position in his company—and it's the "dream job" for you.

The building of your SEP portfolio becomes a way of living. The more you learn, the more you discover about yourself, the more opportunities which you expose yourself to and take advantage of, the deeper and more fulfilling your life becomes. Along the way you learn more about what you like and don't like, about what you want and don't want. You become a wiser investor and a healthier, happier person. And, with each investment you make, you reduce your risk of "losing everything" if one of your investments turns out to be less than what you'd hoped for or needed. To manage your SEP portfolio wisely, you must reevaluate your investments from time to time, add more as you find more in which you are interested and remove the ones that aren't working for you. Building your SEP portfolio is a constant activity and Calm and Sense requires continuous movement in all we do socially, emotionally and personally.

Many of us have a belief that "Once I get a certain thing, I'll be the person I always wanted to be: happy, successful and content." This is *not* Calm and Sense thinking! That type of belief is what I call the "when this, then that" trap. Relying on one thing—or even ten specific things or events—to bring us Calm and Sense is a setup. Why? Because we are never truly satisfied with accomplishments alone. Calm and Sense tells us that when we complete one task, gain one thing or meet one special person, we need to keep doing more of this sort of thing in order to continue to feel satisfied after the newness and excitement of the accomplishment passes. Maybe you have heard the cliché, "Life is a journey, not a destination." Calm and Sense agrees!

Your SEP portfolio is the heartbeat of a Calm and Sense life. The more we engage ourselves in the world around us, the more we learn about ourselves and how to overcome obstacles, identify interests and strengths we never knew we had and overcome the barriers that were keeping us stagnant and to which we have already given too much power.

Equally importantly, Calm and Sense cannot stress enough the power of connecting with other people! We all need people and we all need a sense of belonging. *You cannot imagine how much life there is until you start living.*

Remember how Agnes believed that all was lost when her relationship with Marty ended? How she had invested *only* in her relationship with Marty? When that investment crumbled, so did her world and her image of herself. Had she invested in her SEP portfolio as Calm and Sense advises, when things with Marty were going bad, she would have had support and resources to help her through the rough times. She would not have been SEP bankrupt but would have had people in her life to remind her of her value when she was unable to see it for herself. She would have had activities to focus on instead of focusing on trying to figure out what she could have done differently to have kept Marty. She would have had people and activities in her life that made her feel good about herself so that her entire self-image was not tied to Marty's treatment of her. That is not to say that the pain of losing that relationship wouldn't have existed—it still would have, but she would have had the ability to manage it in a healthy, positive, Calm and Sense way and be able to keep moving forward with her life.

Remember Hank? He built his SEP portfolio and this brought him to Calm and Sense living. Hank had decided he was going to give college another try. I had to increase the goals to be achieved with him (as I did with Agnes), because I felt he was wasting his money seeing me every week to complain about his life rather than looking for solutions. Although Hank was reluctant at first, he and I began working on a plan of action.

Hank was far too disconnected with the world. This was not working for him; it was providing him with more reasons to feel like a failure. Hank needed to get to know more people and to work on his presentation when meeting new people. The first order of business for Hank was to stop relying on *his* way to get things done and trust the Calm and Sense way to guide him forward.

Hank and I took a serious inventory of his passions. Unlike therapists who focus more on problems people have, I like to begin with people's motivators. Hank identified sports, auto racing, auto mechanics, muscle cars, comedy, poker and writing as his major passions in life. This was a perfect start. After that, he and I needed to find ways to connect him to others and to activities that supported these passions.

Since Hank was returning to college "one more time," we looked for activities that could connect him to other people while keeping his passions motivating him. Since he did not feel comfortable joining any teams at school, we agreed that he might like to try sports writing for the college newspaper—a great investment for his SEP portfolio. I told Hank to come back to see me after he had looked into this possibility.

I also gave Hank a little life coaching before I sent him off on his endeavor. He was to *smile* while he walked on campus and whenever he met someone new. "What? I will look ridiculous!" was his initial response, but those were my terms. (On a personal note, smiling often has been one of my strongest keys to success in life!) Hank resisted at first, saying he just "doesn't do that (smile)," but I reminded him that his way of doing things had not yet brought him Calm and Sense, so what did he have to lose? That day, he left my office mumbling under his breath, but he also knew and understood the instructions I expected him to follow.

Hank graduated with an associate's degree in journalism eighteen months later and enrolled in a four-year school pursuing a bachelor's degree in journalism. Hank found a sense of community after joining the college newspaper staff and eventually became the sports editor of that paper. One day he said to me, "You know, that smiling stuff works, Dr. Leo!"

Of course, there was more work involved in Hank's success than simply smiling his way to happiness. He experienced some bumps in the road when learning how to relate to others, manage his anger and find his way, but he stuck with it. Calm and Sense living supports smiles and a healthy sense of humor in everything we do! You see, Hank actually had a very healthy sense of humor but, until he learned Calm and Sense, it had been buried—stifled by his self-doubt, anger and negativity.

Hank's ability to flourish at the newspaper brought him confidence in himself. That confidence also resulted in much more investing in his SEP portfolio as time went on. He became more determined to do well in all of his classes and he made friends at the newspaper, in classes and at sporting events he covered. He was hired to do announcing at the college basketball games and, at graduation, he even won an award for his contributions to the newspaper.

Hank started volunteering at a soup kitchen, after being invited to do so by a young woman he met through the college newspaper. Hank had previously stopped talking to his high school friends, because they were all in college doing well and he felt unworthy of their friendships due to his feelings of shame and embarrassment. Hank reconnected with a few of these high school friends and goes to Atlantic City with them every so often to play poker.

Although Hank still has some work to do regarding his past, he has now learned to accept that a world of possibilities does exist and that it is up to him to go out there and find them. He no longer blames his past or his father for his misfortunes but now thanks them for strengthening him enough to make the changes he had to in order to find Calm and Sense. (We will talk some more about the effects of our past on our present in chapter 7.)

The most incredible change I saw in Hank was evident in listening to the way he spoke of people he now knows and in his ability to see in them what he could not see in himself before he learned Calm and Sense. It is in conversations such as these that I find personal satisfaction and pride for clients, like Hank, knowing they have truly embraced the essence of what Calm and Sense is all about.

When you have Calm and Sense, you want everyone else to have it too! You feel compelled to spread the knowledge to others and help free them from their despair and misery. Calm and Sense breeds Calm and Sense. Perhaps you know someone who appears totally comfortable and content with him or herself, speaks easily to others and does not complain or fret over trite matters. There is something that draws people who have not yet learned Calm and Sense to those people who have. It's not magic—it's Calm and Sense.

Hopefully you too have decided on the value of an SEP portfolio when investments begin to bear interest. What we haven't discussed yet is how to start building your SEP portfolio. Calm and Sense says to begin with investing in your passions. Dividends and interest won't begin to pour into your life until you make the contributions. *You* are your greatest asset! Invest often and fearlessly.

In keeping your social, emotional and professional needs well nourished, you are essentially laying the groundwork for Calm and Sense living. It is important to understand that Calm comes to us when we seek it and heed its call. Remember, the quest for Calm is an ever-changing, constant experience—it is always there for us. This may sound a bit confusing. Perhaps you're thinking, "It sounds like Calm is never truly attained and, even if I am successful, I have to keep looking for it!" The reality is this: When you have Calm in your life, you are continuously driven to seek and find more of it. However, *while* you are seeking more, you feel, dwell in and enjoy the benefits of the Calm you already embrace. So, when you are Calm and you are achieving goals in new social, emotional and professional activities, relationships and perceptions, *you want more and more of them.*

Let me share with you a clear example of how all this works in real life. When I first tried skiing, I was scared silly! Bundled up in big, bulky clothes, two sticks in my hands and long rods clamped onto big robotic-looking boots on my feet, I felt like I looked completely ridiculous as I watched others gliding down the mountain slope with ease and style, speed and confidence. I thought to myself, *How am I going to do that? There's just no way!*

But, being the risk taker I am, I got on the chairlift and watched the bottom of the mountain get farther and farther away as my stomach churned, my fears intensified and self-doubt consumed me. *Why didn't I stay in the lodge, safe and sound with a nice warm drink and big blazing fire?* I asked myself.

An important note: We *must* leave that "safe lodge" in life in order to get to Calm! As Sigmund Freud said, "A cautious businessman avoids investing all his capital in one concern, so wisdom would probably admonish us also not to anticipate all our happiness from one quarter alone." When we play everything we do in life "safely," we deny ourselves the ability to advance, grow and, ultimately, to gain Calm. Sure, we can sit in the "lodge" and be comfortable and protected, but we are only looking out the window at life. We are watching people swoosh down hills, smiling, laughing and enjoying. They then come into the lodge and talk about how "awesome" the mountain was or how they "learned a new way" to maneuver themselves on the slope. We watch them, we hear them, but we cannot truly understand what they have experienced. *If we don't leave the lodge, we are watching life pass by, mere spectators of what we could be.*

Riding the chairlift, my heart was pounding as we approached the drop-off spot. It seemed like time was moving at lightning speed. "How do I get off?" Well, I slid off very clumsily and, with a little push from the lodge staff, started moving toward the hill. *This isn't so bad,* I thought to myself. Then there was the downslope. *Eek! I am going to ski down there?* Well, indeed I went down that hill.

Holding on to my poles for dear life (why, I still don't know—they did not help me much and still don't to this day), I was gliding down the hill. People were passing me to my left and right, much faster than I was going. Just as I gained some momentum, I fell. My skis went flying off my boots and I tumbled around while rolling down that hill.

What was I to do? Well, I got up. A fellow skier helped me collect my skis and showed me how to put them back on my boots. Then I started moving down the hill again. I fell a few more times but made it to the bottom of the hill. Guess what? I loved it! I was determined to get back on the lift and do it again. And that's exactly what I did.

All that day, I could not get enough of skiing! Each time I went down the mountain, I got better and fell fewer times. Skiing was an ultimate rush of fun that I had never experienced until I pushed myself to do it. Soon, I was going down bigger, more complicated hills, because the beginner hills were not giving me the satisfaction I had originally received when I first learned how to ski. I was moved to risk more in order to get more! Today, I am a worthy skier and there are not many high-challenge hills I would not attempt.

My example illustrates, I believe, how Calm works. The better we feel, the more confident we become; the more challenged we are, the more Calm we have! It is a matter of stepping off the sidelines of life and getting in the game. But we never "arrive" at Calm. More correctly, we step into it like stepping into the ocean—gradually gaining comfort, confidence and self-assurance—and continue moving further in as time passes.

The most difficult barriers to overcome on the way to attaining Calm lay in self-doubt and fear of the unknown. But remember, those old patterns of thinking are just that: old. We developed them as children when we needed to protect ourselves from dangers that, as children, we had no way of using Calm and Sense to manage. Indeed, those old defense mechanisms may have served us well during our childhoods, but today the dangers of childhood are gone.

Remember, Hank was wired for letdowns and disappointments, because his father was an alcoholic. He came to believe that he could trust no one, that he did not deserve any good in his life and that people did not like him—because that was his reality as a child. Those old childhood beliefs kept him confined to depression, misery and anger as an adult.

Agnes had been raised in a male-dominated home, wired to believe that the man in the relationship makes all the decisions and that her role was to be subservient to Marty's (her father's?) schedule, plans and demands. That type of thinking caused her to spend almost ten years of her life waiting for Marty to marry her. That is *not* Calm and Sense living!

How were you wired as a child? Can it be that you are still "sitting in the ski lodge," letting life go on in front of you, feeling unworthy? Unloved? Unable to be as happy as other people seem to be? If the answer is yes (and even if it is not), read on.

Chapter 7

You Are Not a Slave to Your Past

It is important for all of us to remember where we have come from: where we have been, what we have endured, whom we have been with, what we have seen and how we have learned to survive. It's equally as important to remember that regardless of the pain, sorrow, losses and humiliation, we *have* survived and are here today! While the past has molded who we are at this very moment, for better and worse, there's nothing we can do to change the past. Denying parts of our pasts doesn't erase those parts from having happened; ignoring the experiences of our pasts doesn't always serve us well as we move forward through life; and focusing on—or getting stuck in—the past doesn't allow us to live fully today. Today, right now, as life is happening, it's what we do with the lessons and experiences from our pasts that shape who we are and who we will be in the future. Calm and Sense tells us that it is up to us to make the best use of the lessons from our pasts and continue moving forward.

If our pasts have been wonderful, it's easy for us to say, "This is my past and I'm okay with it." However, if our pasts have been anything less than wonderful, we often have difficulty looking at them in positive ways. We have difficulty saying, "This is my past and I'm okay with it." Remember: If we have suffered, we have also endured. If we have experienced pain, trauma, hardship, etc., we have endured. We kept moving forward as best as we knew how and continue to do so. Survival is a basic human instinct. We've talked about how, as children, our survival instincts helped us make our way through unpleasant or traumatic circumstances. We've talked about the wiring we acquired during childhood and how we carried that wiring into adulthood where that wiring doesn't serve us well. Faulty wiring and getting stuck in "survival mode" long after what we are surviving is over keeps us focused on trying to fix the past and often prevents us from moving forward, from making Sense of our pasts, embracing who we are today and looking positively at the possibilities of healthy, happy lives.

Our need to feel safe, loved and "okay" motivates us to keep trying to get through a difficult time. Sometimes, when relief doesn't come quickly enough, we feel like we are spinning our wheels, unable to make things better. In that tired, beaten-down state, that frustration and feeling of failure can often lull us into believing we are destined to be stuck in a bad place for the rest of our lives or even lead us to believe we don't deserve better. But when we escape or break free from bad, dangerous, threatening, painful or frightening places in our lives (even for just a short time) and find places of refuge where we feel good and where we find shelter from the previous trouble and trauma, we feel a sense of success and hope and realize that there *is* something better, something to keep working toward. We continue to seek a place of safety, a place of Calm and Sense, a place where the external forces, circumstances, people or thoughts that have troubled us (or still do) no longer threaten us. We seek a place where we can comfortably move from surviving to living. Sometimes the peace and safety we find lasts for a few moments or hours and sometimes for a few days. Sometimes it is a more permanent change. Calm and Sense tells us that whenever we come to this place in a positive and healthy way, we should make note of the things that helped us get there, the things that helped us to feel safe and the things that brought us Calm and make Sense. Then we can and should use those things to help us continue to move forward.

Sometimes, in our desperation to get relief from the traumatic situations in which we find ourselves and in the absence of (and sometimes despite having) positive support and assistance, we find comfort and take refuge in things like alcohol, drugs, sex, shopping, gambling, eating, etc. These things temporarily lull us into a sense of separation from our troubles—into a false sense of safety and well-being. Sometimes we deny that the horrible things are happening, believing that if we pretend they don't exist, they will go away. Sometimes we separate ourselves from all the people and activities in our lives; we isolate ourselves to protect ourselves from continuing to be hurt or to hide our feelings of inadequacy or shame from those around us. Doing these things can help us feel safe for a while but, ultimately, they are not safe or healthy, they don't make good Sense and they take us further away from Calm.

When we are suffering, sometimes we have a difficult time noticing that we are feeling good and that the clouds are lifting and an even more difficult time identifying what positive things happened that made us feel good. Calm and Sense reminds us to take a good look at now instead of focusing on yesterday. It's human nature to want to repeat something that feels good, but you can't do it if you don't identify what it is! We need to focus on today, see the positive in each day and keep moving forward, creating more and more situations that help us feel safe and that bring us further from the pain and trauma of our pasts and closer to lives of Calm and Sense.

Fortunately, some of us are able to recognize that life is happening to us today, that we do have power in the choices we make and that our pasts belong in the past. With that knowledge, we can keep moving toward Calm and Sense in our lives. However, there are some of us who just can't seem to get moving in that direction. What is it that keeps people from searching for and reaching that safe haven, that feeling of having Calm and Sense, even when it's the thing they want most? What is it that makes people get stuck and leaves them unable to rescue themselves from (or sometimes even realize the seriousness of) the situations they are in that are causing them so much unhappiness? Why is it that some people are forever *blaming* their pasts for their situations today instead of moving forward, living in the present and planning for the future?

The lack of Social Maturity and Emotional Maturity are two primary causes. Social Maturity is the ability to engage in relationships and situations free from envy, jealousy, blame, judgment, rage and resentment. It is also the acceptance that others are not perfect, nor responsible for our feelings, success, happiness, well-being or situation. (We will explore Social Maturity in chapter 8.) Emotional Maturity is the ability to manage our behaviors and thoughts by not personalizing others' remarks, actions or impulses that we find threatening, insulting or abusive and resisting the desire to respond with the same. (We will talk more about Emotional Maturity in chapter 9.)

Another factor that plays a role in our inability to move forward is that the people around us, the people who love us, often enable us by comforting us, supporting us and allowing (sometimes even encouraging) us to remain in the "surviving" place instead of helping us move forward to a thriving place.

Yet another contributing factor is that we are overwhelmed with movies, reality shows, court television shows and media coverage that give us examples of people who use the trauma of their pasts to escape being held responsible for their current actions. Our legal system—not intentionally and sometimes detrimentally— is quite encouraging and supportive when it comes to helping people relinquish any sense of personal responsibility for their pasts. In fact, there are countless defense attorneys who are driving around in very expensive cars, living in opulent homes and leading lavish lifestyles, because they are artful in convincing judges or juries that their clients did something morally, physically, legally or ethically wrong *because they suffered greatly as children and knew no other way*. This does not make any Sense! As well (and even more importantly), it feeds people's minds with the idea that if they have had terrible childhoods, they are destined to do bad things as adults or repeat the abuse (on others) that they, themselves, suffered as children and that it's okay to use a less-than-stellar past as an excuse. Negative Nick loves this stuff, because it allows him to grow and tell us with even more authority that we are bad, we can't change and we are stuck. Calm and Sense warns that this is faulty adult wiring. Remember: The more we hear something, the more we believe it. It is even more dangerous when the message is coming from the legal system by which we are all bound.

For example, Charles Manson, Ted Bundy, Jeffrey Dahmer and John Wayne Gacy are all serial killers, notorious for the heinous crimes they committed against humanity. While some of them had very troubled childhoods, some had average, uncomplicated early lives. During their trials for their crimes, a few of them used "insanity" defenses, claiming it was their troubled pasts that led them to do the things they did. None of them, however, had ever been diagnosed by a medical professional with a disorder that prevented them from knowing right from wrong or being able to control their own actions (and not one of them was able to convince a jury that he was not responsible for his actions). The popular media spent a lot of time and effort sensationalizing their crimes and focusing on mothers who were promiscuous alcoholics or fathers who wanted nothing to do with their sons. The message the public received was that a troubled childhood leads to uncontrollable, unlawful behavior. If it is true that adults who suffered greatly as children are incapable of stopping themselves from doing something that is morally, physically, legally or ethically wrong, then everyone who has had a traumatic childhood or past would be committing crimes. This is not the case. Many of us have had pasts that included events that ranged from unpleasant to horrible—but we are not out in the world committing crimes.

Because the media is a business needing to sell advertising, it feeds our morbid curiosities by giving us gory details and juicy bits of history (often completely out of context). That's what sells. We are often bombarded by stories about the things that go wrong—about who's to blame for this and that or where the buck was passed—when hearing or reading about what's happening with survivors of natural disasters (like hurricane Katrina). The hundreds of stories of hope, courage, compassion and giving don't make the front page or the six o'clock news. A story about a man with a terribly troubled childhood who is now building schools for children in Africa or a story about a woman who was raped by her male relatives and is now helping young women in third world countries learn how to grow food and feed their children doesn't sell as many copies or get as high ratings as the negative stories do, so we don't hear about them very often. The media tells us that even if we donate our money, it doesn't get to where we believe it will or doesn't get used for what we hoped it would. The media tells us that even when we try to do the right thing, it doesn't help. Forgetting the details, we are left with the underlying message that if you've had a terrible past, it's all right to continue blaming that for your lack of success, because that's what "everyone else" does. And, even if you try to do something to make things better, it doesn't work. It's no wonder many of us believe we are trapped or controlled by our pasts with no way to truly attain Calm and Sense and joyful, happy lives.

One example, not as well known as the names I mentioned earlier, is Sanford Clark. He was fifteen years old when his mother (predominantly) and father felt he was no good and let his uncle take him to a chicken ranch to "make him a man." There his uncle sodomized him and verbally, emotionally and physically abused him, burning his back with boiling water, beating him and burying him for periods of time under the floorboards with a chain around his neck. Sanford was also forced to dig graves and help dispose of the bodies of the little boys his uncle sodomized and murdered. No one wondered how Sanford was doing until his older sister noticed that something was amiss in the letters Sanford had been forced to send home to assure his family he was well. She went to visit him and was terribly uncomfortable with what she found. As a result of her attempts to rescue her brother from what she sensed was a bad situation, the gruesome and horrific truth came out about Sanford's abuse, the murders and that Sanford's grandparents had been supporting his uncle, enabling him and his behaviors and even participating in at least one of the murders (Sanford's grandmother pled guilty to murder and was sentenced to life in prison). Though he had been involved with the murders, Sanford was spared charges by the district attorney, who believed Sanford was not a willing participant in the crimes. The DA sent Sanford to a school for boys, where he stayed for twenty-three months and, on his leaving, was asked by the DA to live a life of good deeds. Sanford Clark went on to serve in World War II and then worked for twenty-eight years for the postal service in Canada. He married and adopted and raised two sons with his wife, to whom he was married for fifty-five years. The Clarks were involved in many different organizations and supported many different causes. Sanford Clark died in 1991, at age seventy-eight, having lived his adult life honoring the request made of him by the DA.[1]

What makes the difference between a person whose traumatic past has influenced him or her so negatively that he or she does something morally, physically, legally or ethically wrong and a person whose traumatic past does not cause that kind of behavior? Why are some people able to accept their pasts and make their lives better, while others feel their pasts give them permission or a sense of entitlement to act however they wish and take no responsibility? Why do the laws of this country allow for such privilege—and indirectly foster the idea that we are slaves to our pasts?

As to the question about the law, the answer, simply, is that the law allows more leniency in cases of individuals who are deemed "mentally incompetent" or "insane" at the time of their crimes. While this is a very relevant and reasonable defense in a good number of cases (I'll give you an example in just a bit), unfortunately the laws are so broadly written that creative lawyers are able manipulate them to "protect" clients from due punishment—when the clients have a background that includes some kind of abuse or suffering—by claiming their clients "did not know better."

The presence of a true mental illness is what defines legal "insanity." True mental illnesses—like bipolar disorder and schizophrenia, which are biologically based and cause people to have psychotic episodes in which they lose touch with reality—are very different from personality disorders—like antisocial personality disorder, which deals with people's lack of concern for others and may include behaviors like animal abuse, robbery, vandalism, arson or general disregard for others or their feelings or well-being, or narcissistic personality disorder, which deals with people's beliefs that the world revolves around them and where they also have no feelings, empathy or regard for others' feelings or needs—which do not cause sufferers to lose touch with reality. These are, in turn, a far cry from really horrific behavior. People suffering with true mental illnesses begin showing signs of illness in adolescence and early adulthood. They have a documented history of multiple hospitalizations and treatment attempts. Their family and friends are well aware of the condition.

True mental illness is generally diagnosed *before* a person commits an unspeakable crime. It does not come on suddenly—right about the time a person commits an illegal act. When attempting to use the insanity defense for clients who do not have documented histories of true mental illness, attorneys try to present information about their clients' pasts to make up for the fact that there are no existing diagnoses. True mental illness, where a person truly has no control over his or her behavior, is not something that "just shows up" at some point in a person's life without any prior, clearly identifiable red flags. Criminals (and attorneys) who want "insanity" diagnoses after the fact just aren't making Sense. A serial killer who petitions the court to be allowed to act as his own attorney and is found competent by the court to do so cannot reasonably expect, then, to be also found incompetent by reason of insanity with respect to the charges he is facing. These cases are examples of attempts to manipulate the law to excuse a criminal from his or her responsibility.

The story of a client I counseled while employed as a psychiatric social worker at a state hospital illustrates the type of situation for which the law's leniency *is* appropriate. Dave was a forty-year-old male who had been diagnosed with schizophrenia. By the time I met him he had been treated for at least twenty years with various medications and hospitalizations. One of the common characteristics of schizophrenia is auditory hallucinations (hearing voices and other sounds that exist only within the person's head—they have no external source). The voices are sometimes funny, are sometimes mean and sometimes tell people to do things. Medications do not eliminate the voices completely but often "quiet them down" and give the person more ability to identify them as auditory hallucinations and distinguish them from reality. Dave heard voices all the time. He had been taking medication for a while and it was helping with the voices. Then he stopped taking it. This is also very common in people with schizophrenia, because the side effects can be quite unbearable at times.

Off the medication, Dave began to hear voices telling him that his mother was Satan and that she was going to kill him. The voices commanded him (these particular auditory hallucinations are called "command hallucinations") to kill his mother or he would be killed himself. Dave had lived with his mother all of his life and had a very supportive, loving relationship with her. One day the voices were just too much for him to bear and they convinced him that his mother must be killed. Dave stabbed his mother eighty-seven times, cut her body open, doused it with gasoline and lit a match setting her on fire. The fire destroyed her body as well as the house they lived in.

Dave was arrested and brought to jail. Upon his interrogation, the police immediately knew that Dave was in a state of psychosis and needed psychiatric evaluation. Dave openly admitted that he committed the murder and explained why he did it. Later, he was transferred to the state psychiatric hospital for a mental competence evaluation. He was found "incompetent to stand trial" until his condition was stabilized.

After about a month of treatment, which included medication and therapy in a hospital setting, Dave returned to a state of lucidity and remembered everything he had done. He wept often and felt suicidal; it was a very long time before he was mentally stable enough to stand trial and be sentenced for his crime.

Dave's family members forgave him, because they knew that he did not commit this crime of his own free will and accord. They understood and accepted the nature of his illness and, although they were grief-stricken, they realized that Dave was ultimately not responsible for the murder of his mother or the arson of her home. Because there was clinical documentation of a clear history of mental illness and given Dave's history of treatment and hospitalizations and his lack of motive and criminal history, the court also recognized that Dave was not ultimately responsible for his actions.

Provisions for insanity within the law exist for people like Dave, whose circumstances are quite different from and who are clearly in a separate category from murderers like John Wayne Gacy and Jeffrey Dahmer. If you recall, it was reported that Ted Bundy calmly calculated his plans for every woman he kidnapped, raped, tortured and killed. These are not plans that could be made or carried out—or carried out with such consistency—by someone who is legally insane. During Bundy's defense we heard that he never knew who his father was, that he grew up believing that his mother was not his mother but rather his older sister and that his mother was a prostitute. Charles Manson commanded quite a following and manipulated countless people to engage in murder—also not acts that could be planned or carried out by someone who is mentally incompetent. Like Bundy, Manson's past included questionable parentage as well as an alcoholic mother who supposedly sold him for a pitcher of beer to a childless waitress.

The purpose of these examples is to point out that even though the law allows for special cases, our pasts are not death sentences, nor are they excuses to keep ourselves from moving ahead to that safe haven, that place of Calm and Sense. Millions of people overcome horrific pasts, turn out happy and healthy and live responsible lives.

This brings us back to the earlier question: What makes these people different from those who are unable to accept their pasts and make their lives better? The answer is Calm and Sense.

Calm and Sense tells us that to completely "survive" our pasts, live fully in the present and create futures that are happy and fulfilling, we have to be able to look at our pasts reasonably and learn from them. To embrace Calm and make Sense, we have to move beyond blaming our pasts for our circumstances and take responsibility for who we are and what we do today. Only in examining our identities and our origins can we change our childhood wiring, begin to love ourselves for who we are and truly move forward.

It's important to note that a diagnosis of a mental illness does not prevent someone from living a life of Calm and Sense and working toward and achieving great success and fulfillment. There are many examples of people with diagnosed mental illnesses or disorders who have been greatly successful. John Nash, who was born in 1928, is an economist and mathematician whose work and theories are currently used in market economics, computing, evolutionary biology, artificial intelligence, accounting and military theory. He attended what is now named Carnegie Mellon University on a scholarship and was then accepted at Harvard, but instead attended and earned his doctorate degree at Princeton University on a fellowship. Nash was a senior research mathematician at Princeton University, was on the faculty of MIT during the later part of his life and eventually was awarded the Nobel Memorial Prize in Economic Sciences. At age thirty-one, John Nash was diagnosed with paranoid schizophrenia. Having spent years suffering with the effects of the disorder, he spent time in various mental health institutions and trying various types of medications. Despite his constantly challenged mental health and his potential to be a danger to himself and others based on his delusions and hallucinations, John Nash was able to succeed in the field in which he was so invested.[2]

Among others, actor/comedian Robin Williams and former United States president Abraham Lincoln are also examples of people who are famous for the positive things they've accomplished, despite allegedly having diagnoses of bipolar disorder.

I do believe that most people think their pasts are the main reasons they are unfulfilled in life, unhappy and incapable of reaching higher states of self-appreciation and self-love. I also believe that this is the biggest misconception and self-defeating belief any person can have. So many of us think of our pasts in this way: "Since I suffered tremendously as a child or adult, I must have to live a life of misery while everyone else around me does not." Does this make Sense on any level?

Calm and Sense respectfully acknowledges that many of us have lived very hard, challenging and sometimes abusive lives. But as much as Calm and Sense holds our pasts as very important, it also theorizes that our futures are far more important for they allow us to have all that we did not have before. So, let's turn that statement around and re-conceptualize the idea: "Since I suffered tremendously as a child or adult, I am tired of being defeated and I *am* going to do whatever it is I have to do to make my life better *now*!" Calm and Sense tells us that we should be pulled by the future and pushed forward by the past—not the other way around.

Chapter 8

Social Maturity

Joan Rivers' mantra for many years has been, "Oh, grow up!" Indeed, Joan is on to something vital to Calm and Sense. Do you know of people in your life who act like children when it comes to managing problems in their lives? Do you know people who want what they want when they want it? Do you know people who cannot manage anger appropriately? How about people who are insulting, demeaning or are complainers? Partners, lovers or spouses who quarrel over the dishes not being done, the garbage not being taken out, the laundry left on the floor? These are minor examples of an underdeveloped Social or Emotional Maturity.

Social Maturity is defined as the ability to engage in relationships (with acquaintances, friends and intimate partners) and situations free from envy, jealousy, blame, judgment, rage and resentment. It also involves understanding how to honor and respect those in civil, parental, business or spiritual authority. Lastly, Social Maturity is understanding and accepting that others are not perfect, nor are they responsible for our feelings, success, happiness, well-being or situations.

Children cannot meet needs for themselves such as safety, well-being, food, care, comfort and health. So, many of these needs are, in fact, the responsibilities of parent(s) or guardian(s).

As we mature, we learn to become more and more self-sufficient and require less and less from our caretakers; however, some people do not expand socially and remain fixed on the idea that someone or something "owes" them something (success, happiness, wealth, etc.). For these people, when these needs are not met by outside providers, they react as children would: with anger, blame, jealousy, nastiness and revenge.

Social Maturity is a key element in acquiring Calm and Sense and is also a distinguishing characteristic of those who benefit from their pasts rather than blaming them. I have heard it said that prisons are filled with adult bodies that have the minds of twelve-year-olds. I have worked in a prison and can attest to the accuracy of that statement. I have seen grown men arguing and bickering about the most trivial things. Fighting over an apple, a television show, who gets the top bunk in a cell, the "look" someone gave them, the extra thirty seconds one got "in the yard," etc. The issues fought over and those that take such an "important" role in day-to-day life in prison mimic those you find on a grammar school playground.

Many people not in jail bicker and complain about issues in their lives as well: small things, such as who got the window seat at the office, the husband who never takes his shoes off when he comes in the house, the neighbor who seems to have a limitless supply of cash, because she buys a new car every year or takes her family on trips every other week. Some of us feel cheated by these things or entitled to have them. What do we do when we feel slighted? Those lacking Social Maturity revert to childhood thinking. They get envious and angry and want to "get even" or they stew and show hostility toward those whom they believe are getting more advantages than they are.

Socially Mature people do not have time or room in their thoughts for such matters. Nor do those of us who have Calm and Sense working in our lives. We know that worth is not measured by such things and cannot be so...ever. This is the basic concept that people lacking Social Maturity need to understand and accept. What is the point of arguing, worrying or stressing over perceived disadvantages? Remember the Ten Year Rule (chapter 1)? True Social Maturity is demonstrated by taking responsibility and using Reasonable Reasoning to gauge just how important this thing is that you are trying to get, do, succeed in, etc. and taking responsibility for its execution—not believing that someone or something owes it to you or is getting in your way of achieving it.

You may now be wondering, *Are you saying that Social Maturity is wisdom?* I am. Intelligence, they say, can be measured. There are intelligence tests, SATs and various other standardized tests that can be taken to provide an outcome or score of some type that will evaluate how "intelligent" you are when compared to others who have taken the same test. Wisdom, on the other hand, cannot be tested or measured, much like "common sense." Many people who do not have formalized educations or college degrees feel compelled to defend themselves for that lack by saying things such as, "Well, I may not have book smarts, but I have street smarts!" How do they know this? And again, how can it be measured?

Of common sense and wisdom, Ralph Waldo Emerson said, "Common sense is as rare as genius"; Alfred Lord Tennyson said, "Knowledge comes, but Wisdom lingers."

Measuring common sense is impossible. There is no test to take to prove we have it, yet we freely identify it in others and ourselves. We seem to gauge a person's having or not having common sense by the way that person handles things or reacts to a given situation. But on what characteristics do we base this thing called common sense? When we are told to "use our common sense," what exactly does that mean? Specifically defining it, as measuring it, is a very challenging if not impossible task. You either have it or you don't. That leaves common sense open to much speculation and personal definitions of what it actually is. In a sense, the inability to clearly define it leaves one wondering if one actually has it or if it truly exists at all.

Common sense, as I see it, is a shared understanding with others. It is also knowing right from wrong, good from bad, potential from impossible, dark from light and the like. For example, most would say that it is common sense that tells you not to touch a hot stove, not to leave the house without clothes on, not to leave your keys in the car and not to try to jump across the Grand Canyon. These are things we have learned through experience, observation and growing up and they are certainly beneficial to know.

Common sense, then, also guides us in our interactions with others. It tells us that we should not walk up to a complete stranger (or friend, for that matter) and say, "You have the biggest nose I have ever seen! How much tissue do you need to blow it?" If we go to a wake, common sense tells us not to walk in laughing or begin telling jokes to the family of the deceased. These social behavior guidelines, which are shared or "common" throughout a culture or across cultures, are learned throughout our lives either by direct experience or from observing and imitating others. We learn them by watching what other people do and applying it to our own lives. These behaviors are what are known as customs, rituals or social mores. So perhaps "common sense" can be more accurately defined as proper socialization.

But is having this type of common sense enough to bring us to a state of inner peace and safety and to have the love of ourselves that we most certainly need in order to feel good, successful and at peace with the world around us? No. For these things, we rely on Calm and Sense!

Calm and Sense is most certainly measurable and defined. We know we have it when we feel emotionally invincible, confident, determined and peaceful. We no longer yearn for things that we once thought were impossible to obtain and cease believing in fairy tales that imply "when this or that happens or when we meet him or her, then life will be all I want it to be." We exist in the moment, because we know that *now* is all we have to make the most of our lives!

Beyond any book smarts and common sense we may have, only with Calm and Sense and the Social Maturity that comes with it do we no longer feel bitter or resentful for what we perceive others have, compared to what we have. We live and let others live as well. The jealousy and belief that we are getting less than others is gone. There is no longer a competition for "who has the most" and our minds become free of that clutter and worry.

With the Social Maturity that comes with Calm and Sense, we radiate enthusiasm and happiness to those around us. We generate and share real feelings, deeper and more valuable than the imitated and mechanical behaviors of the social mores we have learned. As a result, people want more of us! We do not fear taking risks or challenging old thoughts and behaviors that we used to believe protected us in some way. We take responsibility for our own lives and situations. We accept that regardless of what our pasts consisted of we are not going to be held back by them but, rather, catapulted forward by them, pulled by the future, not fearing it. *This* is being "grown up" and demonstrates both real Calm and Sense and Social Maturity.

Chapter 9

Emotional Maturity

Similar to Social Maturity, Emotional Maturity is the ability to manage our behaviors and thoughts by not personalizing others' remarks, actions or impulses that we find threatening, insulting or abusive and by resisting the desire to respond in kind.

You might be thinking, *Now wait just a minute. I will not allow anyone to treat me like a bag of trash or a doormat and let them get away with it. I won't do that!* Calm and Sense does not advocate that anyone tolerate disrespectful treatment by anyone at any time. That is absolutely unacceptable. The Calm and Sense solution to these types of attacks is to *re-conceptualize*, not retaliate. Who is making these statements to you? What truth do the statements hold? Why are you giving power away to someone so emotionally and socially immature? Why are you allowing the person to control your thoughts, feelings or behaviors? Remember: When you love yourself and have Calm and Sense, you are wearing an emotional suit of armor. People who make judgments, insult others or demean others are not happy people themselves. You have a choice not to allow negativity to pierce your armor and cause you to react in ways that could potentially be dangerous and cause harm to yourself or others, either physically or emotionally.

To illustrate how emotional *immaturity* between a couple may play out, let's look at Ted and Alice. They began a discussion about finances (again). Alice was angry already, because she was previously talking to one of her best friends who had just planned and booked a trip to Cancun with her husband. Alice and Ted had not been on a vacation for several years.

At dinner that night, Alice said, "When are we ever going to go away on a vacation?"

Ted responded, "We can't afford it now."

Alice got more heated and retorted, "You seem to have enough money to go out to the bar with your friends every Thursday night."

"That's different," Ted rationalized. "It's only a few dollars a week, not a vacation."

"You haven't gotten a raise in a long time, Ted; why don't you get a second job?"

"I work very hard and you don't work at all!" Ted exclaimed. "Why don't you get off your duff and find a part-time job?" Ted felt attacked and threatened and his self-image was deflated, because he did not make a large salary. He wanted to take his family on vacation but realized his limitations. However, hearing his wife's comments got his defenses up, because he felt hurt and shame.

"I take care of the house every day, pick the kids up from school, help them with their homework and drive them to afterschool activities. Do you think that's easy?" screamed Alice. "The least you could do is be a better husband and father and realize that your family deserves a trip somewhere once in a while! You know, I was talking to Kelly today. She, James and their kids are going to Cancun next month! They go away all the time! *That's* a hard working man!"

Ted's pride was injured. Hurt is the seed of anger and, as his own self-worth was being challenged, he responded with rage. He yelled out, "I am sick and tired of this crap all the time! If you want to be going on vacations all the time, then maybe you should find another man! It's the same old story with you all the time! You don't appreciate me!"

Ted slammed his dinner dish and utensils on the table, threw his chair back (which fell on the floor), stormed out of the house, banged the door behind him and screeched his car out of the driveway heading to the local bar. Alice screamed after him, "There you go again! Just leaving. Never solving the problem!" She turned to her two children who were not saying a word but looked upset. "Kids, eat your dinner!"

There are *many* problems to address in this scenario, but for the purpose of explaining Emotional Maturity, let's focus first on Alice. She heard about her friend's trip and reflected on the fact that her family never vacationed. She got jealous and envious, so what did she do? She decided to "blame" Ted for not making enough money to take care of his family sufficiently. She insulted him, judged him and attacked his character.

Ted lacked self-esteem. He worked hard every day, went out once a week with friends to the local bar and secretly hoped never to be challenged as a man, father or husband. When his limited income became the topic of conversation, he immediately felt guilt and failure as a man and as a provider. So, when Alice pushed these buttons, Ted's hurt turned to anger—the emotion with which he was most comfortable—and he tried to defend himself by putting blame on Alice: "You get a job, Alice!" Then, hearing about Kelly's husband's "success" and ability to take his family on vacations, Ted felt threatened and insecure, which also came out in anger. Not a man with Calm and Sense or any Emotional Maturity. Both "parents" acted more like children than their own children.

How many of us react to situations in our lives as Ted and Alice did? We resort to blame, insult and rage when we don't get "our way." This is what children do. As adults, if we continue using these behaviors, we have not matured emotionally and we are not moving toward Calm, but away from it.

Sometimes, instead of acting out in anger, we get depressed. We don't direct our negative energy outward (like Ted) but turn it inward. We stop trying, we stop caring and we stop believing we can be successful, that we are worthwhile or that there's any point in moving forward. We give up and engage in lots of negative self-talk. Instead of exploding and running out like Ted, we become depressed and withdrawn. We stop being able to *see* the best in ourselves, let alone *be* the best we can be.

If Ted and Alice had Calm and Sense in their lives, perhaps the situation would have gone more like this:

> Alice: "Ted, I was talking to my friend Kelly today and she told me her family is going on another vacation. You know, I was thinking maybe we could try to save some money and take a trip too."
>
> Ted: "Money's tight, but you're right. Maybe we could clean out the garage and have a garage sale or something. That would give us a head start. Where would you like to go?"
>
> Alice: "Well, we have never been to the theme park and the kids would love it! How much money would we need to do something like that?"

Ted: "I have no idea. Why don't we look online and find out some fares and hotel rates. If it's expensive, maybe we could find a cheaper alternative so we could go someplace else sooner."

Alice: "Alright, let's take a look. Kelly and her family were there last year. I'll call her and get an idea of the cost. They flew, but maybe we could drive."

Ted: "Four days in the car with the kids! That's not a vacation; that's a prison sentence!"

Alice and Ted: "Ha ha."

Farfetched? Not at all! *That* is Calm and Sense working. Each of those two scenarios is absolutely possible, but only one is positive and productive. When we have Calm and Sense, we have Emotional and Social Maturity and *wisdom*. We are secure with ourselves and live in the moment, making the most of our current situations, resources and abilities. Many children act as if the world owes them something and feel that they are the center of the universe—but they can! It is the adult who continues to expect these things and behaves accordingly who has not fully "grown up" and is underdeveloped in these two crucial areas of life.

Temper tantrums, anger management problems, possessiveness, nastiness, irresponsibility and a false sense of entitlement can be found in many adults today. People who break the law and *then* worry about their rights while being tried in court or while incarcerated are emotionally and socially immature adults, similar to people who anger quickly over small things in life like the laundry not being folded, the dishes not being done, toothpaste caps being left off, missing the bus, etc. If we have truly matured socially and emotionally, we are not bothered enough by such small inconveniences to make us either grow furious or completely deflate.

Chapter 10

Identity

Calm and Sense gives you full permission to own your life! It is yours, it is a gift and it rightfully belongs to you and only you. Many of us have lived under false pretenses for much of our lives, wrongly believing that something(s) or someone(s) other than ourselves held the deed to our being, our dreams, our accomplishments and our successes. Calm and Sense tells us that in order for us to be content with our lives and to achieve our goals, we must take responsibility for our lives. Before we can do that, though, we need to identify, at least to ourselves, who we are and who we want to be.

Many of us find ourselves looking in the mirror (either literally or figuratively) and wondering, "Who am I?" Sometimes the question comes up because we feel lost or depressed and really have no idea what to do or why we do what we do when we get up in the morning—or even *how* to find a way to manage to get up in the morning. Sometimes the question comes up because we reacted to a specific situation in a way that surprised us. Sometimes the question lies in the recesses of the mind, festering, nagging and then hiding again. And sometimes the question comes up because we are content with our lives at the moment but know that life is an ever-changing entity and if we sit still for too long, our "content" will surely turn to "discontent."

There are many, many things that can lead us to question who we are, just as there are many different ways that we can respond to that question. For some of us, we experience the question as a guilt-inducing accusation that frightens us into hiding from ourselves. On the other end of the spectrum, those of us who have Calm and Sense experience the question as an exciting opportunity to grow and learn.

No matter what the cause or response, the fact is that many people struggle with identity. Often, this lack of knowing who we are leaves us floating around the harbor, perhaps feeling "out to sea" with no direction. However, never truly knowing *exactly* who we are can be favorable.

Calm and Sense advocates curiosity in self-exploration always. Besides, the less we know about *exactly* who we are, the more potential we have for finding new and exciting aspects of ourselves. You see, for some of us, danger lurks in believing that we know exactly who we are. Once we decide, "This is who I am," that is where we stay. If our images of ourselves are not good ones, we have resigned ourselves to lives that are filled with negativity and will not provide us with all of the things we want for ourselves. If our images of ourselves are good ones, we still hurt ourselves by taking away our rights and responsibilities to grow and change. Calm and Sense says to always leave room for variety, new ideas and adventures in identity. Learn something new about yourself every day. Create something new about yourself every day.

In chapter 6 we talked about the importance of knowing who we are so that we can make wise investments in our social, emotional and professional portfolios. There, too, it is important to be open to new ideas and not to require ourselves to define ourselves completely. Remember, when you make connections with organizations and people to enhance your SEP portfolio based on what you do know about yourself, you are always opening up opportunities for meeting new people, learning new things and discovering new interests you may never have thought you would have.

Another potential trouble area we may encounter in our search for ourselves is getting fixated on knowing fully who we are. For some, especially those who are unhappy with their lives and who do not live lives that include Calm and make Sense, this can become an unhealthy obsession. When we spend too much time trying to identify every detail of who we are, we are not leaving time or mental space to grow and to learn new things. We also don't leave ourselves time to invest in being who we are!

Calm and Sense tells us that we lose the value in discovering who we are if we are not going to *be* who we are. As well, it is fruitless to try to become who we think others want us to be—which, by the way, is most often someone we are not comfortable being.

What are the magical, personal and unique features that you and only you have? What makes you different from others? What are the things about you that draw others to you? What are the things about you of which you are proud, about which you feel good or in which you are confident? We all have these things, each of us in our own ways.

For some of us, though, it's very difficult to identify positive things about ourselves. And without some sense of positive identity, it's easy to fall prey to becoming someone else or becoming whom we believe the world or someone else wants us to be. I believe that many people fall into this category and relinquish much of their true selves to the expectations (both real and perceived) of the people and the world around them. Calm and Sense says stop! Don't fake being anyone. Be who you are. And, by all means, be yourself and please yourself first.

Following the crowd and doing what everyone else is doing is a personality pitfall. However, in a somewhat strange irony, we are encouraged to take from others the traits that fit us best. Dame Edith Evans, a British actress, once said, "I seem to have an awful lot of people inside me." You might be wondering what that all means. Let's discuss.

We need to identify not only who we are, but also who we want to be. We need to identify the things that are important to us and then find ways to incorporate those things into our lives. (Remember: Discover who you are and then *be* who you are.) At times, we don't even realize something could be important to us or be something we want to improve about ourselves until we see someone else has it or someone else do it. Sometimes we do realize it but have no clue *how* to get or do it. Fortunately, we are social beings and (for the most part) meet and interact with people on a daily basis. It is from these interactions with others that we often learn more about ourselves.

Most of us have met people in our lives who moved us, touched us or inspired us in such a way that we want more of them. People who make us feel good about ourselves, our skills and the way we see the world, people who inspire us to become better and people who move us to try something new. These people are our "teachers," our influences and guides who help us to identify who we are and what is important to us as individuals. We want to be more like them in one way or another, so we take on the individual characteristics of them that we admire. We do not *become* them, but rather the traits we admire in them *become us*!

Now you may be wondering, *Are you saying that to become myself I need to find people whom I admire and act like them? Then I wouldn't be me; I would be them, right?*

Calm and Sense never encourages us to sacrifice who we are as individuals by mimicking or copying from others. However, there are ways to incorporate what we admire in and learn from others without negatively impacting our own identities. Let me clarify the two concepts that guide how we accomplish this. The first is that it's always okay to see a trait you admire in someone else and then incorporate that trait into your character. The second concept is what Calm and Sense calls Self-Discovery. Self-Discovery occurs when we encounter people who generate positive feelings within us. I am sure you know the feeling to which I am referring. It's not one of love, lust or covetousness but of mutuality, kindred souls, like minds or pure respect and admiration. It's the feeling of connectedness that comes from feeling great about some aspect(s) of yourself when you are around a particular person or people. The people who inspire these feelings in us are our Identity Fortifiers: They reinforce and strengthen who *we are* by reacting positively to that aspect, therefore inspiring us to be more ourselves! They help us understand our own strengths, motivate us, believe in us, encourage us and inspire us to take a step further. When we are with our Identity Fortifiers, we feel good, we are comfortable in our own skins and we are confident and secure in being ourselves. There is no guessing game, suspiciousness or falseness present in the relationship or exchange of communication with Identity Fortifiers. We feel free to just be and are respected and appreciated.

Identity Fortifiers can appear in our lives anywhere and at any time. They can be anyone: a teacher, a police officer, an associate at work, someone we meet on the train—even a dog (who loves you no matter who you are). Our responsibilities are to recognize them when they appear in our lives and to make the best use of their presences. These Identity Fortifiers are the "awful lot of people inside me" of whom Edith Evans spoke. In truth, we are the result of the many people (and experiences) we have encountered throughout our lives. And while we cannot control who comes into and goes out from our lives and when, it is up to us to decipher what we need from them at the time we encounter them and to take it with us.

Remember, those whose presences or impressions inspire us to believe in ourselves are those who strengthen and clarify our sense of self. But this is merely the beginning of Self-Discovery. Identity Fortifiers are necessary to reinforce what we believe in, what we believe to be right and also what makes us who we are as individuals, but we cannot merely be pieces of many people. So, the question remains: Who are you, really?

Before proceeding further, I need to discuss a few things about Maslow's Hierarchy of Needs (we'll explore this more in depth in chapter 15), a hierarchy that ends with Self-Actualization. Calm and Sense is driven by our individual need to Self-Actualize.

What is Self-Actualization? To Self-Actualize means to become "all we can be," attaining a sense of freedom and independence having mastered some area in life or having a grand sense of competency in something we have undertaken. We may feel a sense of accomplishment in completing a task that makes us want to say, "I did this!"

Maslow's Hierarchy *ends* with Self-Actualization, though, which differs from Calm and Sense. Calm and Sense believes we can and should Self-Actualize over and over again, with each new endeavor we seek out. It is not a "one-shot deal"—it is the constant search for new and self-inspiring motivational activities in life that we continue to undertake to feed our senses of self and keep Calm and Sense alive in us always.

Some examples of Self-Actualizing activities may be completing college, learning a new language, writing a book, learning how to play an instrument, having a family or starting a business of your own. But there are ways to Self-Actualize on a smaller scale too. Consider learning how to feel good about yourself, losing twenty pounds, exercising humor more often than frustration or feeling more confident in social situations or at work. Though perhaps not as "astonishing" as earning a Ph.D. in Thermonuclear Applied Neuroscientific Reproduction of Humanoid Genetics, these examples *are* equally significant, if not more so. For it is these "small achievements" that build character, self-esteem, confidence and courage.

Maslow believed that "lower level" needs (like food, sleep and shelter) must be met before we can move on to the "higher level" needs (like intimacy and self respect) and ultimately Self-Actualization. Reasonable Reasoning asks us that if we are hungry or homeless, how probable or profitable would the attempt to find closeness or intimacy in a marriage be? Calm and Sense believes that if we are not fully onboard with a true love of ourselves and are not past the urge to find negativity, withdraw socially and be self-destructive, we are not ready to take on the bigger challenges that wait for us in life. That is *not* to say that we cannot move *toward* Self-Actualization *while* we work on the necessary smaller, yet significant tasks in our lives. By all means, as human beings we are capable of making magical things happen in our worlds all the time. Greatness is the reward of self-confidence! If we don't believe in ourselves, then how can we expect anyone else to?

So, while we may find our Identity Fortifiers along the way, just finding them is not enough to gain full Calm and Sense. We must then *believe* what they offer us and put it to work. It is then that we begin to carve out our own niches as people—who we are and what is important to us personally, socially, emotionally, spiritually, professionally, etc. This includes resisting the "old wiring" that tells us "I can never do that!" or "My life has been one disappointment after another. I can never be happy." New wiring must be created that says, "I *can* do this" and "I *will* discover how to reach my goal."

I want to be very clear about your intrinsic value here and now: you *are* already someone! You *do* have values, strengths and dreams! Calm and Sense does not require reinventing the wheel of your life, it just says you must get the wheel oiled up and rolling in the right direction.

You may want to add some new features to your wheel of life—maybe some fancy rims or lug nuts or perhaps some interesting hubcaps or a new shine. Maybe you envision new tires altogether. Whatever it is, the fact remains that you already have a wheel of life with which to work. Calm and Sense wants you to improve it where improvement may be needed. Where and how you do that is up to you. The trick is to start discovering and creating the person you have always wanted to be. Perhaps you are not sure of just who you are. That's okay. Many of us can easily get so caught up in the daily grind of life and routine that we function mechanically, becoming overwhelmed and "stressed out," watching the world go by while we suffer silently. (That's *not* okay.) We dream of a better life, better friends, things to do, better self-esteem, more happiness, more meaning, etc., but are so busy with just getting through the day that we stop taking action to acquire those things. Then we find ourselves falling back into "if" thinking (more about this in chapter 15) or envious tendencies: "If I had more time..." "If I had more money..." "If I had a spouse who didn't work so many hours..." "If this, then that..." The obvious problem here is that somewhere along this path of hope we cease to take action in making things happen. Why?

There are seven fundamental myths that keep people from having Calm and Sense in their lives:

- Without lots of money, I cannot live the life I want; therefore, I can never be happy.
- Without a perfect partner or perfect relationship I can never be happy.
- I don't know how to be happy.
- The world owes me something and I never get a break; therefore, I can never be happy.
- People don't like me; therefore, I can never be happy.
- I am never going to be perfect; therefore, I can never be happy.
- My life has been a series of failures and disappointments; therefore, I can never be happy.

With which of these myths can you identify?

In my line of work, people never cease to amaze me with the strengths they have but do not even realize that they have. However puzzling it is at times, it is equally fulfilling to me when my clients begin to *see* and *believe* in the strengths that have been present in their lives for so long, yet were lying dormant like an ancient volcano ready to explode, spewing streams of enlightenment.

I have also seen in my practice many clients who readily go miles and miles out of the way to make other people happy. This happens all the time. Yet, when it comes to taking care of themselves or actually believing they have done a good job or done a good deed, they dismiss it immediately! "It's just what I do (for others)," but not for themselves. I often hear myself telling my clients, if you treated yourself even a fraction as well as you treat others, you would have Calm and Sense.

In your search for self and identity, Calm and Sense reminds us that it is *vital* to take a deep, thorough, *honest* look at who you are, where you have been, what you do well, who the vital people are in your life and how you got to where you are. You must also listen to your heart and to your Identity Fortifiers. When people compliment you, stop dismissing it as someone "just being nice" and allow it to boost your character. Calm and Sense gives you full permission to believe the good things people say about you!

You see, the *true* reasons most people fail to believe they can be happy or have Calm and Sense is because they don't believe they deserve to be happy. They do not love themselves enough or they fear leaving the lives they are currently living, however unhappy they may be, because their lives provide false senses of safety as it is all these people know to be true. When we learn to expect less, that is what we receive. Conversely, when we expect more we usually receive it. However, sometimes we don't. It is at those times that we feel justified in saying things like, "See? I gave that Calm and Sense thing a chance, but it didn't work!" And it is at those times that I say to you, "If you really had Calm and Sense you would not be so quick to give up and reinforce negative thinking." Calm and Sense requires consistency, belief and patience. Calm and Sense also allows and even *encourages* mistakes, because in every mistake there is a lesson to be learned *if* you are ready to learn it!

Many of us fail to realize and understand that *true* happiness does not last forever and it is not a constant presence in our lives. It comes and it goes, waxes and wanes, goes down deep then comes up for air. We have great days, good days and not-so-good days. That is life. That is *normal.* The misconception that being "happy" should mean *always* feeling happy is just not reality. We all want and truly deserve to be happy, but during those times when we are not euphoric we should not be alarmed and so quick to say, "See? Happiness doesn't really exist for me."

It is more practical, then, in our search for "happiness," to instead be searching for Calm and Sense! Calm and Sense *is* a constant and *includes* happiness, but also frees us to live comfortably in times when we are not joyous. Calm and Sense keeps us comfortable and content at all times and reminds us of our self-worth and that we are fine all the time.

Chapter 11

Time Keeps On Ticking

The list of promises we make to ourselves as to *when* we will be happy is as long as a ride from Houston to Singapore by rowboat (and equally as laborious)! "When I meet Mr. or Miss Right, *then* I'll be happy!" "When I get the perfect job, *then* my life will be all I ever dreamed!" "As soon as I pay off all my bills, *then* I will feel secure!" In general, people get caught up in the false belief that people, possessions, riches or titles somehow define and dictate balance and well-being. These "things" certainly do affect our lives in countless ways, for better or for worse. However, keeping our lives "on hold" or our true senses of inner peace on "standby" for these acquisitions is not Calm and Sense thinking.

We are all given a life and it comes with an expiration date. None of us knows exactly how many minutes, hours, days, weeks, months or years we have been given to live life. Too many of us seem to be forgetful of this fact. We cannot create more time. That is why time is our most valuable resource. It is treasured, because of its limitations and our inability to create it. I often remind my clients that life is not a dress rehearsal; it is the *real deal*. Showtime! Every single second of our days counts and it is *our* responsibility to *make* them count, because *now* is the only time of which we can be sure!

Numerous studies examined terminally ill people who were literally days or moments away from death. One question which was most often asked in these studies was, "Knowing your time is nearing, what would you choose to do more or less of if you could start over again?" Overwhelmingly, the top two responses have always been, "Laugh more and worry less." Very few people near death have ever responded to that question by saying, "I wish I had made more money, met the right man/woman, made sure all of my bills were paid, been the CEO of a Fortune 500 company," etc. Laugh more and worry less. A great mantra for living and one Calm and Sense encourages all of us to say, think and *do* daily.

Waiting for "something" or "someone" to enter our lives and "make us happy" is like sitting in a garden with a chestnut in one's hand, doing nothing but waiting for it to become a mighty tree. One will spend a very long time waiting for that to happen! The truth of the matter is that the chestnut needs someone to plant it; it can handle the rest of the job of growing all by itself. Such is life. We must "plant seeds" all around us in the "garden of life." We plant a seed of friendship here then go to another part of the "garden" and plant a seed of education there. As we wander around our "gardens of life" weeding, watering and planting, we eventually begin to see our seeds growing little by little, day by day. If one particular plant needs a little more water or sunlight, we make the necessary changes and move on. We don't just sit waiting for the seed to plant itself, water itself and remove the weeds that may be hampering its growth by itself.

When you make good use of your time in tending your garden, before you know it—and without waiting for one certain seed to grow and magically make your garden all you envisioned it to be—you will have all kinds of beautiful plants, flowers, trees and bushes all around you. Calm and Sense believes that variety *is* the spice of life and the more we "plant," the more we naturally have. A tree of wisdom, a rosebush of love, a mighty oak of happiness, perhaps a money tree...

The more activities, friendships, hobbies, projects, etc., in which we involve ourselves, the more we feel complete, the more people with whom we come into contact, the more we learn about ourselves, the more *alive* we feel and the more identity we establish on our own terms. The trick is to keep searching for new ideas (planting new seeds). Do not wait for or count on any one "magic" person, thing or event (plant) to suddenly make "all the difference" in your life (garden). Most importantly, use the time you have to enjoy *all* the beauty that grows around you!

Time is nonrefundable, valuable and limited. Calm and Sense says to cherish time and use it wisely, as if today was your last day on earth. What if it was? Would you be satisfied with all you have done and created so far? Would you think of people you "should have" called or talked to or loved more? Did you write that book? See that waterfall? Learn how to scuba dive? Take your grandfather fishing? Plant that garden? Have you laughed much and worried little? Neither all the money in the world nor any other possession can buy us time. There is no one who can make more time. Calm and Sense urges and implores you to start tending the "garden" of your life *today.* Begin to sow and therefore reap!

Calm and Sense living is living *now*, in the present, not "someday" or "when I have the time." You *have* the time, but only right now. And for how much longer, none of us knows for sure.

Calm and Sense says that when you plant your seeds now, you must also tend to them now. You cannot sit, watch them die and then give up. Calm and Sense does not believe in the word *try*. Trying is an excuse not to do something. We either do something or we do not. Trying implies potential failure and Calm and Sense knows no failure. We may stumble; we may fall. A baby falls many times when he or she is learning to walk, but each fall is a step toward success, not a journey to failure. So it is with living in Calm and Sense.

We *learn*; we do not *try*. We do not waste valuable time putting our efforts into something with a preconceived idea that we can or will fail. We make good use of our time by *doing,* with the confidence that even if the outcome is not what we had hoped, we have still learned and, therefore, progressed and succeeded. Embracing Calm and Sense, we are committed to feeling happier and more self-confident, free from self-defeating, negative thoughts and behaviors. We are wearing an emotional suit of armor and do not allow any person, thing or negative thought to have power over our success.

My parents used to tell me, "Tomorrow never comes." It took me two master's degrees to figure out what that means. Tomorrow never does come. We are always in today! There is really no such reality as "tomorrow." Tomorrow is an imagining, a projection, an idea. Once that time that was "tomorrow" gets here, it's today. In other words, today is the tomorrow of yesterday. Our reality is always based in today. Calm and Sense is rooted in present thinking and believes there is no better time to make positive changes in our lives than *now,* because "now thinking" initiates immediate change and commitment.

Ask yourself what is keeping you from taking that leap from an unfulfilled life to one of rich self-satisfaction. How many times have you promised yourself that you are going to make changes or do things differently, only to be sidetracked by distractions in your life? There will *always* be distractions! Calm and Sense is your emotional navigational system that will continuously remind you that staying on track will lessen the impact of all those troublesome distractions along the way.

Chapter 12

Where Are You? Where Are You Going?

So, where are you in relation to what you want to do with your life? Do you know? Where are you going? Many of us get stuck, because we cannot figure out how to get where we would like to be or we don't believe we deserve to have the lives we dream for ourselves or we're too lazy to make the effort. And many of us get stuck because of fear.

Calm and Sense requires that you begin to replace fear with curiosity in order to begin to move forward with your life.

I would like you to think of some of the world's most important, influential people—living or deceased, male or female, ancient or modern. Now select one of these people to focus on. Think about what qualities he or she has or had that qualifies the person for this category (important, worldwide, influential). Now imagine that very same person being a bundle of nerves or doubting every move he or she ever made, always giving up if he or she failed to accomplish something, being snooty or snobby with other people or constantly feeling like the world owed the person something and if it wasn't delivered, the person would carry on and cry like a baby blaming everyone except him or herself for not receiving it. Would you have chosen that person at all if even *one* of those negative traits was apparent in his or her rise to prominence?

In acquiring Calm and Sense, we must first begin to conceptualize what fear truly is. What do people fear? What do you fear? Say, for example, your answer is snakes. A lot of people fear snakes. What would happen if you could replace that fear of snakes with a *curiosity* about snakes? What exactly makes them so scary to you? You don't have to necessarily like snakes to be curious about them, but to *fear* them is far less interesting or beneficial to you than being perplexed by them. Fear gets in the way of Calm and Sense all of the time!

Another example of fear: Are you afraid of meeting new people? That is another very common fear that keeps many people from benefiting from relationships, friendships or opportunities. What is the fear based on in this situation? Ask yourself, "Why am I so afraid of meeting new people? Why am I so afraid of possibly meeting the most wonderful person in the world or the person who may offer me the dream job I always wanted or the greatest friend I have ever had?" Yes, it is okay to get angry about answering this question and confronting this issue. Anger, when used properly, is one of the best accelerants to light the fire of change and Calm and Sense relies on change, new ideas and different ways of viewing ourselves and the world around us!

Does fear lie on *you* like a slab of stone, holding you down, helpless, powerless, trapped in a life of despair? Do you often hear yourself saying or thinking, "If I could only do/think/be/find..."? Well, here is the good news: You can! Little by little, as you learn how to use Calm and Sense in your life, you will begin to notice how little power fear really has at all. The one and only reason you fear anything is because you are reinforcing it by believing in it.

What kinds of things do we really fear? Rejection is a very popular answer. Rejection from whom or what? Where did this fear originate? Fear of crowds? Public speaking? What is so truly frightening that we, the most advanced species on this great planet of ours, cannot overcome? Cavemen feared fire until they learned how to control it. Now, thanks to our ancient relatives, we can heat our homes, cook our food, run our automobiles, sing around campfires, roast marshmallows and have romantic "mood lighting" if we so choose! That is taking fear and turning it into curiosity. Where would we be today if our ancestors did not face and overcome that which frightened them? Where are you today if your fears are limiting your potential? One of my clients, Jay, was an eighteen-year-old man who grew up in a home where negativity and gloom were served up as regularly as bread and butter. Jay's parents taught him from an early age that good things in life come only to the "lucky and fortunate" and the "rich rule the world at the expense of the poor people." Jay had a very small circle of friends in high school but did not associate with anyone whose family had "more than" his did, because he was ashamed of his parents, the home in which he lived, the clothes he wore and the car his parents drove. Jay did not look poor, impoverished or destitute at all. He just was a normal looking teenager but without the designer labels attached to his wardrobe.

For most, the adolescent years are all about fitting in and impressing peers, but Jay was steady and selective in those with whom he kept company. His self-esteem was never fostered or nurtured while he was a child. He remembered his parents being paranoid and worried about what people's true motives were. "What do they want with us?" was a common question in his home. More destructive than that was Jay's parents' belief that people were judging them. If Jay was invited to parties (Jay was invited to *many* parties), his parents said things to him such as "Why do you want to go there? Those people don't like you; they just want to make fun of you" or "They are no good for you." Fitting in became the least of Jay's problems. His identity was being kept from developing. His sense of worth never had a chance to flourish with the constant (and constantly reinforced) fear of being judged as "less than" everyone else.

Jay's parents were, not surprisingly, very self-absorbed. Jay recalled his parents never asked to see his grades from high school. There were also times when he missed school for weeks and failed classes and his parents didn't know. The school's guidance counselors called Jay's home looking for him. With both of his parents working, it was easy for him to "cover" by having his older brother take the calls, say he was Jay's father and claim that Jay was sick.

Jay was not a bad person. In fact, he was very caring, sensitive and intelligent and put himself out for anyone who needed him before thinking twice about it. He wanted so desperately to be liked and accepted that he spared his own needs and feelings for anyone who asked or demanded anything from him. His difficulty with attending school resulted from his lack of belief in his own abilities due to his parents' continuous self-absorption and negativity toward life. Jay believed that all of his classmates were smarter than he was, were better dressed than he was, were more "together" than he was and had better families than he did. He withdrew and became depressed. He wanted to date girls, but he did not have the confidence he needed to ask one out on a date. Jay sometimes wished that he could "save a girl from a would-be attacker and show her" what a good guy he was. If this happened, then she would notice and like him. This type of thinking illustrates just how far removed Jay was from any sense of self-respect or how to relate to other people.

Jay went out of his way to be nice to others with the hopes that his kindness would cause people to like and accept him. He was quiet and shy and kept silently patient.

During one of our sessions Jay shared a story with me about an experience he had when he was in second or third grade. A classmate named Juanita was a very threatening female bully. Juanita was not afraid of anyone or anything. All the children feared her and kept their distance. Juanita ruled the playground. One day, Juanita approached Jay on the playground with a snowball she made and told him to "eat it." Faced by his peers and the fierce stare of Juanita, Jay simply obeyed, took the snowball and ate it. That incident, according to Jay, set the stage of shame for many years to come. On the one hand, he avoided a brawl with the big, bullying Juanita; on the other, he suffered shame and humiliation in front of his peers.

I will get back to Jay's story a little later. It is important to point out here what Calm and Sense would encourage anyone to start doing immediately: I know from working with countless clients throughout my career that we do not see ourselves as positively as those around us do. This misunderstanding or inability is one of the most important aspects to overcome in order to gain Calm and Sense. We do not give ourselves nearly as much credit, respect, accolades or love as others who know us do. It is almost as if when we receive a compliment, we dismiss it as a mistake. "That can't be for me!" Turn this around, however, and I bet you can easily compliment someone in your life who has helped you, done a good job or shown some type of positive achievement done in a fine manner.

Sometimes we get caught up in false, negative thinking such as, "No one knows me or appreciates me" or "Why doesn't my boss see the hard work I'm doing?" My question to you is: Are you allowing others to know and appreciate you? Do you know and appreciate yourself? Without a firm and solid sense of self-appreciation and self-respect, compliments and appreciation from others fall upon deaf ears. We are unable to accept from others what we cannot give to ourselves. As a result, we continue to block the positive and seek out the negative. Some say seeing is believing; Calm and Sense says believing is seeing. That belief begins right now. Tell yourself at this moment, "I am excellent at so many things and I cannot wait to make a list of them!"

In order to begin seeing Calm and Sense work in your life, you need to begin working Calm and Sense into your life. Right now (not next week or next month), take some time and begin a true, deep evaluation of where you are in your life. Pay close attention to how you got to where you are, who or what helped you get there and what things or thoughts are recurring in your mind that cause you to feel unhappy, stuck or buried under that "slab of stone" known as *fear*.

Before you take another step, step back into yourself.

Let's get back to Jay who was stuck, unhappy and often daydreamed and fantasized about "winning" a girl's love, fitting in with the "cool" people at school and being a rock star...someday. But, soon enough, his reality brought him back to the present. As Jay got older, though, he began to think and experience things through his own eyes and mind. His parents' negativity and pessimism had already caused much damage as had the bullying from other kids. Jay lacked confidence, direction and self-respect. He felt like he did not fit in anywhere. Then he began getting high on marijuana.

Jay and his small circle of friends smoked marijuana daily. Jay loved the feeling it gave him and the perceived ability to "understand" more about life and people. Jay even started going to school more often, because the drug gave him a false sense of courage. When he smoked, the altered state of mind caused Jay to think less about the hurt, uncertainty and disbelief in himself. He even made new friends when he had pot to share.

Jay became so dependent on marijuana to "feel good" about himself that he did little unless he was high. That included going to school, going out with friends, listening to music, going to the movies, etc. Besides, being high was better than where he was (emotionally, socially and personally).

Before continuing with Jay's story, let me explain a little about how marijuana affects the brain. On its own, your brain naturally produces serotonin and endorphins. These brain chemicals are "natural" antidepressants and (for most people) they exist in your brain at a fairly constant level on your average day. Your brain knows when it needs to produce more or less and how much more or less to keep things in a natural equilibrium and it does so when necessary. Sometimes you have emotional experiences that cause your brain to produce more and some that cause your brain to produce less. For example, when you are very excited about something (like falling in love), your brain produces more for a while. These natural brain chemicals are what produce that "natural high" feeling when you are happy.

Tetrahydrocannabinol (THC) is the active chemical in marijuana that produces the "high" feeling. When someone smokes marijuana, THC is absorbed into his brain and tricks his brain into thinking it does not need to create its own serotonin or endorphins anymore, because there is plenty there already (from the marijuana). Therefore, while the brain is being supplied THC, it decreases the levels of serotonin and endorphins it produces. When the person stops smoking marijuana, the brain recognizes that the level has dropped and that it has to start producing more serotonin and endorphins again. However, it can take days or weeks for the natural serotonin and endorphin levels to refill themselves. During that time period, the person who smoked pot feels edgy, depressed and anxious and, in most cases, wants more pot (because the level of chemical that made them feel good—both innate and inhaled—has now gone down and he wants it to go back up again *now*). Can you see how this dangerous cycle works?

As much as Jay believed that he had found the answer to all his problems, what he didn't know was that his problems were only compounding. When Jay had no pot, he felt much worse than he had ever felt before he had begun using it. Guilt compounded things, because he knew smoking really was not a good thing to do and he knew using it could get him arrested or into even bigger trouble.

It is no wonder there is an epidemic of substance abuse and depression around the world today. People lack Calm and Sense and they resort to artificial, harmful, addictive, illegal remedies to feel better about their lives and who they are as people. Having Calm and Sense—that all-encompassing, secure, soothing, confident feeling—is so powerful, so liberating, so life changing! It is more addictive than any drug of which I have ever heard. It's also free and legal.

As you are thinking about that and the "remedies" you have tried in the past or may be using now, let's discuss Lynn's story.

Lynn was an attractive, thirty-eight-year-old mother of two children (ages three and one) who had never been married but had been living with Michael, the father of the two children, for about four years in a house she purchased herself several years before meeting him. Lynn had a good job in the billing department of a major national insurance company, where she had worked for almost twenty years.

Prior to meeting Michael, Lynn had a number of unsuccessful relationships and many one-night encounters. Many of her relationships were with men who were married or who were emotionally and socially unavailable to her 99 percent of the time.

On the surface, Lynn projected an image of being a very self-confident, outgoing, successful young woman with an excellent sense of humor and a penchant for partying. Everyone who knew her wanted to be more like her. She had a great job, a well decorated home of her own, personality and beauty. She certainly seemed to have it all.

Inside, however, Lynn was suffering with a bankrupt sense of self-worth. Why, one may wonder, would someone with so much going for her involve herself with married men who would not and could not give her what she truly wanted? Because Lynn, for all her surface assets, did not believe she truly deserved to be loved! She settled for second, third or fourth best all of the time. However, she *seemed* happy.

Lynn's story is a very important one, because it illustrates the misinterpretations most of us carry around as a measuring tool for our own success. We all see and know people who seem to have it all: the looks, the home, the job, the friends, the cash, etc. "Boy, what I wouldn't do to trade places with him or her!" one might say. Calm and Sense supports the old saying, "You can't judge a book by its cover."

For example, my first vehicle was an old car. I paid two hundred dollars for it before I had my driver's license. I found some old license plates in my parents' basement and put them on the car just so I could drive it the short, ten-minute drive home. I thought, *Who will know*? Well, that old car ran out of gas about four blocks from where I bought it.

Quickly, I parked the car, took the plates off it so the police wouldn't "run" them and find out they didn't belong on that car and tow it and I ran home for gas.

Upon my return to where I left the car, I found it missing! Chances are, if I had left the plates on it, the police would not have bothered with it. What I did not know in my youth was that without the plates the car became an "abandoned vehicle."

Well, after appearing in court and with the assistance of a family friend who was a police officer, I was let off with a fine and hefty lecture from the judge. I was lucky.

The point of my story, though, goes further. I loved that car with all my teenage heart! I paid for it with two hundred dollars that I had scrimped and saved. I worked on that car night and day, inside and out, top to bottom and made it purr like a kitten and run like a stallion. It *looked* like something pulled out of a lake, but that car was fast and furious, dependable and durable, sound and secure.

My best friend's father took him to a used auto lot about the same time I got my license. His dad bought him a beautiful luxury car! The wheels shone, the interior was spotless and the dashboard was clean and slippery.

But, wouldn't you know, that car broke down two days after my friend got it. It broke down many times over! It seemed like that car had a curse on it. All the shine, all the chrome, all the grandeur couldn't keep it running—but it sure did *look* good.

On the other hand, my old eyesore never missed a start. It always ran on all eight cylinders, held oil and got me everywhere I needed to be—every time. I had that beloved car for six years and it was still running like a champ when I had to get rid of it, because emissions laws changed.

Are you comparing yourself to a new or old car? What *seems* better often is not. The care and preparation I put into my car made me very proud of it. Even though it wasn't the best looking vehicle on the road, I knew every time I needed it, it was ready, willing and able to be there for me. My car was healthy on the "inside" and it was because I personally saw to it that it was. My friend's newer one was a false dream. Not cared for on the "inside," but a little paint and polish on the outside does not a car make!

Had Jay or, more importantly, Jay's parents understood this concept, all of his family's Calm and Sense would have kept their self-esteem secure in what "really matters" in life.

In Lynn's case, she was like my friend's luxury car. She looked great from all angles and was admired by many. Sadly, though, she was not firing on all cylinders. She was not taking care of herself. She was hurting deeply and did her best to hide it, just like the salesman did at his used auto lot with all those "cream puffs" on his list: polished them up with cheap soap and car wax, but didn't do the real work under the hood.

Calm and Sense does not require transformation to any other person but to our true selves. Our true selves include the selves that are currently lost, trapped in old thinking, tangled in old "wiring" and doubting the abilities we already have inherent in us. It is *not* just conforming to any other person's way of living. Changing ourselves to conform to another person's way of living or to fit into another person's life will not, does not and cannot bring Calm and Sense.

How many times have you or someone you know altered your/his/her identity to "fit" with the identity of someone else? This is quite common in relationships (see chapter 20) and usually a person's friends or family are the first to notice that "s/he has not been her/himself since dating Mr./Miss X..."

This "personality morphing" is a sign of insecurity and self-doubt. Calm and Sense pledges to help people *never* change from (or move further away from being) the true people they are. Think about the irony of personality morphing for a moment and why it simply does not make Calm or Sense. If you meet someone and he or she is attracted to you, why in the world would you feel the need to change yourself one bit? If you do, you "become" someone else and the other person may not be attracted to you at all anymore.

It was Valentine's Day when Lynn was "let go" by her married boyfriend of many years. A month later, Lynn met Michael on one of the many dating Web sites on the Internet. There was something about Michael that Lynn found attractive. Perhaps it was his shared interest in alcohol consumption, his looks or his sense of humor. Or perhaps it was the fact that he was not married. A month after they met, Michael moved into Lynn's house. Friends and relatives were a bit disconcerted. "So soon?" they worried. It didn't take long before things in Lynn's life began changing very quickly.

There was the "redecorating" of her once inviting home. Now a huge, flat screen television set hung from the quaint living room wall; track lighting replaced the coziness of her lamps; her basement became a "bar" room where she and Michael played nude darts through the night and drank to excess. Not only did Lynn's home change in its appearance and lose its sense of her personal charm, so did she, in many ways, lose her identity and spirit.

Despite this, Michael encouraged the morphing process and manipulated Lynn into becoming the person *he* wanted her to be. This is a very dangerous situation for a person who does not have Calm and Sense yet, because that person is vulnerable, feels unworthy and undeserving and lacks major self-esteem, love and respect. A person in this situation doesn't have the foundation on which to stand up for him or herself. Lynn initially believed (consciously) that Michael had her best intentions in mind, so she gave herself to him in every single possible way she could.

As a result, Lynn's credit score plummeted. In the name of "love" she indulged all of Michael's demands for things—including a forty-thousand-dollar pickup truck with a snowplow attached to it. Michael was going to begin a snowplowing business in the winter and do power washing in the summer months. Well, he *was*... but that never happened. Consequently, that same truck, purchased in Lynn's name, was being "hidden" from the repossession people who had been trying to collect it for more than twelve months of nonpayment. The truck was only one of many examples of Lynn's "love" for Michael that continued for four years.

Lynn was behind on mortgage payments for her home; they had gone without phone service, electricity, heat and water numerous times. Michael hadn't held a job for longer than two weeks since he and Lynn met. He reported to her that he got jobs, but then there were always stories about a boss who was a jerk, the company's business was slow, "they will call me when they need me again" and so on.

Early on in the relationship, Lynn brought Michael to meet her family and friends. After meeting him, most knew there was "just something about him" that didn't seem right. Sometimes there were visits when Michael abruptly stood up and left, saying he "got a bad vibe" from a friend or family member of Lynn's. Soon enough, Lynn did not see her family and friends anymore. She got pregnant and gave birth after their first year together. As their child grew older, Michael continued going out until all hours of the night, not working, being verbally (and possibly physically) abusive to Lynn and certainly not being a dad. Lynn made excuses for Michael routinely.

At one point, Lynn said she was done with Michael. She asked her sister Sheila to loan her money so she could take care of a few things and get Michael out of the house. Throughout their lives, Lynn and Sheila were very close. But even that relationship had deteriorated by the time Lynn asked for the loan. Sheila declined to loan Lynn money until Michael was out of the house.

Apparently, Sheila had a bad feeling about things, because about a month after Lynn's request for money in an effort to "get Michael out," Lynn was pregnant with a second baby. Michael was going nowhere (in more ways than one).

Looking at Lynn and her life at this point, rather than seeing her as the gorgeous, bubbly, successful and admired woman that she "was," we probably would judge her life and position to be pathetic and see her as a worn and defeated woman living in a situation in which no one would ever want or choose to be involved.

This brings me to another very important aspect of Calm and Sense thinking: learning to separate self-worth from circumstances. You are *not* your situation. You are *not* your circumstances. Your situation and your circumstances are not *you*. Situations and circumstances are things that happen in life. Sometimes choices we make determine the situations and circumstances we face. However, even if the situations and circumstances we face are the direct result of choices we made and even if the situations and circumstances we find ourselves in affect our lives in big ways, *who we are* is not defined by them.

Just because we see and know people in our lives and assume they must have or be doing something right does not always mean that they actually are. Looks can be—and often are—deceiving.

If Lynn truly was the person people perceived her to be, she would have never allowed her life to be taken over, manipulated and controlled by Michael—or *anyone*, for that matter! Calm and Sense empowers us to detect undesirable circumstances, people and situations and *avoid* them, not involve ourselves in them. Had Lynn had a clearer understanding of who she was as a person, with self-respect, self-love and self-appreciation, Michael probably would never have gotten past the first date. Lynn's family and friends quickly picked up on Michael's character. How did Lynn miss it?

How do we "miss it" when we become too involved in situations that feed Negative Nick and leave Positive Pat starving? We miss it, because we are busy filling in the empty spaces we have not taken care of by ourselves, hungrily taking in what our partners are feeding us, no matter whether it is good or bad for us. Feeding Negative Nick makes it much easier for us to believe that we don't deserve lives of our own or to make decisions on our own. In that mind-set, we can't see clearly. And in that place, we often miss seeing what's obvious to others.

With regard to personality morphing in relationships, not all of our potential partners are like Michael. What if *you* met a person who already had Calm and Sense and *you* started to "morph" into everything that person was, leaving behind your friends, your sense of self, your interests, your passions, your hobbies, etc. The person with Calm and Sense would recognize this in you and think, *You are not the person I thought you were. You are changing to please me. This is strange! Don't you have a life of your own?*

And this is *imperative* in your acquisition of Calm and Sense! You must have a life that is yours, wholly and totally! Handcrafted and personally made by you, for you and defining the uniqueness, individuality and essence of you and only you. When you don't have this, it is too easy to be drawn into the definition of a life someone else has made for you and away from Calm and Sense. And without Calm and Sense, it's too easy to be lost on the road of life and not know where you are or where you are going!

Chapter 13

Believe in Yourself

As a therapist, I have learned that helping people believe in themselves is truly my most useful skill. Once you have mastered the ability to believe in yourself, you can achieve anything! Can you recall being a child and learning how to ride a bicycle? Therapy is to life as training wheels are to bicycling. Do you remember the day or moment when you just *knew* that it was time for those training wheels to come off and you could ride freely, confidently and "all by yourself"? It was a grand, proud moment for you, as well as for those around you, wasn't it?

For me, there is no greater joy than watching my clients challenge their fears, accept some assistance, use the instruction and finally "get it"! I often tell my clients, "The real therapy is not occurring in my office; it's occurring in your life, in real life." Calm and Sense living is like riding a bike: once you learn it, you never forget. For most people, getting started is the most difficult part. Why? Because so many of us have trouble believing in ourselves.

In searching ourselves for who we really are, most of us get stuck and are quick to come up with excuses that keep us from our own individualities. We find reasons not to believe in ourselves, because it seems easier than believing that we are and we can. We are a generation that desires and expects "quick fixes" for everything from a headache to improving our lives! Calm and Sense living requires us to slow down and dismiss the rush, to demonstrate patience with ourselves and with our growth. We did not get to where we are overnight and we should not push ourselves hastily. There is a Chinese proverb that states, "With time and patience the mulberry leaf becomes a silk gown." Calm and Sense says, "With patience and curiosity, the person you will find is the person you are destined and driven to be."

Impatience is destructive in many ways when you are learning to live in Calm and Sense. There are no shortcuts to Calm and Sense, nor should there be! The search for ourselves is not a trip we want to rush. We want to see all of the sights, hear all of the sounds and not miss a lesson, person, thought or step we need to get there. Besides, all of our "rushing" in the world has actually distracted us enough already. No one has ever won that race. It's time to step out of the competition.

Impatience can also be detrimental to Calm and Sense because it is, in many ways, a setup for failure. When we are looking for instant results all of the time, we miss the small accomplishments we make along the way. It is indeed the many small goals and changes we make in our lives that bring about Calm and Sense collectively. "If we miss the slights we lose our sights!" Self-care and Calm and Sense demand patience, persistence and perseverance. Many of us have been neglecting to give ourselves those gifts throughout our entire lives. The time to start is *now*! It is also time to start reminding yourself that *you are worth the wait.* If you begin practicing what you have learned so far, Calm and Sense is already trying to find you.

Let's return to Jay's story. Jay became increasingly depressed. As time passed, his pot smoking continued, but it was no longer providing him with the relief he used to get from the substance. The biggest lie of narcotics is: "Use me and I will help you feel better and more 'yourself.' I'll always be there for you!" (That is, until you need more or something stronger.) Jay withdrew from friends and family and spent most of his time alone in his room listening to sad music, desperately wanting to go somewhere, anywhere, away from where he was. Escape was nowhere in sight. He felt guilty, imperfect and out of touch with the world.

Jay was in English class one day and, as was usual for him, he was high. Many times Jay "dozed off" during various classes, but perhaps because Jay wasn't acting out or had teachers who were not perceptive enough to think that a student who sleeps frequently during classes might have a problem of some sort, no one bothered him or made an issue of it. But on this particular day, Jay had a substitute teacher for English class who *did* "bother" Jay when the teacher observed him sleeping in class. The substitute knew about drug symptoms and sent Jay to the school nurse. (This is proper procedure in schools these days if a teacher suspects a student is under the influence of a drug.)

Upon examining Jay, the nurse felt she had enough medical evidence to support calling Jay's mother to come pick him up and take him for a drug test at the local diagnostics center.

In that phone conversation, Jay's mother hurled some accusatory words at the nurse. She told the nurse, "My son would never do such a thing!" She commented irritably that she would have to "leave work and lose pay" in order to come and get her son. Her ire continued when she came to the school, got Jay and took him to the laboratory.

At the lab, Jay tested positive for cannabis (pot). Jay's parents lectured him on how he had "disgraced the family" and "would never amount to anything." They also repeatedly asked him, "How could you do this to *us*?" instead of focusing on what their son was doing to himself. (Remember, Jay's parents were very self-absorbed.)

When the school administrators learned about the test results, they again followed proper procedure. The administrators informed Jay's parents that he would have to be seen for a mandated substance abuse evaluation and assessment and then follow whatever recommendations the therapist made. At this point I met Jay. He was "mandated" to see me.

I found Jay to be intelligent, sensitive, insightful, funny and respectful. Jay saw himself as a "loser, ugly, boring, shy and stupid." He didn't like himself, know himself or believe in himself. Jay needed an Emotional Makeover and he needed it immediately.

Do you need an Emotional Makeover? Take a few moments and listen to what your thoughts are telling you. Our thoughts dictate to us our belief in who we are. (Remember, in chapter 2 we talked about Sense and I provided you with details on how to take control over and eliminate destructive thinking and self-talk.) Now, let's consider how you currently see yourself. Do you find it easy to point out your flaws and your undesirable feelings about who you are? Do you believe in yourself? In your abilities? Do you believe you deserve the life you envision for yourself? If you answered yes only to the first question, then you sound like a candidate for an Emotional Makeover.

Therapy does not create anything for people that does not already exist. Therapy deals in *fact* (e.g., I am healthy; I am strong; I am compassionate) and eliminates fiction (e.g., the clothes I wear define who I am;

the amount of money I make determines whether or not I deserve to be happy; I am not attractive enough to find true love) from people's lives. Many of my clients, and perhaps you as well, spend much—if not most—of their time living in fictional views of who they really are as people. They see the things around them as defining who they are. They see their lack of attaining particular goals as proof that they are not capable. It's difficult to really believe in yourself when you don't even have a clear, realistic, factual view of who you are. Calm and Sense demands fact, evidence and proof of our being. Calm and Sense does not encourage or support pity, penalty or perjury for who we are or who we may have been in the past. Once we can see clearly who we are, we can't help but begin to believe in ourselves.

Calm and Sense, like good therapy, does not pull us back into the past. Instead, Calm and Sense allows the future to pull us forward, letting the past push us ahead, moving ever further away from the convoluted thoughts, destructive behaviors and beliefs, unsatisfying relationships and false, fictional lives by which we used to believe we were surrounded. Calm and Sense propels us away from the false beliefs that others are somehow better than we are or that we are weak, slaves to our pasts and unable to ever get ahead or feel good about ourselves. Calm and Sense helps us to identify our true qualities, skills and characteristics so that we can experience today and move into the future with unshakable belief in ourselves.

As you read the information in this book, are you beginning to feel the future's pull and the past's push? Allow yourself to experience it. This feeling is real. Remember: You cannot change your past, but you *are* the author of your future. That's the promise of Calm and Sense. You have only the future to which to look forward. What would you like your life to look like tomorrow? In six months? One year? Ten years? Imagine and begin. Harness the power of the present and journey with confidence into the future. You can do it. Believe in yourself!

Chapter 14

Live in the Moment

Where does your journey begin? Right here. Right now. Calm and Sense requires us to always *live in the moment*. In doing this, we form our destinies.

Calm and Sense believes that our futures are *now*. Every day, every moment, every situation we find ourselves in forms for us our destinies. For many of us and because we are a generation that demands instant gratification, if we do not see "immediate results" coming from our efforts, we lose interest or belief in what we are doing.

This is a human characteristic that has evolved with time and technology. Calm and Sense is compelled to address it. In a life where most things are a "click," pill, push or text away, we have lost a tremendous amount of what ancestors called "patience." Most of our demand for quick fixes does not come solely from ourselves. We have become "conditioned" to expect immediate results through our exposure to technology, jobs, friends, families, the healthcare industry, etc. What technology and the world have *not* taught us, however, is what the Dutch have been saying for centuries: "A handful of patience is worth more than a bushel of brains."

I stress patience throughout Calm and Sense, because I truly desire that my readers and clients find it and practice it dutifully and willingly. Why? Because patience is the foundation of maturity and its value reaches far beyond the moment in which it is practiced. I understand well how we all want results as quickly as possible and I agree that results are what keep our motivation high and our interests peaked, but some things are not to be rushed and are well worth the wait. *You* are worth the wait and the more patience you allow yourself and others in life, the quicker you will see Calm and Sense embrace you.

Too often I have seen my clients "give up" prematurely and miss opportunities in their lives where results were within reach. I have heard "I should have waited" or "I couldn't stand it anymore, so I did this or that again..." which brought only more disappointment, despair and "old thinking" back into the picture instead of belief in Calm and Sense. This is why I and Calm and Sense implore you to "stop and smell the roses" when you feel the past pulling you back instead of pushing you forward.

Additionally, patience reduces stress and blood pressure and will immediately benefit your well-being mentally and physically. Stress causes hair loss, heart attacks, ulcers, acne and a host of other medical problems. So, if you *must* have immediate results to motivate your practice of patience, consider those immediate "benefits." And if you *really* get stuck, remember the Ten Year Rule (chapter 1) to gauge your response to a trying situation.

Remember your wiring that existed to protect you from things in your *past*? Now is the time to begin to "disconnect" some of those faulty connections: the ones that spark sometimes, because the wiring is old and frayed; the wiring that "shorts out" from time to time, keeping us in the dark from who we truly are. In order to avoid any future blackouts or possible fires in your thinking, it is time to reevaluate the necessity of your circuits and get started on your Emotional Makeover!

Jay was living a life of destructive, negative, self-defeating and fictitious beliefs about who he was as a person. I have provided you with a factual history of Jay's life. I added nothing and left nothing of either positive or negative weight out of its narrative. Can you detect any evidence that could substantiate any of his self-loathing?

You may respond, "Well, he *was* smoking pot and probably doing other drugs, wasn't he?" Yes, he was. However, is that in itself a reason for this young man to believe he was ugly, unworthy, stupid, boring or unlovable? The sad fact of the matter is that Jay was conditioned to believe these things by the messages he received from his primary caregivers (his parents) growing up and through his formative years into young adulthood. There did come a point for Jay when he said his parents' "negativity" didn't affect him "that much anymore," but the "wiring" was already installed and friction ran through his brain constantly like electricity through a lightning rod!

Somehow, Jay suffered silently. He did not act out his hurt and anger but rather pointed it toward himself. This internalization of anger and resentment reinforced his parents' constant criticism and he, in effect, became what they said he would be. Conversely, some people act out hurt, rage and resentment by becoming violent with others, condescending, controlling, bitter and mean. Remember Juanita, the girl who bullied Jay on the playground? She was just a child, but all the children feared her bullying behavior. Was that her fault? Doubtful.

Since Calm and Sense works to separate fact from fiction, truth from lies and evidence from hearsay, the first step to helping Jay find Calm and Sense was to take his accusations of himself to the superior court of Calm and Sense thinking.

Jay lacked a person or people in his life whom he could truly trust and look up to. He had no Identity Fortifiers (see chapter 10 for more information about Identity Fortifiers). Ideally, when we are children, our parents or other adult figures in our lives provide role models. But that "person" or role model can appear at any time. Do not be fooled into thinking, "Well, I never had a good role model as a child, so I never received the benefit of guidance, support and trust." That person, that role model, can materialize at any time during the course of a life and, in fact, will materialize over and over again with various people we meet. All Calm and Sense requires is that we seek him or her in all we do.

It was my honor to "materialize" for Jay. As he began to trust me and because I didn't ignore any of his obvious or subtle calls for help as his teachers and parents did, my meetings with him began to help him gather strength and the ability to get a clearer picture of who he *really* was as a person. This person was in clear contrast to the one he had previously "thought" himself to be. Jay's previous self began to slowly file itself away into the fiction section, while his new self bore brighter, more colorful pages in the nonfiction category where it belonged.

Calm and Sense encourages us to surround ourselves with people who truly have our best interests in heart and mind. It is only by these relationships that we can gain an honest reflection of who we are, what our strengths are, how we make a difference in the world and why we deserve to be loved and appreciated. Many of my clients are (or were) surrounding themselves with people who do (or did) not support them emotionally and would only continue reinforcing the negative thoughts they had of themselves. People without Calm and Sense seek these negative relationships unconsciously, because it is truly all they know. It is comfortable in a destructive way, because they do not yet understand that they deserve more and better.

No matter who you were or what you did in the past, Calm and Sense assures you that you can change your future one moment at a time! What I taught Jay is what Calm and Sense teaches everyone: *We are all good people and deserve love, value and respect.* If you tell yourself this eleven times a day, every day, as practiced by many Eastern religions, you will begin to feel the power of Calm and Sense very quickly. They are powerful words and have brought countless people I know out of despair and self-doubt. I recommend beginning to use them immediately.

Jay did and soon Jay was challenging his own destructive thinking and began using the "looking for evidence" technique I taught him whenever his self-doubt arose. "Show me the money!" became his mantra in sessions with me as he began to joke about his old ways of thinking. He had a great sense of humor and began using it more freely. Jay also was a truly gifted person and, not surprisingly, had a keen sense of empathy and understanding of others who were suffering.

Jay completed high school and entered college. His plan was to study psychology (a proud moment for me, I must say) and enter the healing profession. There was no doubt in my mind that he would do well. His intelligence, respectfulness, *patience*, sense of humor and confidence were well uncovered at this point. Gone were the doubts, sadness and feelings of alienation.

Jay's parents did not change much, nor did they participate often in Jay's treatment. By age eighteen, however, Jay had become a capable young man and did well even without their support. Jay made a profound self-discovery about his parents that I use to this day with clients who have unresolved issues regarding their parents. Jay said, "I have come to believe that given the problems they (his parents) had (emotionally, socially, physically), they did the best they could. I think if anyone can come to that conclusion about their parents and truly believe they couldn't have done any better, then there is no reason not to forgive and love them. They did bring me life. They are my parents, for better or worse."

I have borrowed Jay's nugget of wisdom numerous times to help my clients put that possibility to the test. Did your parents do "the best they could"? Can you absolutely believe that? If so, then you have made a major breakthrough emotionally and understand that parents are not always perfect, prepared or positive role models. In many cases, our parents did not have Calm and Sense. This leaves us responsible for doing a bit of "self-parenting" to fill in the gaps. You may be wondering, *What about parents who blatantly abused their children? Do they deserve forgiveness? Did they really do the best they could have raising their children?*

Those are excellent questions and they bring us back to the story of Michael and Lynn. With two young children, Lynn continued to stay with Michael even though he was controlling her every move, not working, spending more money than they could afford, emotionally abusing her, sending pictures of his "private parts" to someone from his cell phone (Lynn found these pictures), breaking the law by "hiding" a truck for which a repossession agency was searching and leaving the house every evening and returning home at 6 A.M. Meanwhile, Lynn put the children in daycare every weekday while she worked and Michael stayed home.

Lynn said she saw little, if any, of her family and friends anymore. Sometimes she professed her decision to leave Michael "for real this time," but it never happened. Because of her decision to remain in such a destructive relationship, she lost the support of all the people who loved her most. Lynn's family and friends no longer provided her with pep talks or strategies about how she could make it on her own and free herself from Michael. If Lynn wanted to rebuild her life, she had to prove it "for real this time."

Lynn met with me off and on for about eight months. True to form, she "talked the Calm and Sense talk" but did not choose to "walk the Calm and Sense walk," much like her promises to friends and family to leave Michael which never resulted in any action. Calm and Sense requires a commitment to change, courage to face and conquer fears and the desire to truly want a better life. Calm and Sense is always there for the taking, but you must be ready to take it.

Lynn's story, at least at this point, does not have a happy ending. She chose to stay with Michael and to enable the lifestyle he was living while sacrificing all she had to do so. Is this a parent her children will one day be able to say did "the best she could?" Maybe.

Sometimes people are not truly prepared to make their lives better. As hard as it is to believe this, many people fear success, because they do not know it. Failures are easy when they are expected and when people set out to fail, failure is what they will find. My belief is that Lynn deeply feared that she could not become the person she truly is. I also believe that many people who remain in lives of despair, like Lynn's, do so because it is comfortable despite being destructive.

Self-doubt is fueled by sabotaged efforts. Sabotaged efforts are the creation of people who fear success. With each "failure" one can at least say, "I knew I would never be able to do that." It's a dysfunctional process that reinforces the negative thoughts and beliefs that people carry about who they are. But, at least to them, they can rely on it in a world where they cannot rely on anything else of value. Lynn erroneously believed that she may not have had much, but at least she had the ability to know what she could not do. And she believed she could not take a leap of faith or make the commitment to Calm and Sense, because she felt "the devil she knows is better than the devil she doesn't." Her living in the here and now consisted of survival.

How do you feel about your current existence? When you peer into your mind at a snapshot of yourself right here, right now, what do you see? If you don't like what you see, the time to start doing something about it is *now*.

Chapter 15

Surviving

Survival is something we all pursue, on many levels, in many different ways. Some of us define survival as staying above a certain level of income. To others, survival literally means staying alive in circumstances where their physical well-being is challenged on a daily basis. Some would say that survival means getting through one stressful day at a time as a single parent on welfare and ending each day with everyone healthy, fed, clothed, tucked into bed and safe. Still others might see survival as guiding their staff toward generating enough sales to keep their company afloat and therefore keeping their jobs as company executives. No matter what our definitions of survival are, we all face some of the same challenges when struggling to survive: identifying our needs, managing them appropriately and confronting fear with courage.

I met Annie on a very hot, humid, rainy day in July. I had reservations about scheduling the appointment, because she hadn't shown up at the first two we had scheduled. The phone number she had initially given me was "not in service" when I called her. A few days later she called to reschedule and then missed that appointment as well. When people miss appointments and don't notify me in advance, they have taken up time slots that could have been used by other people in need. I had my doubts after Annie didn't show for intake appointment number two and her phone still was "not in service." When Annie called me for a third try she was very apologetic. There was something in her voice that alerted my intuition and told me to give her one more chance. So I did.

Annie arrived rain-soaked and shaking. She fumbled with her umbrella and jacket, obviously nervous and somewhat embarrassed. As I tried to settle her down and helped her get comfortable, I noticed she was wearing a long sleeve shirt on what was a very hot and humid day. I could understand the raincoat, but the clothes puzzled me.

Despite arriving wet and disheveled, Annie was a stunning twenty-eight-year-old woman with dark hair, blue eyes, high cheekbones and a slim figure. She could have been a model with her unique, exotic looks, but her trembling voice told a story of desperation and tragedy I had never encountered in all my years as a therapist.

Annie was born in a coastal town to Linda and Frank, a young married couple who were both age twenty-nine at the time of Annie's birth. Frank owned a fishing boat that took people out to sea for bluefishing every day. He had inherited the family business when his father passed away. Frank was well acquainted with the charter boat business, having worked with his father for many years on the same boat. Frank was a good captain, paid his crew generously and lived an honest life. He was happy for what he had and was always willing to help out friends who needed him.

Frank had been raised by his father; his mother had passed away from cancer when he was only six years old. Frank's father never remarried and had no other children. He always called the sea "Mother, because it provides me food, structure, nurturing and a home for my family."

Linda attended college and graduated with a degree in social work. She was employed by a social service agency for a number of years, until she decided that she wanted to start a business of her own. Approaching age thirty, Linda also started thinking about raising a family and wanted to do so in a "calmer" environment.

Linda moved to the same coastal town as Frank and opened a candle shop downtown. By this time, Linda's father had passed away after having had three massive heart attacks; Linda's mom was in an assisted living residence. Linda was an only child.

Frank met Linda at a chamber of commerce meeting, as they were both business owners in the town. As the story goes, it was love at first sight. Both twenty-eight years old, they married and began a life together. A year later, Frank and Linda celebrated the birth of their daughter, Annie: their pride and joy!

Annie remembers a "great life" as a child, running the beaches, riding with her dad on his boat (now renamed *Princess Ann*) and spending time with her mother making candles in her shop. Annie enjoyed school and had lots of friends, two dogs, two cats and a hamster.

When Annie was nine, she and her parents were driving to an amusement park they had been to many times before. They were all excited for a day of fun on the boardwalk. Annie remembered the wild anticipation of cotton candy, the Ferris wheel and all the other rides she and her dad would enjoy together (her mom was a bit squeamish when it came to the rides). Suddenly there were screeching tires, screams and a very loud bang.

Annie's next memory was waking up in a hospital room with big white lights over her head, machines beeping around her and tubes in her arms and nose. There were strange people in strange clothes walking around her, looking at her. "Where's my mommy? Where's my daddy?" she asked. Annie was never to see either of them again.

This began the tragedy of Annie's life. There were no relatives who came forward to care for her. During the next years she was in and out of foster homes. Sometimes she was in one "for a while" and others "not long at all."

Annie remembers being sexually abused by various foster fathers from the time she was eleven years old until she turned fourteen. Annie said they told her, "This is what your mommy and daddy told us to do to you, so you better listen and behave." Her fear was so great that most of the time she just froze, like captive prey trapped by savage beasts.

When Annie was fourteen years old, she and another girl in one of the foster homes ran away. They wound up on the streets of a nearby city and were quickly approached by "a really nice man" who promised to help them both. He fed them, bought them clothes and introduced them to alcohol, marijuana, cocaine, methamphetamines and ecstasy. Annie felt the drugs helped her escape her fears and pain. *This is much better than it was in foster care!* she thought as the drugs slowly lured her deeper into euphoria. Nice clothes, a nice place to live (actually, it was a seedy motel, but Annie thought a place where she wasn't a maid was great), good food and drugs. *I can do this!* she thought. Then came the catch.

The "nice guy" who "saved" her came for repayment. He began to abuse Annie sexually and to teach her how to make money by prostituting herself. Now fully dependent on drugs, fearful of going back to the foster home where she would definitely be "punished severely" for running away and without family to help her, what was she to do?

Annie also had a fear and distrust of police. After all, it was the police who escorted her to many foster homes and she regularly saw police bringing other children back after they ran away. She did not believe the police were going to be of any assistance to her.

So began Annie's life as a street walker in the dark alleys of the city. She was turning tricks, doing drugs and being beaten and was trapped in a world that several years ago she could never have even imagined existed.

We'll return to Annie's story soon. Consider the feeling you get when you learn that someone to whom you are attracted is also attracted to you. Then you begin dating and all of a sudden life is wonderful! "Problems" you had that felt big and troublesome somehow don't seem so big and bad anymore. Bad habits you may have been "trying" (remember trying does not exist in Calm and Sense) to remedy, such as overeating, drinking too much, biting your nails, etc., vanish miraculously. Call it love or call it lust, these emotions pack some very strong power!

It is also true that when we suffer significant losses in our lives, all of our other "problems" don't seem so troublesome anymore. Consider the loss of a parent, child, beloved pet, friend, etc. Nothing bears as much significance as the loss of a loved one.

We experience moments in our lives when something terribly painful (e.g., the death of a loved one, the loss of a job) or amazingly wonderful (e.g., falling in love, getting a prized promotion) happens. Those events are so emotionally intense that they have a way of putting everything else we were worrying about into a clearer perspective. While experiencing the new, intense emotion, we are instantly and temporarily freed from the things that had been troubling us most. Even though these moments of liberation come as a result of extreme happiness or extreme sadness, it is often only through them that we witness how our thinking can and does suddenly become focused. Because of the joy or the crisis, when we are overcome with high levels of happiness or sadness, there is no more procrastination, self-doubt or resistance to living in the here and now—we move into "survival mode." We have no choice but to deal with the reality of our priorities and we dismiss or put on hold the other stressors like a problem boss or an unpaid bill. They become secondary to the matter at hand. Calm and Sense says we all need to live in the here and now and we should not be waiting for some intense emotional event to get us there! The challenge of Calm and Sense is to harness that ability, use it every day and gain emotional freedom, self-satisfaction and self-determination from it in all we do.

For most people, the newness and excitement of falling in love eventually fades. We also eventually come to accept loss in our lives as we go through the grieving process. When the emotional intensity subsides, our lives return to what they were and we often find ourselves again struggling with the inability to focus, make decisions or even feel good about ourselves. We find ourselves participating in "if" and "when" thinking again, procrastinating, blaming and making excuses not to do something, instead of continuing to live in the here and now. We know now, though, that the ability to focus and to live in the moment *was there* and that we *could do it*. When you have Calm and Sense, you also have the tools to continue to have self-esteem and live in the present—all the time! You don't need a major, emotionally intense event to force you there.

"If" Versus "How" Thinking

Unfortunately, Annie did not have this perspective when she lived a life of deep, dark fear as a prostitute for seven years. All the while, through the depths of depression, anger and self-disgust she experienced, she always told herself, "There has to be more to my life than this." She remembered viewing the ocean—the sea which her father called "Mother"—and tried to focus on that vision, seeking answers. She remembered her playful hamster and the smell of her mother's cooking. These thoughts brought her momentary comfort, but she slowly sunk deeper into uncertainty. "How did this happen to me?" Annie pitied herself and, as sad as she was, she was also angry and bitter. She was angry with her parents for "leaving" her; she was angry at the world and at herself as she wondered why she survived the car accident when her parents did not. Countless times she wished she had died with them. "If only..."

There are two things of which we can be guaranteed in this life: death and change. Nothing else is owed us or granted to us. Calm and Sense is not about death; it is about change. A lot of people say, "I don't like change." What does that indicate? My professional experience tells me that it reflects an inner fear. Fear of change. This is puzzling, however, because for all the people who say they don't like change, there are as many who wish they could change their lives.

Calm and Sense requires an openness and an invitation to change and adaptability in our lives. To truly be able to adapt to change and not fear it, we must become "how" thinkers, not "if" thinkers. "If" does not propel us any further than a hurricane can budge a boulder. "How" can teach us to make the boulder move on its own by carving it into a wheel.

How do we become "how" thinkers instead of "if" thinkers? "*If* I could only have a better job, relationship, more money, less sadness" versus "*How* can I get a better job, a better relationship, more money, be less sad?" The word *how* automatically propels us to action and our plan has sprung wings. "If" allows the power within us to be overshadowed and made ineffective by some other source of power outside of ourselves. "If" leaves us totally dependent on something or someone to come along and grant us our most desired wishes, lifestyles, needs, etc. "If I could win the lottery" or "If I could find a genie in a bottle." The wise and truly motivated do not know much about "if"; they believe in and seek "how."

Here's another great difference between "if" thinking and "how" thinking: "If" cannot be taught to us, ever! So, while you are waiting on ifs to come around and you get stuck, what do you do? "I've been waiting around to see *if* I can improve my life by getting another job. So far, nothing has been happening. Can you show me *if* I will?" No one can.

On the other hand, here is the way it works with "how": "I've noticed you seem to be very happy in your relationship and career. I would love to know *how* you do it! Can you teach me *how* you do it?" You see, someone *can* give you specific instructions or specific suggestions of how something can be done. And, in a deeper sense, Calm and Sense *is* the "how"!

Calm and Sense encourages us all to learn *how* to be who we want, get what we need on our own, enjoy beneficial relationships and believe in ourselves. If you are a "how" thinker, you can always find assistance and you can *always* succeed. "If," on the other hand, leaves you stranded, alone, waiting and wishing. "How" propels you into action! "How" also allows room for guidance from others if needed.

As you read these two statements, pay attention to your immediate reactions to each:

- If I could have anything in the world I wanted...
- How can I get the thing I most want in the world?

Do you notice the difference between the two? The first statement is wishful thinking. It instills a sense of fantasy. The second statement is action-producing thinking. It immediately sets your thinking into action to create reality.

Now read the two statements out loud. Listen to your tone, volume and energy. When we say the first statement out loud, most of us will find that the power behind it is somewhat like a lazy river. When we say the second statement out loud, most of us will find that there is more strength and determination behind the words. That's the difference between "if" and "how" thinking.

Unfortunately, many of us get caught up in the "ifs" of life and do not get to the "hows". "Hows" are what direct us to the new and exciting things in life that Calm and Sense requires to keep our SEP portfolios active, updated and growing. "Hows" also lead us to ideas, people, places and activities we may have never even thought we would enjoy. "If" thinking leads to false feelings and beliefs that life cannot get better. "*If* I could only be thin *then* I would be happy!" "*If* I didn't grow up in such a dysfunctional family *then* I would be 'normal'." The ifs can go on and on without helping us move forward one bit; it's the hows that start us moving toward the changes we seek.

Imagine Benjamin Franklin (as the story goes) standing outside in a thunderstorm observing the lightning in the sky and thinking, *If I could harness that power from there down here, maybe it would be useful.* Then imagine Ben shrugging his shoulders and walking back in his house. Where would we be today? Luckily for us, Ben was a "how" guy. He thought, *How can I get that power from up there to down here?* Then he flew a kite in the sky—because he figured out a way to get where he couldn't—and got the shock of his life, which ultimately lit and powered the world. Now *that* is the power of "how."

Annie had been living with "if" instead of "how" thinking for too long. By the time I met Annie, she had been arrested numerous times for prostitution, shoplifting, loitering and various drug-related offenses. She had spent time in jail as well, with no sentence ever lasting more than ninety days or so. She had lived with various men off and on, none of whom, she said, "ever gave a damn about me really or ever told me a stitch of truth." She was truly used and abused by many and had the scars to prove it.

Remember the long sleeve shirt I mentioned Annie was wearing when I met her that awfully hot and humid summer day? That shirt was Annie's way of hiding the telltale signs of a tragic life. Underneath the sleeves, Annie's arms were marred with track marks from needles, scars from self-abuse and suicide attempts and bruises from the physical abuse she had been receiving from Brent, her most recent "boyfriend."

I learned that Annie's missed appointments with me were because of threats she had received from Brent. He had repeatedly threatened her and beat her when she did not "obey" his demands and he had a very strong resistance to her wanting to "go talk to somebody." That "somebody" was me.

I was very curious to find out how Annie had found me. She explained to me that she had sought assistance at a church and the pastor of that church, a good friend of mine, referred her to me and set her up temporarily in a shelter.

Annie was an intriguing person. She was a riddle and she was mysterious. Her angelic face did not match her battered arms; her Calm and well-carried demeanor did not seem in place with a "street smart" and savvy prostitute. Her soft-spoken voice was not what you would expect from a woman who had served jail time and had been hardened by life on the streets. Though far from "innocent," she was innocent in her speech and bearing. Annie had the charm of a nine-year-old girl, which is where I believe she "left" herself when her parents were killed. The life she had lived from that moment on belonged to someone else, not to her, not to Annie.

When I interview new clients in my practice, I always ask the question, "Why now?" I want to know what has brought that person to me at that specific time in his or her life. I want to know what, if anything, he or she has already tried to do to help him or herself. Every person I treat has a different answer to this question. The answer, no matter what it is, provides me with information and explains many things about the person. Each person's answer to this question helps me determine the course and purpose for that person's care and gets us started moving in the right direction. For many people, as it was with Annie, therapy is a "last resort," turned to only when other methods do not bring about the desired effect or results.

So I asked Annie, "Why now?"

"I miss my parents," she replied. At that moment, her answer was puzzling and childlike but came to make perfect sense the more she explained. With tears in her eyes (and in mine), Annie recounted the story of her childhood I shared with you.

Broken, battered, addicted, lonely, homeless, penniless, friendless, orphaned, depressed and lost. That's how Annie described herself. But then Annie said something wonderful. Annie asked me to help her learn *how* to get her life back! "*How*" is the magic word that causes us to take action and make change.

Annie never once said, "*If* I can get off the drugs..." or "*If* I had a place to live..." "*...then* I would feel better!" She never said, "*If* I can get out of this relationship..." She just did it. She took the leap of faith. She got away from Brent and was finally free and able to come and see me. All those other things—getting off drugs, finding a permanent place to live, etc.—were important and not to be overlooked, but she knew that and so did I. She also knew that in learning *how* to get her life back, she would also learn *how* to do those things as well.

Assessing and Prioritizing Our Needs

In life, from time to time, we all have the tendency to look at each and every "problem" we have. Collectively, as a large group comprising many individual issues, these "problems" can seem overwhelming and impossible to overcome. Annie had the innate perception to know that making her life better would also entail mending the various individual problems she had. Annie was able to see that many of the individual issues she was struggling with were all part of one bigger issue. You see, when we become distracted by too many problems, we lose sight of the ultimate goal, which is to live more comfortably, peacefully and meaningfully and without disturbances from outside situations, people or circumstances.

Calm and Sense tells us to scale down our problem finder! Instead of looking for all kinds of little, individual things that we identify as problems in our lives, we should focus on the singular issue of who we are now and how we can become the person we most want to be. With that mind-set and with that singular goal, our "many problems" will be solved as we move along.

You may be wondering, "Where do I begin?" That's a fair and reasonable question. The answer is that you must assess your immediate needs.

According to renowned psychologist Dr. Abraham Maslow, all of us have what he referred to as a "Hierarchy of Needs." This hierarchy begins with physiological necessities such as food, water, sleep and oxygen and ends with our need for Self-Actualization. Here is what Maslow's Hierarchy of Needs looks like, starting with the most important and basic needs:

- Physiological Needs (food, water, sleep, oxygen)
- Safety Needs (shelter, stable environment)
- Love and Belonging (support and affection from others, intimacy and a sense of belonging)
- Esteem (self-respect, mastery, accomplishment)
- Self-Actualization (fulfillment of potential in life, wholeness)

Dr. Maslow believed that humans must accomplish and acquire these needs, in succession, in order to reach and satisfy the next need.[1] In other words, if you have no food to eat (a physiological need), a place to be protected from the weather (a safety need) is not the priority; food is. If you live in an unstable, hostile environment (a safety need), it is of little value to seek a romance (a belongingness and love need) until a stable environment can be established and so on, leading to the most important need in life, which Maslow believed to be Self-Actualization. Self-Actualization is, in effect, the fulfillment of all the preceding needs. Having them all frees us to find wholeness, completeness and true fulfillment in our lives.

Let's get back to the question of "Where do I begin?" We've already discussed that you must assess your immediate needs. Depending on your circumstances, you may feel like you have an overwhelming list of needs and also feel as if many of them qualify as "immediate." How do you truly determine which of your needs is immediate? This is where Maslow's hierarchy provides the most value to Calm and Sense. When looking at our list of needs, no matter how long or short, and grouping them according to Maslow's categories, we can clearly see which are immediate and which are not. Immediate needs are those that fall in the Physiological Needs category. If you have no concerns in that category, then your most immediate needs would be the ones that are in the Safety Needs category and so forth.

In Annie's situation, once she left Brent, she identified that she needed food and a place to stay to be and feel safe. What point would it have made for her if she had begun her journey to regaining her life by seeking to fulfill her need, for example, for a satisfying, loving relationship? None. That would have led to frustration and a continuation of the cycle out of which she was trying to break. Both Calm and Sense and Dr. Maslow tell us that it is impossible to truly satisfy needs that are higher up on the hierarchy until immediate needs are addressed and met.

Sometimes, in our attempts to address an entire list of needs instead of identifying which are the most immediate or even after having identified what our most immediate needs are, many of us "need jump," attempting to meet one need but quickly giving up and attempting to meet another and so on. We end up frustrated, disappointed and discouraged. Remember Lynn (chapter 12)? Until Lynn was truly able to feel safe at home, other attempts to mend her life were constantly interrupted and sabotaged by recurring problems in her relationship with Michael. Annie, on the other hand, got it right from the start. She knew that her need to separate herself from daily abuse and manipulation was her most important need to be addressed in order to "get her life back." She was not conscious of it at the time, but she instinctively knew that whatever she had tried previously to help herself never seemed to work and only compounded her feelings of despair and failure.

In chapter 5 we talked about the concept that a child's first need is *safety*, not love. Such is the case with adults as well. We must address our needs for safety first. Once we have satisfied that, we can begin to find solutions to our other needs much more readily and easily.

Let's look at Annie's circumstances again. Now she was in a situation that was safer and more manageable. Her immediate needs for shelter, food and clothing were met and she could begin to find Calm and Sense in her life, free from the distractions that were keeping her stuck in a life she knew was not really hers.

Annie's situation is somewhat extreme and certainly you may be saying to yourself, "I am not homeless. I have a job and I never went to jail or supported a drug habit as a prostitute! What need should I start with?" My experience has taught me that there are three things that keep people from finding Calm and Sense in their lives. All three of these things are fears and where there is fear there is a threat to your safety in some form. That means that the things that are keeping people from finding Calm and Sense in their lives are based on the basic need for safety. The three fears I'm referring to are fear of the past, fear of the present and fear of the future. With these fears, we include fear of being alone, fear of not being accepted, fear of not being "good enough," fear of rejection, fear of failure, fear of being indigent, fear of the unknown and fear of success.

While these fears seem to operate tirelessly in our thinking, our need for Self-Actualization (as identified by Dr. Maslow) pushes us to make the changes we subconsciously know we should make but do not. However, in moving forward or attempting to move forward, we sometimes reencounter the fear of not being safe and we stop our forward progress in an attempt to protect or regain our feeling of safety. Bouncing back and forth between these conflicting drives often causes us to remain in bad situations, because we identify them as "safer" than the unknown. We feel that we "know what we have" and choose to feel safe in that instead of taking risks that would put us in uncharted waters, even though we may find utopia in those seas of uncertainty.

It takes courage to change, but the rewards are endless! Even if we do not succeed every time, we do learn something every time. With each new risk we take, our courage gets stronger and stronger.

Chapter 16

Worry and Fear

There are two main reasons that people stay "stuck" in situations or lives that continuously cause them to be unhappy. What if I told you these two reasons had absolutely no scientific benefit to the wellness of mankind or to you as a person? What if I told you neither of these two things ever made a person's life better or more fulfilling? What if I told you that these two things keep people from reaching their full potential and can actually cause people to suffer severe medical problems causing death? Would you eliminate them from your life?

The two culprits—the most useless powerful emotions that impede Calm and Sense—that keep people from living in Calm and Sense are *worry* and *fear*. I'm sure you are familiar with both of these and the effect they can have on your life.

We worry about far too much! Finances, jobs, friends, looks, relationships, homes, cars, hair, wars, crime, illness, death…the list can stretch onward. What is it that causes us to worry anyway? What good can come from it? None. Worry is a stifling emotion that has never prevented a single thing from happening, yet we can't seem to stop doing it.

If worry had some actual benefit or provided any tangible, grounded proof of its necessity in our lives, then it could be validated and justified as a proper means to deal with the world and our lives. But it doesn't. In fact, worry causes stress. Stress causes many other undesired things in our lives that only lead to the potential of more worry. More worry equals more stress. Does this make any sense? Not to Calm and Sense.

Calm and Sense uses acronyms to help us refocus negative thinking and replace falsities with fact. Best of all, they make perfect Calm and Sense! The first Calm and Sense acronym I want to share with you is WORRY. Calm and Sense says WORRY causes us to react **W**ith**O**ut **R**eal **R**eason **Y**et. This is exactly what we do when we participate in worry and it is always in vain. What would cause so many people to engage in such a futile emotion? One that has no bearing, relevance or power to bring any good to our lives? Why is so much of our valuable time given to such a useless and unproductive action?

The reason we worry is because it provides us with a false sense of security and control. Often, people think about all of the worst possible things that *might* happen, believing they will then have the answers to these situations beforehand. You might be thinking, *Well, this does not sound like such a bad idea.* I too once believed that if I expected the worst, then I would never be disappointed. The problem with this type of thinking is that you can never truly come up with *all* the possibilities. We certainly miss many possibilities and they are usually the ones that occur after much worrying. Then we hear ourselves say, "I never thought *that* would happen!"

As human beings, we are designed to be on the alert for trouble and it is our nature to pay more attention to warning signs rather than positive news. People encounter problems when worrying becomes more of an obsession and less of a survival tool. Some people fret over money, relationships, health, jobs, kids, etc., *all the time*. This is not Calm and Sense living.

What is one to do about WORRY if it is what we do **W**ith**O**ut **R**eal **R**eason **Y**et?

Plan. Productive use of worry can push us into some form of beneficial action. Suppose you are worried about money (or a lack thereof). Instead of getting stuck worrying and feeling powerless, devise a plan of action. What do I need to do to stop this worry and safeguard my assets and myself? Get your "how" thinking in motion! Make a list of what you spend and then eliminate what you can: start cutting down or cutting out what's not really necessary, set up a bank account and have it automatically save a small amount of money from your pay each month, etc.

Worried your job is in jeopardy? Make an appointment to meet with your boss. Have a heart-to-heart discussion with him or her to address your concerns. Worrying that you may lose your job will not prevent it from happening. If you really are in danger of losing it, it is better to know sooner than later. That way, you can get yourself ready and prepared to seek other employment beforehand. The point here is that worry is a *call to action*, not a mystical way to prevent the inevitable.

Kathleen McGowan reported in a *Psychology Today* article that a group of worriers were asked to write down all their concerns over a two-week period. By the end of that time period, 85 percent of the things about which each participant worried turned out fine. Many people believe their worrying (*just* their concern—not any action) can prevent something bad from happening.[1]

Most studies also show that people worry repeatedly over the same issues. Some studies also say that worrying is a very strong form of procrastination that keeps us from engaging in a difficult task. It makes good Calm and Sense, then, that those of us who worry incessantly (or even "more than we would like to," because we find that it is disrupting our lives) should write down our worries whenever they occur. The resulting list of worries can benefit us in several ways. In keeping a running tab of the things that are keeping us from taking action, we have an actual list of the things we need to begin to work on or to let go. Also, we can look at the list from time to time to see what actually happened regarding each particular thing we worried about. In doing this, we will find that most of them never amounted to much, if anything, and we can learn to see the futility of continuing to strain our emotions over things that never occur. We can reduce the worry and move on.

Look at your worry time. Which do you spend more time doing: worrying about something or getting something accomplished? Remember that Calm and Sense is based in *now* thinking and *present* action! If you find that your present is being consumed by thoughts of *what if* or *when I*, then you are not living with Calm and Sense and you are spending too much time worrying and not enough time doing.

In case I haven't yet convinced you to cut down (or, even better, eliminate) your worry time, here is some information about how chronic worrying affects your health: it is associated with heart attacks, elevated blood pressure, musculoskeletal aches and pains, gastrointestinal disturbances, ulcers, skin eruptions, eczema, asthma, respiratory problems and, ultimately, dying younger. Now *that* is something to worry (and *do something*) about! Recall the studies of terminally ill people who said they wished they had "laughed more and worried less."

Roughly one quarter of the world's population meets the criteria for a diagnosable, worry-related anxiety disorder at some time in their lives.

For these people, professional treatment is necessary to help them get back to a place where worry does not control their lives. Looking at the amount of worry time in which the rest of the population indulges, roughly half of us are spinning our wheels and fighting the worry demon on a daily basis.[2] Again, along with this, by the year 2020, it is estimated that depression will be the second most common health problem in the world. Recent figures show that globally 450 million people suffer from mental disorders, with 154 million suffering from depression.[3] In the United States, 20.9 million adults or about 9.5 percent of the population age eighteen and older in a given year have a depressive disorder.[4] These are startling figures and a call to action for all of us! Calm and Sense tells us that we all need to cease the worry, fear, stagnation and feelings of isolation or jealousy of others. We can find and have all we need if we begin to seek it, accept it and believe in who we are.

"Why are so many people unhappy these days?" "What is going on?" "Was it always like this?" I am asked these questions over and over and the answer is "No." It was not always like this. The short answer to the question about what is going on these days and why people are so unhappy is that we (all people) are becoming more and more disconnected from one another. Family, neighborhoods, churches and various other social structures previously connected people and gave them more meaning and stability in their lives. Unfortunately, many of these institutions have gradually broken down, leaving us lacking reassurance and support. Most people avoid asking for reassurance, because they believe it will make them seem weak or needy. Asking for help of any kind is never a sign of weakness. The bottom line is that we simply do not experience enough human moments. As a result, people worry alone, which is the worst way to worry!

The second culprit and enemy of Calm and Sense is *fear*. Calm and Sense tells us that FEAR is **F**eeling **E**mbarrassment **A**nd **R**isk. Fear produces embarrassment, risk or both. Embarrassment is rooted in insecurity. Risk is rooted in physical safety. Fear without action, like worry, is debilitating for all of us. It keeps us from trying new things, expressing who we are and truly believing in ourselves.

Often we choose not to speak up in front of friends, coworkers or even strangers, because we feel we may be embarrassed by our words or that we won't fit in. We tell ourselves, "I never know what to say!" or "I could never do that!" Calm and Sense asks *why*? When we are comfortable with and confident in ourselves, we don't fear not "fitting in," because we don't need to "fit in" to anything but our own skin. We love ourselves for who we are and are okay with the idea that not everyone will like us or think that we "fit in" with them. What really is there to fear anyway?

Calm and Sense tells us that when we take action, when we begin to do the things we "fear," we find that the only real negative aspect of the thing we feared was the fear we felt about facing it in the first place! From a place of confidence and Calm and Sense (as we discussed in chapter 6) we acknowledge that fear is just an emotional barrier. Then, when we take steps to pursue what it is we fear and we succeed, we build our self-confidence and learn more about what we are truly capable of when we allow ourselves to step outside of our "safe lodge" and live life! The next time we encounter something that might earlier have caused us to feel fear, it is much easier to sidestep that barrier and keep moving forward. We rewire ourselves not to take on the emotion of fear when we encounter something new or challenging, because we have replaced that unhealthy, unproductive emotion with confidence and self-assuredness.

Now you may be wondering, *Are you suggesting that I join a circus and learn to walk a tightrope or jump on the trapeze and swing over a lake of fire filled with man-eating piranhas in order to feel better and have Calm and Sense in my life?* If that's what your heart most desires. But for the rest of us (myself included), no. You may also be wondering, *Well, I want to lose weight and I heard about this great new product online and I want to take it, but I also read that someone died taking it! I am afraid it could hurt me too, but I really want to try it. Should I just ignore my fear?* No. Calm and Sense does *not* advocate doing things that are physically harmful or dangerous to your health. Fear serves a positive purpose in our lives by alerting us to possible dangers, like the instinct you have not to step into oncoming traffic. The fear I am talking about here is the kind that prevents you from doing things that you could otherwise safely be doing; the kind that causes emotional turmoil and health problems and that renders you powerless to move forward with your life and attain the goals you have set for yourself. Calm and Sense does *not* advocate ignoring your sense of fear when that fear is caused by a very real threat to your safety.

Calm and Sense offers seven guaranteed ways to feel less fear in your life:

- **Lighten up and have a sense of humor.** Victor Borge, the famed musician-comedian, once said, "Laughter is the shortest distance between two people." Too many of us are so fearful of failure that we sabotage ourselves by putting doubt in the way of our success. Sometimes an embarrassment today makes for a very funny story tomorrow. Remember that and also remember that no one is watching and waiting for *you*, all by yourself, to fail at something. There is no committee that sits up all night planning for your demise or trying to figure out how to embarrass you. People are generally supportive, curious of others and rooting for the success of their peers. (Don't you do that?) A mistake is only that: a mistake. We learn from it. We can make light of it with a joke and share a laugh at our own expense once in a while. Men, take note that a sense of humor is the number one thing that attracts women. More than looks, if men can keep women laughing, they increase their chances of dating them by a high margin. (More on that in chapter 25.) Humor is not something with which we are born, but do not let that stop you from developing a lighter side to viewing yourself and the world around you. Remember, the overwhelming wish of the terminally ill was to *laugh more and worry less*!

- **Learn to look outside of yourself.** Basketball coach John Wooden said, "Things turn out best for the people who make the best of the way things turn out." If you endure a scary or frightening situation and it goes bad, before immediately blaming yourself for the entire "failure," be sure to look at the whole picture. Sometimes things go wrong that we have or had no control over whatsoever. It's not always "all about you." Sometimes you do your best and something else, something outside of your control, causes imperfection. That is life. If you analyze a situation that went poorly and find that it *was* due to something you did incorrectly or happened to overlook, avoid feeling shame. Shame tells us that something we did failed because of something we *are*, not because we are good people who simply made a mistake (i.e., because of something we *did*). There is a huge difference between who we *are* and what we *do*. Not acknowledging that allows us to continue feeding Negative Nick and promotes further fear and lack of confidence.
- **Stop blaming yourself.** This type of emotional behavior is so destructive and debilitating that it may be the leading cause of the fear we have! Self-blame has also been found to be a major contributor to depression in many people. The more you blame yourself for

problems, the more fearful of success you become and the more depressed you get. Self-blame erodes our self-esteem and causes us to fear ever trying something again. Many people are so critical and demanding of themselves that they set impossible expectations. This produces a double blow to our Calm and Sense. First, if we believe we can "never do anything right" then we never have the courage to do it. We choose to "play it safe" and do nothing. Then, because we did nothing, we feel like failures, learn to dislike ourselves and become more depressed. Calm and Sense calls on us to accept who we are and to believe in our potential. Again, taking risks allows us to free ourselves from self-blame. As we try to challenge the fears that bind us, slowly we learn that we are not so bad after all. There *are* things we are quite capable of doing and with each accomplishment comes more self-confidence and less depression.

- **Expect progress, not perfection.** We all have probably heard the saying, "Rome was not built in a day." Neither will we ever master the art of perfectionism. Still, we set ourselves up to fear new situations, relationships or lifestyles, because we insist on doing them perfectly! Babies fall many times as they learn to walk. But they keep trying and we cheer them on with enthusiasm and joy as they *progress*. We never expect them to stand up suddenly one day and walk around the block. They practice, they learn, we encourage them and we see every fall they take as a step closer to their ability to walk "all by themselves." Do we give ourselves such support and encouragement as we "learn to walk" in life or do we allow fear to keep us "crawling," never achieving the skills we need to truly feel empowered? We must learn to expect mistakes and accept them as positive lessons as we strive for Calm and Sense in our lives. We must also extinguish all of the unnecessary fears we have. We must stop insisting we "can't," because we won't be able to do it "perfectly" the first time. Perfectionism can be exhausting and causes us to become our own worst critics. As in studies of worry, studies of perfectionists render similar results: It is a futile expectation that hinders growth and potential. Children who grow up in homes where parents demand perfection in grades, sports, etc., grow up to be adults who are disappointed, frustrated, angry and severely lacking in self-esteem. Doing a "good job" is not enough; making a million dollars a year is not enough; having problems in a marriage causes great stress and trepidation, because it is "not perfect." Why? Because life gets harder and simply no one is perfect! Learning that *progress* shows us that we are moving toward improvement reassures us and motivates us to continue—but we have to begin somewhere. That somewhere is with an understanding that we want and deserve better lives. We want to fear less and live more.

Making mistakes is a part of life and is essential to the growth process—be it a toddler learning to walk or an alcoholic who has chosen to stop drinking but "slips up" along the way. The alcoholic may remark, "See? I can't do this! I'm too weak!" But what he *really* is saying is either "I can't quit drinking perfectly" or "I am not ready to quit drinking yet." If he was drinking daily and now drinks twice a week, that is progress! He is learning to live more with less alcohol. We too need to assess our readiness for change as well as perfectionist traits. Which is holding you back? Are you ready for less fear and more living in your life or are you afraid that you can't be the "perfect person" immediately?

- **Have a direction.** The Latin philosopher Seneca said, "Our plans miscarry because they have no aim. When a man does not know what harbor he is making for, no wind is the right wind." Many of us fear attaining or attempting to attain a goal merely because we're not quite sure how to get there. We may one day have a fleeting thought of becoming a writer, lawyer, banker or parent, but we allow the thought to disappear. Why? We fear we do not know *how* to get where we want to go. Certainly, lack of navigation would keep anyone from venturing out into the dark night of a blizzard! We need a plan, a roadmap and a sense of direction in order to feel confident and secure. Sometimes the seeker easily dismisses the goal, because the route to arriving seems overwhelming and unattainable. That is also a form of fear. Is your life "too much work"? Are your goals "not that important"? I certainly hope not! If you desire something, it is your responsibility to find a way to make it happen. Do not let fear or a lack of direction dictate your ambitions. Dreaming of personal growth and success is not enough: We also have to act! We have to plan and then carry out our plans with passion.

  The adage "Where there's a will, there's a way" holds true. When you are moved by a dream, goal or desire, begin planning how to accomplish it immediately. Challenge any fears you may have by taking action steps to achieve it. If you're thinking, *I don't think I can make much of my life; I don't even have a high school diploma*, listen to this: Success is *not* measured by academic degrees. Want proof? Bill Gates, one of the richest men in the world, was a college dropout. John D. Rockefeller didn't graduate from high school. Neither did Andrew Carnegie and Henry Ford. More examples are Robert DeNiro, Humphrey Bogart, Sean Connery, Walt Disney, Quentin Tarantino and Patrick Stewart. All quit high school before graduation. And although their books are required reading in many schools and universities, Charles Dickens, Joseph Conrad, Herman Melville, George Bernard Shaw, William Faulkner and Jack London never finished school either. These very successful individuals certainly charted their courses using Calm and Sense and did not fear that a lack of education would embarrass them nor cause them any grave danger. Dream and find direction!

- **Help and be with others whenever you can.** Human beings are social creatures, but we have lost a great amount of our opportunities to socialize. We have become reclusive, self-contained and self-entertained beings in a world where technology has turned our homes into movie theaters, work places, communication centers and concert halls. We can communicate with people across the globe from the comfort of our dens, but when it comes to that human contact that we all most definitely need, there is little of it to be had. In the process of technological growth and advancement, we have actually moved backward as well. Fewer people join fraternal organizations, many children do not play outside with other children much anymore, we can "shop from home" and our senses of community have been all but lost to self-containment and isolated activity. In a very sad way, many of us have lost a lot of our abilities and confidence in simply "being" with other people. We shy away from such encounters. Some of my adolescent clients don't know how to telephone friends' houses and ask for their friends! Instead, they text or e-mail, never actually speaking to their boyfriends, girlfriends or friends' parents. This deterioration of socializing has led us to a fear of being with and communicating with others on a personal, in-person level.

  To combat this, Calm and Sense tells us to make connections with people and organizations. Join a club or fraternity, volunteer time at a hospital or senior citizen facility, begin a neighborhood watch organization, extend yourself however you can and in any amount that you can manage. Remember to expand your social, emotional and professional portfolio and invest in yourself (see chapter 6). The benefits of this are many: You will meet interesting new people and any connection with one group of people branches automatically to other groups of people. You feel good about doing good things and people appreciate it. Increasing your social network is always a good plan in life, for personal, professional and human reasons. It also will "freshen up" your socialization skills and help you sharpen your sense of humor and awareness of yourself. You will notice an increase in your self-esteem and confidence and you will gain a more secure feeling of your place in the world. If you have children, this also sets a good example for them to follow. Princess Diana said, "I'd like people to think of me as someone who cares about them." Indeed, they did. Do you want such an attribute? Involvement with others also serves to help us in times of need; it lessens fears of alienation and feeling "lost" in a world of billions.

Calm and Sense provides a means for and also relies on your continually gaining confidence, self-worth and self-esteem. It also helps and relies on your continued efforts to reduce fear by stepping outside of your comfort zone and becoming more present in "real-life" situations, connecting with people who may need your help or with people who work together to help others. Kindness to and compassion for others results in a strong sense of character and decreased fear.

- **Learn optimism.** William Shakespeare's character Hamlet said, "There is nothing either good or bad, but thinking makes it so." The truth is that viewing our lives and the world around us in a positive light creates feelings of and belief in hope and certainly diminishes our fear. The power of positive thinking has been around since the start of time. Imagine the negative thoughts you may carry around with you. If those thoughts are self-defeating and limit your emotional growth in any way, begin to exercise your ability to increase your supply of options in what you are telling yourself. However you may be "punishing" yourself, understand this: You have the choice to continue beating yourself up or to think otherwise and prove yourself wrong! Imagine you are going to take your emotional beliefs to a court of personal truths and you must defend the reasons why you are not a "good" or "worthy" person. What evidence would you provide to the judge and jury? Would you win your case or would you lack supporting evidence? Suppose the opposing lawyer in this case (which is also you, but now you are thinking positively) had significant evidence to prove you *are* a good and deserving person and that all your evidence to the contrary is simply nonsense. You would be sentenced to "life without negativity"!

Your ability to see things—especially yourself—in a positive light is absolutely a learnable skill. Redirecting negative thoughts when they occur requires attention, practice and diligence. For many of us, these "thoughts" have been playing in our minds for a long time. If that is the case, do not despair! Keep fighting the negative by replacing it with the positive. In no time, you will begin not only to *feel* better, but also to truly *believe* the good you hear. After all, if we tell ourselves something enough times, we will believe it, good or bad. Calm and Sense says to make self-talk good all the time!

It is important to understand that our limitations can be drastically reduced, if not totally eliminated, by overcoming worry and fear. Calm and Sense requires living in the *present* and allowing worry and fear to exist somewhere else—somewhere that is not accessible to us. Spend your moments in pursuit of Calm and Sense thinking, planning and doing.

Chapter 17

Finding Courage

Courage is being able to give ourselves wholly and fully to others as well as to ourselves. It is the belief that we are capable of finding, facing and challenging what we know to be right, what we need to improve, what we deserve from our works and what we do not yet know but need to understand. It is when we act with courage that we reap rewards of self-understanding, self-reliance and self-esteem and are able to be of benefit to others.

Calm and Sense says COURAGE is Ceasing Our Unfounded Resistances And Gaining Endurance. Next time you feel unable to face a new task, person, situation, challenge or encounter, be courageous.

After all, what are we to gain by being afraid and believing we do not have the courage to face unknown people, circumstances, challenges or behaviors? When you think of your role models or heroes or of the people who have made great differences for the betterment of the world, the one essential characteristic they share is having courage in order to accomplish their heroic goals.

L. Frank Baum, author of the timeless and classic story *The Wizard of Oz*, illustrated the three basic major components of a mentally healthy person with Calm and Sense. The Scarecrow wanted a "brain" so he could think, have foresight, gain and retain knowledge and grow wiser. The Tinman needed a "heart" so he could love, feel, empathize and connect with care and true concern to himself and others. The Cowardly Lion, the "King of the Jungle," longed for "nerve" or *courage* to be who he truly was meant to be and not to fear that which he wanted to challenge. He knew that the lack of that "nerve" or courage was holding back his true "roar." Like him, our "roars" are stifled until we have courage—until we *choose* not to fear those things that cannot hurt us!

Dorothy brought these three essential human characteristics together so they could work in harmony to help her truly find that there is "no place like home." Separately, these three personality traits could not accomplish much. However, working together effectively as a team, they were able to overcome their obstacles. We too must understand that Calm and Sense requires us all to have courage, love (heart) and good Sense (thinking power). With these characteristics firmly in place, what is there really ever to fear?

Triumph is the reward of courage!

When we choose a life of routine, void of change and filled with worry and fear (chapter 16), we are not using our Calm and Sense and our inner needs to feel whole and complete as people (Self-Actualization). This pushes us into destructive, self-defeating ways of thinking. It is also the root of major depression, which will be the second most common health problem worldwide by the year 2020.[1] Sadly, these numbers are ever increasing.

Courage is important, because it allows us to step outside of our "safe lodges" more easily and to challenge our fears and the things that keep us from moving forward in our lives. Most people who lack courage have not yet tried to be courageous. Maybe you were raised like Jay (chapter 12), who never learned courage as a child, because his parents did not demonstrate or provide a role model of it for him. It did not mean that he lacked courage; he just did not know how to use it. We are all capable of being courageous, but fear locks many of us into believing we can't. We think, *I could never do that!*

One reason for *thinking* you don't have courage certainly can come from the lack of learning how to use this quality growing up. Another reason for thinking you do not have courage may be that you experienced some past event or situation that caused you to feel mortified or embarrassed when you extended yourself outside of your normal comfort zone. Now you just can't bring yourself to do it again or even allow yourself to believe that you can. This kind of withdrawal can result from a relationship where you "took a chance" and gave of yourself freely and without trepidation. Then you found out that you were being lied to, cheated on, used, manipulated or just not truly loved in return. Perhaps you took a class and when you answered a question, the class laughed or the professor ridiculed your answer. Maybe you were overweight as a child and were constantly teased and harassed. Maybe a sorority or fraternity you pledged in college humiliated you and told you "you weren't good enough" to be "one of them." These types of traumatizing incidents are painful. In our instinct to survive, we retreat, never willing to suffer such great pain again. As a result, we lose trust in others and, even worse, in ourselves. It becomes safer to "stay put" and not be courageous.

However, it is in that "staying put" that we lose our abilities to grow. Complacency does not generate Calm and Sense! We must become more curious about fear and less compelled to retreat to places where we stagnate emotionally and socially. Fear can be a great teacher. When we challenge our fears we build courage, develop an understanding of what was holding us back and gain the ability to bravely face our challenges, other people and even ourselves in ways that are more productive and beneficial to our lives.

Hiding from anyone or anything will never solve any problem, bring us any new answers, establish healthy self-esteem or win us any respect from ourselves or others. Courage and confidence go hand-in-hand. Most people have heard Franklin D. Roosevelt's famous "There is nothing to fear but fear itself" statement. But what does that really mean? It means that the only thing we *should* fear is being afraid to do something, because that stops us from accomplishing our goals. We must identify our fears, challenge them and conquer them. If you feel you truly must fear something, make sure you have sufficient evidence to support your case. Be aware, though, that most things we believe we *should* fear (like asking for a raise, speaking in public, sharing our true feelings with a friend, sticking up for what we feel is right or returning to a life of uncontrolled drug use) can be resolved at least to a point where we are not constantly living with a fear of those things that stop us from living our lives. Remember, if it will not kill you, it will only make you stronger!

Depression attempts to force us into reclusion and seclusion. It attempts to take away our courage. When we are depressed we fill our minds with many non-truths and nonsense such as not being "good/pretty/smart/strong/rich/thin enough." Calm and Sense says "enough is enough" to all of that. Fear only being fearful and then banish all the rest from your mind. Let your true "roar" be heard!

Chapter 18

Making Your Own Happiness

We sometimes sacrifice far too much of our power or relinquish it to others. Too often, we allow other people to dictate what we think or feel about ourselves or our lives. Oftentimes we give this power to people whose values or roles in our lives do not warrant our allowing them to impede our Calm and Sense and dictate how we feel. Yet we still do. I often hear things like, "My coworker makes me so mad!" and "Every time I see my sister she has something nasty to say and that makes me feel so bad!" What I say is this: Stop, look and listen to *your* Calm and Sense. If a child "insults" you, does it hurt as much as if one of your peers, partner or family member does? Probably not, although it might. Why?

It's easy for us to excuse children for their lack of moral understanding with a general sense that they "don't know any better." Adults, on the other hand, should know better. But there are many socially and emotionally immature adults. (Chapters 8 and 9 discuss Social and Emotional Maturity.)

If you are truly happy with who you are, you will never feel the need to insult or demean another person. There is just no reason for it. People with Calm and Sense are total people, happy about who they are, content with what they have, curious and courageous enough to improve their lives. They do not benefit whatsoever from judging or criticizing others. They just don't need to.

People lacking Calm and Sense have not found that inner peace, that sense of self that causes people to be at ease with themselves and the world around them. They insult, judge and criticize other people due to the inner turmoil and self-loathing in their own lives. Demeaning others is how they make themselves feel better. By projecting all their own inadequacies onto other people, they don't have to identify those inadequacies as their own. Socially and Emotionally Mature adults with Calm and Sense do not do this. Again, there is simply no need.

Additionally, those of us who are living Calm and Sense lives cannot be affected by other people's insults and negativity. We know who we are and we like ourselves. We wear that "emotional suit of armor" all the time and no one can penetrate it. We begin to see that those very unhappy, unfulfilled people are suffering emotionally, are socially immature and have to find something to criticize or insult in others all the time in some dysfunctional, unhealthy attempt to make themselves feel better.

Calm and Sense gives us back all of our power to safeguard ourselves from negativity and emotionally unhealthy people. No one has the authority to make you feel anything! If you believe they do, you are allowing them to.

What does all of this have to do with happiness? I'll get to that soon. For now, though, let's return to Annie's story.

It was during her most recent stay in jail that Annie made her decision to leave behind the life she was living. She was speaking to a fellow inmate one evening over a game of checkers and found in this other inmate a source of inspiration and strength. This woman's name was Ruth; she was seventy-five years old. Perhaps Annie perceived her as a mother figure. She was, in fact, one of Annie's Identity Fortifiers (see chapter 10 for a description of Identity Fortifiers). Ruth was serving time for a shoplifting charge. She told Annie, "For a piece of meat that cost five dollars and fifteen cents, they want to give me three meals a day, healthcare, a bed and time to play checkers with you! They say crime don't pay. Ha!"

Annie found Ruth wise, harmless and warm. As they talked, Ruth noticed Annie's ravaged arms as well as her outer and inner beauty. "Child, I'm just an old woman trying to get by. Sometimes I win, sometimes I lose, but you got the power to win all the time! What in the world is keeping you here?" Annie replied, "I have no money for bail." Ruth laughed and said, "Child, that's not what I meant. I meant keeping you here at this place in your *life*." Annie told Ruth of her addiction, losses, abuse and life on the streets. "I don't know how to make it on my own, Ruth. How could I ever survive?"

"You got to find the courage to make it, girl! The life you've been living here is harder than the life that waits for you out there. You understand what I'm telling you?" Ruth responded. "You're sticking needles filled with junk in your arms, you're putting your pretty hands, lips and whatever else on the dregs of society and cuttin' your arms up like a piece of roast beef!" Annie began to sob as she recounted this conversation to me, much as she sobbed when it actually took place.

Ruth continued, "You are a young girl. Look around you! You see these women in here, all sickly and wrinkled? All fightin' and screamin' 'cause one wants to watch *Jerry Springer* and the other wants to watch *Days of Our Lives*? Where do you think these ladies is goin'? I see somethin' in you that makes me wonder what you doin' in here. Them ladies in here been drinking the same poison you have all their lives and eventually it'll kill them. You got a chance if you want it! You don't look like no fast-food French fry left under the heat lamp too long yet, girl. What would your mama say if she seen you now?"

Annie knew at that moment exactly what her mother would say and she heard her mother talking through Ruth right then. Annie repeated to herself, "The life I'm living *here* is harder than the life that waits for me *there*."

What life are you living "here"? Is it hard? Do you struggle with people you know, your job, your lover, yourself? Do you wish it would all "go away"? Are you going to find the courage to change and the ability to keep fear from dictating a life of miserable complacency? Are you going to take back your rights to the power over your own emotions? Will you ensure that the criticizers around you waste their arrows of insults when your emotional suit of armor blocks them and shatters them to pieces?

Are you ready to take a long hard look at your life, determine what you want, where you want to go and who you want to be? Are you ready to take full responsibility for making it happen? Are you ready to cease blaming others for your life? Are you willing to accept your past with all of its imperfections and use it as fuel to propel you forward rather than hold you back?

If you are, then you are ready to have Calm and Sense in your life. You are ready to make your own happiness.

Annie took that leap of faith. She realized that she wanted and deserved better and that she had been punishing herself for many years in many ways. Through therapy, Annie came to realize that the reasons for her self-punishment were rooted in guilt over her parents' deaths, anger for their "leaving" her, all of the sexual abuse she experienced throughout her life and a deeply wounded sense of self-esteem. To reinforce Annie's understanding that she truly deserved a better life and that she hadn't done anything for which she should be punished (by herself or by anyone else), I asked her to identify what it was that she had done that was so horrible and deserving of punishment or that warranted surrendering her right to a healthy, happy life. The sexual abuse she suffered as a child was not her fault; however, like most children who are sexually abused, she believed she was responsible. The prostitution and drug use came *after* the guilt and anger, as a form of self-punishment disguised as a means of "feeling better." Together, those ingredients were enough to send Annie along a path of self-destruction—not only physically, but mentally and emotionally as well. Annie *believed* she couldn't do better, did not deserve better and was a terrible person. Because she believed that about herself, she *became* that person.

Human beings can become the best or the worst of themselves depending on what they *believe* they can or cannot do. In acquiring Calm and Sense, we must identify and assess what it is we are allowing or have allowed to get in our way and keep us from moving forward. This may include a horrifying history of neglect, abuse or depravity, a harrowing experience at some point in life or numerous other possibilities. With physical pain, like when we stub a toe, it hurts terribly when it occurs, but after the crescendo of pain the feeling begins to decrease. We feel the pain getting less and less after the "ouch" moment. Unfortunately, the mind does not work this way.

When we experience threatening situations or ones that cause imbalances in our emotional stabilities, we tend to play the events over and over again in our thoughts. We imagine different outcomes, criticize ourselves over what we *should* have done and question why it happened at all. Instead of moving forward from where we are now, we often insist on battling the past, as if at some point our efforts will result in a different outcome. Annie battled her past constantly and with each new reminder of what she did or did not do or why she "had to have this happen" to her, she subconsciously found more and more reasons to justify her lifestyle. Worse, she found more and more reasons to believe she was a horrible, worthless person, deserving of nothing.

At the opposite end of the spectrum from people who believe they deserve nothing (like Annie) are people who have overblown senses of entitlement. These people think the world and every person in it owes them something, because they are just "so wonderful" or because they have suffered so much already. They internalize, *I certainly must be entitled to whatever I want now!*

Remember Hank, in chapter 1? He had this false sense of entitlement. Those people are suffering from some cause but have more work to do to identify what it is. As much as childhood deprivation causes us to expect nothing in life, growing up in homes where we got everything we wanted all the time teaches us only to want more. That is not the lesson of Calm and Sense. Calm and Sense assists us in gaining the ability to *feel* and *believe* we *are* worthy, capable and deserving of lives of emotional peace, self-respect, value, love and dignity—but never at the expense of others. There is a vast difference between appreciation and arrogance.

The significance of Annie's story in explaining Calm and Sense lies in its utter contradiction. Annie was an innocent child who suffered the largest loss a child could ever experience: She lost both of her parents in a car accident that she not only witnessed but also survived. Since she had no able relative to care for her, she wound up in foster care where she was abused in appalling ways. To most of the rest of us, it is clear that none of this was her fault. However, Annie eventually came to believe that this was all her own fault! As a result of that faulty belief, she began to punish herself.

As we've discussed, it took a "golden moment" for Annie to make a decision to change. Annie's moment occurred when she met a fellow inmate, an Identity Fortifier with whom she connected and whose words she took to heart. The key to Annie's true success, though, was that Annie stuck to the plan! She admitted that she had wanted to change many times before but was just not ready. There was always an excuse, some reason why it "couldn't happen just yet." This time, it did. Why? Because Annie was truly ready.

Money and Happiness

Pop music icon Michael Jackson was a man from a family that had and has riches in cash and real estate. Would you say that Michael Jackson's last ten years of life were happy? Do his parents, brothers and sisters seem happy? What about his children? Calm and Sense believes it's not cash that creates contentment! Despite all the riches "the Gloved One" had, he seemed to live a life of despair, ridicule and suffering. Money could not save him. Nor, apparently, could it bring him happiness. He was addicted to countless drugs and narcotics and because of past allegations about his private life, lived the life of a recluse. Calm and Sense does not consider that happiness. Do you?

There are many more examples in the world of people (famous and not) who have lots and lots of money but not true happiness. Why, then, do so many people believe that *if* they were rich *then* they would be happy? It is simply a fairy tale! It is "if" thinking at its finest! When we equate wealth with happiness, what we are truly doing is saying that we are unable to rest or feel peaceful, because we have debt and bills to pay. We are choosing to allow our worries and fears to restrict our abilities to experience happiness when it comes our way. Remember, WORRY means **W**ith**O**ut **R**eal **R**eason **Y**et; FEAR means **F**eeling **E**mbarrassment **A**nd **R**isk. But is true happiness really about not having bills to pay? Really? Will not having debt help you love yourself and others more? That does not make Calm and Sense.

When we have bills, we also have a place to live, food to eat, a car to drive, perhaps a family to feed. We are paying for the things we need to live! If money is tight, don't worry—take action. Spend less and perhaps work more, but do not fall for the fantasy that unlimited money will bring true happiness.

The true "wealth" of happiness lies in self-acceptance and loving what we have more than having what we love! Still not convinced that money can never bring you happiness? Read what some people who can enlighten us on the subject have to say:

- "I have made many millions, but they have brought me no happiness." John D. Rockefeller (American oil magnate)
- "The care of $200 million is too great a load for any back or brain to bear. It is enough to kill anyone. There's no pleasure in it." William H. Vanderbilt (American businessman)
- "Of the billionaires I have known, money just brings out the basic traits in them. If they were jerks before they had money, they are simply jerks with a billion dollars." Warren Buffett (American investor, industrialist and philanthropist)
- "I was happier when doing a mechanic's job." Henry Ford (American founder of the Ford Motor Company and father of modern assembly lines)

Remember our earlier discussion about how many very rich and "successful" people are the unhappiest people in the world? John Cheever, an

American novelist and short story writer, said, "The main emotion of the adult American who has had all the advantages of wealth, education, and culture is disappointment." Studies show that having money or things does not make us happy. Albert Einstein was a genius, but look at how he dressed and groomed himself. He was not caught up in appearance or material things. The man was happy making mistake after mistake until he discovered some very important scientific findings—findings which ultimately benefited the world. He also said, "The most beautiful thing we can experience is the mystery." The "mystery" of learning, of seeking, of trying, of never giving up in the quest for what we truly, deep down desire. We must keep trying, keep making every effort to get where or what we want, no matter what roadblocks we encounter. We cannot make excuses. We cannot give up our efforts if someone tells us we "can't" or "shouldn't." If we believe in ourselves so strongly and desire our goals so passionately, then we will stay focused and determined to accomplish our goals.

Einstein had Calm and Sense. He did not worry about how he presented himself; he did not fear how other people perceived him. Those things had little importance in his life. So will they have little importance in our lives when we learn to use our Calm and Sense. We must keep our eyes on the road ahead, learn from the miles we have put behind us and not look back. Find your passion—even if it is to learn how to truly love yourself—and *go for it*! Experiment with different things, challenge and cease the negative self-talk, rewire your thinking and update it to today's requirements and specifications. Do not fear change; embrace it! Laugh more and worry less. Plant seeds of friendship, interest, opportunity and love around you and enjoy all of your harvest—not merely one tree. Invest generously in your social, emotional and professional portfolio. Seek new challenges and relationships. Possibilities are everywhere and the rewards are plentiful, if and when we seek them and recognize them.

There you have it, straight from the mouths of the "rich and famous." There is no Calm and Sense in the belief that money brings happiness.

Love and Happiness

"I'm so lonely! *If* I could find the right man/woman *then* I know I could be happy!" That is a very tall order and, quite frankly, an unfair expectation to put on any one person, isn't it? First, can you imagine being the one to hear from a new love interest that "You have saved my life from an existence of misery and sadness. I was never happy until I found you!" One might think, *What? You have* never been happy *before me?* This is a red flag of sorts. It delivers a message that "if we don't work out, I'm going to become clingy and desperate and make you feel horribly responsible for my pain." Who would want such a tremendous burden or responsibility? Most people with Calm and Sense want partners who have their acts together and who radiate confidence and enthusiasm in themselves and the world around them. *That* is attractive! A partner who is comfortable with who he or she is; someone who is able to take the world and its problems lightly with a dose of humor. Someone with Calm and Sense!

I am going to elaborate in more detail what a romantic relationship secure in Calm and Sense requires and looks like in part 3, but briefly let me say that if someone is expecting a person, any person, to come along and make him or her happy, that person and that relationship are destined to doom from the beginning.

Relationships and loved ones *do* make us happy...sometimes; that is expected and desirable. But so do balloons, lollipops, dogs, sunny days, ice cream cones and certain songs we hear. Our *true* happiness, or Calm and Sense, can only come from inside ourselves and spread outwards. Our loved ones *contribute* to well-being and comfort, but when we put all of our "happiness eggs" in one basket, what happens when we have an argument or disagreement? We blame that person for our unhappiness. Remember Agnes and Marty (chapter 4)?

Relationships sometimes end. Relationships sometimes experience troubled waters or raging storms. But if we are truly happy people (i.e., we have Calm and Sense) *before* the problems come, we can certainly manage the storms or the dissolution of any relationships much more effectively.

So, you don't know *how* to *be* happy? This is a wonderful one of those "How" questions Calm and Sense loves and encourages. You say you don't know how to be happy, but you do know how to be miserable? People who claim not to know how to be happy are either not *ready* to be happy or are not *willing* to be happy (or gain Calm and Sense). Which is it? Are you not ready or unwilling?

Remember, Calm and Sense requires change and risk taking. It requires courage and commitment. If you want something strongly enough, you can get it! Isn't your happiness worth taking some risks? If not, what is the alternative? Remaining unhappy? If that is what you choose to do, then no book, person or idea can ever sway your thinking. Life is not about waiting for the storms to pass; it's about learning how to dance in the rain!

Are you someone who is convinced that "when your ship comes in," happiness will be delivered to you? We learned earlier that the world owes us nothing. What we *can* expect from life, if we decide to let life steer our courses, is change and death. That's all. No one has ever been delivered a package of happiness. You are responsible for making things happen in your life; you are responsible for making your own happiness. Perhaps you are asking yourself, "Well, how in the world do I do *that*?" Roy Goodman, an American politician, made a relevant comment: "Remember that happiness is a way of travel, not a destination."

We are a nation flooded with unrealistic expectations and false impressions of exactly what "happiness" is. The media bombards us and advertising shows us that happiness equates to people having good times, in beautiful places and with all the benefits of material items beyond realistic means.

On old commercials Ed McMahon delivered larger-than-life checks for millions of dollars to "lucky" sweepstakes winners. People probably thought to themselves, *Well, their problems are gone for good now!* A "larger-than-life" check. Why? Because it was. It was "unreal" and some research on lottery winners shows that many wind up more "unhappy" than "happy" in the long run, because no one or nothing can make a person happy by *delivering* anything to the person. We have to live our lives as real, regular people, content with who we are and what we have. We must keep moving forward and fulfilling the needs we decide are important to us—not those deemed important or "happiness-producing" by external forces.

Calm and Sense believes that many people who claim to be *unhappy* have not had realistic expectations of what happiness truly is—especially if they are waiting for its delivery by any person, place or thing. Calm and Sense recognizes that *happiness* is a pleasure in life, like laughter. It comes from certain times, experiences, achievements, people or occurrences that cause us to feel it for a certain amount of time. Then it subsides into our memories until the next experience that causes it to come around. Most important, though, is this: We can find happiness in the smallest of things as well as in our perceptions of life's events. Here's the catch: We can do this *only if we are open to receiving it*.

We also need to be able to identify whether we are using Calm and Sense thinking when we visualize what happiness is and how we might attain it. Or are we expecting things as children do: "I want that toy!" "I want to go out to eat!" "If I don't get my way, I'm going to throw a hissy fit, break something or stop talking to Mommy and Daddy until I get what I want!" That is *not* Calm and Sense, but it is a good example of socially and emotionally immature people.

"So then," you might ask, "how can I find Calm and Sense and *be* happy?" You must, as mentioned earlier, acknowledge and truly understand that happiness is *not* a destination and that no one lives in a constant or persistent state of happiness. That is the best place to start. Dispel the media's interpretation of what a happy life is supposed to be. Stop comparing your life and character to others around you. You don't really know what another person's life actually consists of as much as no one else knows yours! Remember Lynn (chapter 12)? Everyone *thought* she had the world at her disposal. Happy, attractive, successful, outgoing, etc., but behind her facade was a life of misery, self-loathing, disappointment and sorrow.

How do you find happiness? Take a moral inventory of your assets and think of times in your life when you felt happiness. Now think about those times. How did happiness find you? How did you find it? What changes in your life do you think need to occur now to add to the potential for more happy moments in the present?

Perhaps you need to see more of your friends or family. Perhaps you need to see less of your friends or family and, instead, have some "you time." Smile more often when you meet people (it worked for Hank). Say hello to strangers just for the sake of saying hello. Buy a goldfish. Bring a plant to your office. Join a club or organization. The secret is to do something different or differently. Something that you enjoy, something that combats the belief that you "do not know how to be happy," because there is no book that teaches such things. We laugh without instruction, we cry without classes, we feel because we are human and we know happiness when it comes our way.

If you spend more time searching for the goodness around you and less on what troubles you, you are already using Calm and Sense living and happiness will appear to you far more often and be much more easily identified when it does.

The World Owes Me Something

What is it people are "waiting" for? Riches? Success? Love? To feel better about themselves? To somehow feel they have "made it" in something they do or wish to do? What is WAITING? Calm and Sense says WAITING is **W**illing **A**ll **I**nitiative **T**o **I**dentify **N**o **G**ain. There is no "happy ending" in the waiting game if we are waiting for some great experiences to come and change our lives. We must identify what we need or want, plan how to get it and then do it!

The world owes us nothing, but we can expect change and death. Anything else we need or desire must come from our determination and work to achieve our goals.

We have all heard "the best things in life are free." There is another old saying that goes, "Riches serve a wise man but command a fool." Calm and Sense tells us the same. The best things in life *are* free. For those of us who can see, hear, smell, taste, feel, laugh, love, share, help, walk, run, hug, hold a child, experience a thunderstorm, tell a ghost story around a campfire, throw a rock into a lake, watch a sunset, listen to a senior citizen recount and share his or her wisdom, learn new things and have the *ability to make changes in our lives*, we are beyond wealthy! We are rich with treasures.

Calm and Sense says that the belief that we need "things" to feel good or successful really comes from the need to feel understood and cherished. If you hold and value calmness and sensibility yourself, you will naturally exhibit these qualities to others around you and then receive them in return. The first step, though, is to find value in *you*. Calm and Sense tells us we will not find happiness anywhere until we find love and "happiness" in ourselves!

"But," some might say, "people don't like me. How can I like myself?" Buddha once told one of his followers: "You yourself, as much as anybody in the entire universe, deserve your love and affection." The praise of others is most welcome when it crowns rather than when it bolsters self-worth. When sense of our own value depends on the views of others, it slips out of our control, rising and falling like the bead of mercury in a thermometer.

In believing that "people don't like me. How can I like myself?", Calm and Sense says you have it backward. If you don't love, let alone *like* yourself, people may have a hard time *liking you,* because they most likely don't truly *know you*. Remember Hank? He walked around with an angry face and a guarded posture that immediately repelled others from him. He did not love or respect himself and it showed! He wore it like a shield and it worked. What "shields" are you wearing?

Jenna is a client who came to me because she did not want to be lonely, isolated and afraid of making friends anymore. Jenna was a twenty-seven-year-old woman who lived a very lonely life. She and her cat lived in an apartment and she commuted by train every day to her job at a large financial institution in New York City. Jenna was an attractive girl who wore dark colors and dressed in several layers. In the psychological world, this could very well indicate a person who is "hiding" or "protecting" herself from anyone "knowing" her or gaining access to her "inner self."

Jenna was guarded and reclusive. It took a number of sessions for me to gain her trust and for her to begin to feel comfortable opening up to me. Her story was of a young marriage (she was eighteen, he was thirty-three) and a very sordid one at that.

Jenna did not have the healthiest self-esteem to begin with. However, at the impressionable age of eighteen, she was drawn by the attention of an older and apparently successful man. Her father had never given her the love and nurturing she needed when she was growing up, so she sought it elsewhere and found it in her husband.

When the marriage started to get rocky, Jenna tried to convince herself that all marriages have difficulties in adjustment at the beginning. But as her husband's incessant blaming and ridiculing continued, she began to internalize the criticisms. Emotionally, she felt responsible for all the problems they were having!

Jenna was emotionally abused and manipulated by her husband for four years. He told her awful, horrible things about her and insulted her every move. He said she was ugly, was terrible in bed, could not cook, could not clean a house, was stupid, immature and unappreciative. The list of insults went on and on. He was never satisfied with anything she did. He did not allow her to see her friends or go anywhere without him, yet he was free to come and go as he pleased.

You may wonder why and how someone chooses to stay in such a terrible situation. The truth is that unhealthy people make unhealthy choices! Jenna lacked Calm and Sense. She had no faith in herself and internally blamed and punished herself as much as her husband did. A part of her felt she deserved what she had and another part of her truly believed that she could save her husband from his misery and save the marriage as well.

While spending four years in an emotional torture chamber, Jenna lost contact with all of her friends, because she was not allowed to have them. Her family did not intervene. Jenna said her family was the type that "didn't get into one another's business." She was totally dependent on her husband for any social, emotional and financial support.

Jenna was alone, her own worst enemy and desperately trying to satisfy a man who truly would never be satisfied by anyone. He, himself, was an emotional disaster, blaming her and the world around him for his own unhappiness. There was little hope of a happy ending here. Indeed, the ending was anything but happy.

Jenna woke one morning to find a note on her nightstand. It was a suicide note from her husband, who made it clear that because of all Jenna's imperfections and inabilities to "make him happy," he had killed himself. Because of her. The note went on to say that he felt she never loved him, thought only of herself and he hoped she would "live with this memory the rest of her life" in order to feel his pain. Jenna found her husband hanging in the living room.

Jenna dressed in layers of dark clothes to protect herself as well as to punish herself. She feared ever being with another man again; she felt unworthy of friends, love or even being liked by anyone. She lived a life of dark solitude with her cat and opened herself up to no one. She was frightened and truly believed that no one could or would ever really love her—let alone *like* her—again. It took all the fortitude she had to get up each morning, dress and commute to work. She always looked down when walking and even on a beautiful spring day with the sun shining brightly, she walked as if she was walking through a blizzard of sleet, with fast, sharp steps to avoid the pain. The pain she avoided was the pain of ever being approached by another person.

Wearing dark sunglasses, Jenna kept her face down and in a book, magazine or newspaper when in public, never daring to look up and make eye contact. At work, she spoke only when spoken to and gave short, pointed answers. She rarely ventured out of her cubicle and her eyes remained fixed on her computer screen for the better part of her eight-hour shift.

Jenna complained to me that by the end of each day she was so emotionally drained from keeping her cover and fearing human contact, she went home and fell immediately to sleep. Each day she dreaded the next, knowing she would have to do it all over again!

When a person exists in such a state, it is not surprising to hear that he or she has no friends or that he or she feels unloved. Jenna made sure of her isolation. However, there are those of us who act similarly, though perhaps not to such an extreme. Are you making eye contact with the world around you or do you scuttle past people through life? Do you smile or frown? Do you strike up "small talk" with coworkers or people with whom you commute or do you avoid them? You see, Calm and Sense says it takes liking or showing interest in others to have others like or be interested in us.

Before you quickly dismiss others as "not liking" you, it is important to take a good look at how you are coming across to them. Are you tight-lipped? Guarded? Curt with answers? Are your conversations "all about you"? Could you be more relaxed, laid back, easily approachable, jovial and showing interest in others? These are key elements to Calm and Sense in relationships and friendships (read more about this in part 3).

Jenna was emotionally exhausted, battered and bankrupt when she came to see me. Her methods of "survival" were breaking down and she felt committed to a life of solitude and isolation. Then her "golden moment" came. One morning, on her commute to work, she forgot to bring some reading material. She did not have her tool of distraction; she had nowhere to hide! She panicked and struggled with her anxiety as she thought, *How in the world can I get through this train ride?*

For Jenna, it was a serious problem. Feelings of panic filled her mind and her heart raced. She truly felt naked and vulnerable, even faint. What was she to do now?

Then it happened. The most frightening, heart-pounding, sweat-inducing of all Jenna's nightmares came true. Someone tapped her on the shoulder. She took a deep breath and lifted her head halfway up, but not enough to look at the "intruder" who dared approach her. She saw the hand of an older man. He was holding a newspaper and he said to her in soft-spoken words, "I see you don't have anything to read today. I'm finished with this. You can have it."

With that, Jenna looked up at the man's face, gently took the newspaper from him and said, "Thank you." That was the entire encounter. But it got Jenna thinking. In taking the paper she actually *looked* at the old man for a brief second. She realized she had never seen him before. She also realized that he certainly must have seen her many times before as he realized she always had something to read. He may have seen her for days, weeks, months or years, but *he had noticed her* before and cared enough to sense something was awry with her that morning. And so he helped her. The old man's kind gesture generated a spark of feeling cherished and understood in Jenna. That "golden moment" was all she needed: a touch of Calm and Sense!

The small gesture by the old man touched Jenna in such a way that she felt that the world was not such a scary and threatening place anymore. After that she slowly worked on treating herself with love and care and paying attention to her feelings instead of hiding from them. She started to *look* at people when she walked to the train station, on the train and in stores. She began to smile more and she liked what started to happen.

People smiled back. People said, "Good morning!" and she said, "Good morning!" Jenna began to engage in small talk on the train. She felt empowered more and more with each new risk she took. Her mistrust in people began to lessen; her self-esteem began to rise.

Of course, deeper issues Jenna had from childhood and her marriage were addressed in more detail during our sessions, but Jenna had to find the courage to address who she *was* and learn who she *could be*. She addressed her past anger and self-loathing and was able to move forward, leaving the past where it belonged—in the past.

After several months of therapy, Jenna was using Calm and Sense regularly. She adopted two more playmates for her cat and also started talking to her family again. She got a new job where she could "start over," made some friends and talked about dating again. Gone were the layers of dark clothes and sunglasses too. Jenna freed herself enough to dress in style and walk with confidence. She learned to love herself and allow others to "like" her too!

Perfect Happiness

Perfection is a fantasy. It is also a form of procrastination and avoidance. Many people get caught up in the pursuit of happiness but rarely find it, because they are putting unrealistic expectations on what they believe happiness is supposed to be! Many people have the erroneous belief that they are supposed to feel happy *all the time*. No! I mentioned this earlier, but it is also relevant here, because it relates directly to what many people believe "true" happiness is.

Calm and Sense believes that if we were all "perfectly happy all the time," we would be bored out of our minds. There is no dark without light; there is no warmth without cold; there is no wet without dry; there is no joy without sorrow. According to Calm and Sense, the trick to understanding happiness is this: We must realize that we have absolutely, positively no way to guarantee it and we need to accept that, like a warm summer breeze, happiness comes our way, then blows away. When it does, we can remember that moment or period of time and the feelings we had, but we need not fear the absence of it, because it returns again and again.

Every so often, life reminds us that what makes us happy today may not make us happy tomorrow. Many people forget this and get caught up in the search for "perfect happiness" and how to attain it. We change, the people around us change, life changes. Looking for happiness only in the places we found it before does not guarantee we will find it. Think about this: Does the truck or doll you cherished as a child bring you the same happiness today that it did when you were a child? Probably not. The memory of the happiness may provide you with a momentary feeling of happiness, but if you actually started playing with your cherished childhood toy again you would most likely not find the same depth of excitement and joy. Have you ever experienced the ending of a relationship? At the beginning, the relationship was fireworks, hummingbirds and bliss. At the end? Well, it looked nothing like that at all. Why do relationships change like that? Why can't we pick up our childhood doll and feel the same things we felt many years ago? Because *we change.* We know that change is one thing that is guaranteed in this life. The good news is this: It is absolutely acceptable to change! As we change, many of the things that make us happy change too. Calm and Sense urges you to accept this concept and understand how happiness, like life, flows like a river. It does not sit still like a lake.

You see, it's the *imperfection* of happiness that makes it so exciting and enjoyable! Happiness can come anytime or anywhere. To enjoy it, however, we must be able to identify and relish the feeling while we have it. While there are things we know will bring us some degree of happiness—things like a puppy, an ice cream cone, a favorite song or dance, a roller coaster ride or a favorite meal—the big picture of happiness comes and goes with new and different people, places, feelings and things.

Calm and Sense says that when we love ourselves, we have less of a need for people, places, feelings and things to "make" us happy. When we love ourselves, we are in a constant state of acceptance of ourselves and realize that just being who we are *is* happiness. When situations arise that elevate happiness, well, that's just the cherry on an ice cream sundae.

Failure, Disappointment and the Belief That There Is No True Happiness

I don't know anyone who has not experienced failure and disappointment at some time in life. Neither do I know anyone who has enjoyed failing or being disappointed. For those of you who are convinced that you have "only failed" and "been disappointed" at your endeavors to find happiness, I ask you this: From what you see as your "failures" or "disappointments," what have you learned and what can you now do differently? Calm and Sense believes that when we make mistakes (Calm and Sense does not like to use the word *fail*), we become experts at something. When we make mistakes, we know more than the average person who has not tried what we have. When we make mistakes, we have learned something about something. What have we learned? At the very least we have learned either what to do or what not to do in certain instances. Those are lessons in Calm and Sense and they foster *wisdom.*

Calm and Sense believes to FAIL is to Find Another Important Lesson. In essence, to *fail* is also to *succeed*, because when we learn anything we succeed. The key is to keep ahead of our impulses to dismiss our attempts to find happiness as futile if they do not immediately bring results. Our searches for ourselves can be very painful at times. Trying to get beyond our pasts can be difficult endeavors and it takes courage to make changes in our lives. But to relieve the pain of the proverbial thorn in the foot, we must first endure the greater pain of pulling it out.

If we *believe* we will fail, we will. If we *believe* we are not good enough, we never will be. If we cannot love ourselves, we cannot love others *and* others will have a difficult time loving us. If you are feeling that your life is not happy because of your inability to feel good about who you are or what you do, then listen to what Calm and Sense is telling you! It is time to do something different, not to resign yourself to a life of sadness.

Evaluate your Emotional and Social Maturity levels. Do you accept responsibility in your life or do you blame people, places and things for your troubles and shortcomings? Have you developed and matured with wisdom or do you still react as a child might, wanting what you want when you want it? Do you make necessary changes in your life when things do not go your way or do you blame or expect others to "fix" things for you?

If you don't answer these questions positively, then it is time to use some Calm and Sense in your life today. In doing so, you will first learn and accept that you live in the here and now, not the when or then. Commit now to a future that makes Calm and Sense and renew that commitment every day. The gift of your unique self awaits you and in that, happiness.

Part Three

Calm and Sense in Love and Relationships

"You don't have to go looking for love
when it's where you come from."

Werner Erhard
American entrepreneur, lecturer and author

There are so many questions and so many issues when it comes to relationships. By far, I see more people in my practice because of issues in their relationships than because of any other issue. What is it about relationships and love that causes so much happiness as well as distress? Calm and Sense knows.

In this section, you will learn how to use Calm and Sense in your relationships with loved ones. You will learn how to be a better partner, wife or husband. You will learn how to recognize the reasons a relationship is or is not "working" and how to identify potential pitfalls, repair irrational expectations and gain a healthier understanding of yourself, your partner's needs and your own needs as well.

There are two imperative aspects to Calm and Sense in love and relationships that must be understood in order to have *any* Calm and Sense in your relationships. These two truths are the pillars that support the successful union of two people and if both parties have learned and fully accepted them, a love that lasts forever is certainly likely: *you must first love yourself* and *you cannot change anyone but yourself*.

Chapter 19

You Must First Love Yourself

The first truth in relationships is this: You must have a relationship with yourself before you can have one with another person. You must romance, woo, date, go "steady" with and marry yourself before you can succeed in a love relationship with someone else!

I bet many of you are thinking, *What do you mean, woo and marry myself?*

The essence of Calm and Sense living rests upon the principles of self-acceptance, self-love and self-preservation. When you have mastered these, you are a self-contained unit—you are content, confident and comfortable in your own skin. Complete and whole. A huge misconception many people have is the idea that they need someone to *make* them whole and happy. This could not be further from the truth.

If you feel that you need someone to cure your loneliness, sadness or feeling of "incompleteness," you are not ready for a relationship yet. These feelings are indicative of needing more Calm and Sense in your life.

And now maybe you're thinking, *We all need someone in our lives to make us happy. We can't be happy alone all the time.*

Yes, as human beings we all need other human beings. We need human interaction; we need someone else to help us pass on our genes; sometimes we need an extra pair of hands to help us with something.

That's not what I'm talking about. I'm talking about the erroneous concept that, as individuals, we are not complete without partners.

Are you a person who fears being alone? Do you need to be constantly doing something, to be constantly with someone? Are you uncomfortable just being alone? Do you panic when you are single? Will you endure a not-so-great (or even downright horrible) relationship, because it is better than being alone? Does this make Calm and Sense? Is this truly loving yourself and accepting only beneficial and mutually satisfying relationships in your life, including the relationship with yourself? Absolutely not! It is *settling*. Calm and Sense tells us that when we are truly ready for a relationship, we do not ever want to "settle"; instead, we want to "settle down." There is a huge difference between these two things.

Calm and Sense tells us that ALONE means A Little Oneness Needed Every day.

Even the word itself, "al(l) one," has at its core the idea that "one" *is* an "all" or a whole.

Calm and Sense tells us that before we are fully equipped to truly love others, we must have both a sound and solid understanding of who we are and a true acceptance of ourselves. To do this, you must spend time with yourself. So many of us, though, don't like to be alone. Some of us even *fear* being alone. Too many of us see time alone as being "*by* myself" instead of "*with* myself." Why do people have such problems with being alone? What I have found in my work with so many people is that the fear of aloneness is the result of insecurity and people's resistance to discover who they really are! It is only in "dating" ourselves that we come to appreciate our partners and love them.

Insecurity causes much destruction and contributes to the deterioration of our relationships and of ourselves. This emotion, according to Calm and Sense, must be addressed and conquered before we set forth into a loving relationship of any kind, because it is the result of a lack of self-love and appreciation. Many mistakenly think that a relationship will bring the sense of security for which we are truly longing. The truth is that an insecure person will not gain security from *any* external source, including another person.

Calm and Sense has an acronym for INSECURITY: Intense Need, Sensing Everything Can Unravel, Reacting Irrationally Toward Yourself (and others).

What this acronym also stands for is a call to action to correct it. Using Calm and Sense language, when we are INSECURE, we must Identify

Needs So Emotions Can Understand Rational Explanation. Until we correct our insecurities and the feeling of being insecure, this type of thinking keeps us in a constant state of fear, worry, panic and disarray. We are constantly on the defensive, looking and waiting for something to happen to disrupt the relationship. That's no way to live and certainly no way to enjoy a relationship!

At this point, it is crucial to understand that the lack of a feeling of security in our lives affects not only our relationships but *everything* we do. Calm and Sense says SECURITY is Seeing Everything Clearly Utilizing Realistic Intentions Toward Yourself (and others).

A lack of security limits us and traps us in an emotional prison whereby we lose hope, belief in ourselves, determination and a general sense of worthiness and well-being. Because these effects are so detrimental to every aspect of our lives, it is imperative that you ask yourself if you are feeling insecure and, if you are, what is causing you to feel this way.

In addition, it's important to understand that we create our own insecurities by feeding our minds with falsities about who we are and what we can and cannot do. As I have mentioned throughout this book, we are all searching for safety in our lives. It is a basic human need. Once we have become adults and are able to reasonably care for ourselves, it is our responsibility to tell ourselves we *are* safe and to do whatever it is we need to do to sustain that safety zone. To tell yourself, "He makes me so insecure" or "I get insecure when I don't have this" is neglecting your right and responsibility to keep yourself safe and secure. That job does not belong to anyone or anything other than yourself.

Insecurity brings about jealousy, rage, abuse and overall feelings that we are not truly loved by a partner. Why? Because we have not yet learned to truly love ourselves. We have not had that all-wonderful, glorious and loving affair with ourselves. When we have learned to truly love ourselves, then we are at peace with ourselves, the world and, if we are in a relationship, with our partners. If our partners have insecurities and our Calm and Sense detects this, we leave. It is as simple as that, because those of us with Calm and Sense "settle down"; we do not "settle." We know we are okay being alone if we have to be and that a relationship is only an enhancement to our already fulfilled lives.

Calm and Sense requires that we find a way to "date" and "marry" ourselves before we consider looking for or allowing partners to come into our "relationship." It is imperative that we do not panic when we are alone and that we understand and accept that a relationship with ourselves *is* a relationship. We are never alone with ourselves. Still, many people have a very difficult time with this concept and steadfastly feel the "need" for "someone, anyone" to make them feel whole.

Calm and Sense reminds us to not panic! What happens when we panic? PANIC puts Pain And Nervousness In Control of our emotions. In doing this, we relinquish our Calm and Sense and act irrationally. This is why those who fear loneliness and being single have an extremely difficult time finding true, lasting love. They "settle" instead of "settle down!" Calm and Sense says slow down and take the time you need to find security with yourself.

The experience of aloneness is a wonderful journey of self-exploration, self-acceptance and self-reliance. When you don't take the time to get to know and love yourself, it's easy to watch time pass and allow feelings of desperation to set in. Calm and Sense reminds us that desperation is the seed of regret. When we act purely out of desperation, we make mistakes. Imagine you want to be a surgeon. Now imagine you want it so badly and so immediately that you are willing to lie about your education and experience in order to convince a hospital that you are actually a qualified surgeon. Now imagine that you have somehow been able to pull it off; you are officially a surgeon on staff at a busy hospital. You've had no medical school education or training and you have no real experience operating on people, but you have surgeries to perform—just as you wanted. Now what do you do?

That is an extreme example, of course. Life and death situations are not something most of us in our healthy minds would try to fake, but this example serves to illustrate a point. In real life, desperation can cause us to fake our way into many situations, like relationships. In the excitement of starting a new relationship or getting to know someone with the potential of starting a new relationship, we tend to put our best foot forward, so to speak. In doing this, often the people we introduce ourselves as are our ideal versions of who we would like to be or the people we think that others want us to be or to whom they would be attracted. In this emotional environment, it's easy to be positive and come across as a well-grounded, interesting, funny, cooperative and caring person—a person another individual would certainly like to get to know and perhaps enter a romantic relationship with.

The beginning part of a relationship always seems to be the most exciting, fun and stimulating part of the relationship. Both parties are on their "best behavior" and do and say things so very romantic and flattering that they, well, "fall in love!" But, alas, this bliss often comes to an end. After some period of time, people get back to being their real selves instead of the "ideal version" of themselves they were working hard to be when they first began the relationship. Each partner discovers that the person he or she is now looking at, spending time with, waking up next to or living with is not exactly the person he or she fell in love with or the person he or she thought the other was. Then the struggles begin: the misunderstandings, the lack of communication, the loss of all that wonderful stuff that "we used to have in the beginning." Most of us have had this experience in one or more of our relationships and, sadly, many of us believe that is the way all relationships are destined to be.

Those of us who live a Calm and Sense life know differently. We know that the excitement, romance and fun we experience when we meet someone and start a relationship goes on and on *throughout* the relationship, because we are both our true selves all along and what we see and fall in love with in the other person initially is truly what we get…and still have. People who live lives of Calm and Sense do not enter or begin relationships acting as anyone but themselves and do not spend time in relationships with people who are doing anything less than being true to themselves as well. As a result, the emotion is genuine, as is the excitement and fun—all of which continue throughout the duration of the relationship, especially as the two individuals grow closer over time.

The person who is truly prepared to begin a relationship with another person lives a life that embraces Calm and Sense and, therefore, does not ever feel pressured or desperate to "find someone." This person is quite satisfied and content alone, if that's where he happens to be, and he knows that any relationship he enters will only enhance his state of Calm and Sense, not disturb it.

Having Calm and Sense also benefits the holder by helping him or her identify others who have it (Calm and Sense) and tell them apart from those folks who are "faking" it. People with Calm and Sense have such strong feelings of self-love and self-respect that they always seek to protect their well-being from any potential negative influences. People with Calm and Sense take very good care of themselves.

The art of learning to love yourself must include the ability to be alone for a significant amount of time, free from the feelings of desperation, loneliness and panic that you are "not complete." Only when this is accomplished can you hope to have healthy relationships with others.

Chapter 20

You Cannot Change Anyone but Yourself

The second truth in relationships is that you cannot change anyone but yourself. The tendency to try to change others is another form of insecurity within relationships I see most frequently. I often hear people say, "I can change him if I do *x*, *y* or *z*!" and "If only she would do what I say!" Why do people think that they can *change* someone or that a relationship is about saving someone else from some form of danger or pain?

If you have fallen in love with someone, why would this person need to change? If he or she was worthy of falling in love with, what is there to change? If you were not happy with whom the person is, what was it that you fell in love with? What was it or who was it that you *believed* you could turn them into? People with Calm and Sense don't want or need to change who they are and certainly are not in the business of changing anyone else. Entertainer Billy Joel sang, "Don't go changing, to try and please me...I love you just the way you are." *That* is the idea.

By the same token, anyone with whom we are involved romantically should not be attempting to change us. If you find yourself falling prey to making changes to please a partner, Calm and Sense recommends a relationship reevaluation right away. We cannot become something other than ourselves for anyone.

Someone might object, for example, that "My wife hated *Grateful Dead* music before we met, and I'll admit that I forced her to come with me to some shows, but now she loves them as much as I do. Are you saying I made her change and this is a bad thing?" Of course not! Partners learn from each other all the time and sometimes even unlikely interests are discovered to be mutually enjoyed by two people. Calm and Sense does not discourage those types of changes; in fact, they are encouraged.

The types of changing you should be on the alert for are those that are more manipulative and self-serving for one person instead of mutually beneficial to both. These types of changes can include a partner insisting that good friends you have had for years are no good for you anymore or your partner saying, "Your family doesn't like me, so they must not want you to be happy." It also includes comments like, "That skirt makes you look like a hooker. If you really loved me, you wouldn't dress like that!" These are a reflection of a person's own insecurities and are self-serving and demeaning. You may happen to think that skirt looks absolutely adorable on you: "How dare he tell me something like that?" Calm and Sense says, "Exactly!" Wear what you want and keep your friends and family close. If they love you but seem to have an issue with or concern about your partner, maybe they are seeing something you haven't yet been able to recognize or accept. Remember Lynn (chapter 12)? She made lots of "changes" for Michael, lost contact with all her friends and family because of their concerns and allowed Michael to take total control of her life.

If your Calm and Sense is working, your self-esteem is also where it needs to be. You will find requests to change to be uncomfortable and insulting; you will detect insecurity and manipulation and you will not tolerate it.

Both women and men can also get caught up in the Rescuer Role. You take on the Rescuer Role when you believe someone you have met needs you, your help or both in some intimate or dire way and *only you* can provide exactly what that person needs. The truth is, though, that is another sign of insecurity. In reality, the more "needy" person is the one who sees him or herself as the Rescuer. Taking on this role puts the Rescuer in a position of power over the other person (the Receiver), even if only temporarily. The Rescuer often thinks, *Without me, s/he would never have gotten that job, stopped snorting cocaine, gotten out of jail, had a place to live, etc.*

In the beginning, this kind of relationship gives the Rescuer a purpose and a feeling of being needed. This is usually mistaken for love and speaks to the Rescuer's unmet needs of self-love and lack of Calm and Sense. The Receiver—being a person who is also lacking in those areas—will usually take the help, in whatever form it's being given, any way he or she can. It is important to understand that in a relationship like this, to accept the Rescuer's "gifts" and also condone them as a means of "falling in love" demonstrates the Receiver's lack of Calm and Sense and puts his or her motives into suspicion. Why? Because those of us with Calm and Sense do not mistake helping others or martyring ourselves with romantic love.

Let me bring you back to having a relationship with yourself first. When you have done the work of learning to love yourself, you feel secure in your "marriage of one," you have acquired Calm and Sense in your life, you do not need anyone or anything to help you put your pieces together anymore and you do not need to save someone else and call it romantic love.

This is not to say that being a friend and doing charitable work for another person is discouraged or a sign of weakness. Being a good friend, helping people when they need it and performing charitable work are all Calm and Sense components of being the best person you can be. But charitable work and good deeds do not make a romance!

Here's what could happen when you "take someone in" under the guise of romance. In my practice, I have worked with many people who have shared this scenario with me and I have seen a good number of men and women who had not yet learned Calm and Sense and fell prey to both sides of the "Rescuer Game."

Peggy had been married to Pete, who came from a very wealthy family. Peggy and Pete had a daughter together; Peggy also had an older daughter from a previous relationship. Peggy had come from a poor family and lived a life of urban stress. As a child, Peggy was beaten and sexually abused by her father. Peggy's mother was of little help and did nothing to protect her children from their father's wrath.

Throughout her childhood, Peggy learned that there was little, if anything, she could do to win her father's love; however, having sex with him seemed to get her some attention. Nothing Peggy did was right and her mother was subservient to her father's wants, needs and demands.

An attractive girl, having won a state beauty competition in her late teen years, Peggy learned that men paid attention to her when she dressed provocatively and acted flirtatiously. This led to many encounters with men who doted over Peggy, giving her the same attention she received from her dad but not true love and respect.

Peggy had no real love for herself, nor was any truly given to her from others. Over time, she learned to mistake male attention and sex for love. She was able to get all the attention she wanted, but she was unable to see that the attention was not for her—it was only for what she could provide! This left her empty, angry and full of self-hatred on a subconscious level. She never felt "quite right" or truly loved by anyone. Her relationships were all about what men could get from her (in her case, sex). Because she didn't know better, Peggy continued participating in this vicious cycle of "false love" that consisted of receiving attention from men who wanted only to have sex with her (which she mistook for "love") and being abandoned by them. This always left her feeling unloved, unwanted and angry (subconsciously at herself) and in a more desperate search for the next man who would make her feel better by showing her attention and sticking around longer than the previous ones had.

Sadly, this cycle repeated itself over and over. The men came and went from her life. When Peggy tried to get a relationship going further, the men were nowhere to be found or were not interested in anything more from or with her. That's when she met Pete.

Peggy met Pete at her place of employment and they got "friendly" more than once or twice in the broom closet—which was where her second daughter was conceived. At his family's insistence, because she was pregnant with his child, Pete married Peggy. His family, being the "uppity" socialites they were, did not accept Peggy. They called her "white trash" and made various other offensive judgments about her and her oldest daughter. Despite this, they somehow thought it would look better if the couple was married when the child was born.

Peggy's marriage to Pete lasted three years. It ended, also at his family's insistence, because of the vast differences between Pete's background and hers.

Peggy never felt accepted by Pete's family and, according to her own account, honestly never "really wanted to marry him in the first place." She admitted he was "out of her league"; she felt more comfortable with the rough and tumble crowd of tattooed bikers and barflies than with the martini-sipping, designer clothes-wearing upper echelon of country club society. Peggy shrugged the marriage off like any other "relationship" she had encountered and went back to living the single life.

Back in the "bar life," Peggy met Bart and found him to be the "man of her dreams." Bart was unemployed, on probation, living "with friends" (really in his car) and was more than two years in arrears in his child support payments for his nine-year-old daughter.

This was the man for whom she said she had been waiting. How did she know this? Because he stayed around for more than a week or two after having had sexual relations three times. He kept calling her and didn't disappear like all the others had.

Peggy allowed Bart to move in to her home a month after meeting him. She thought, *We've been together a month! This man is really interested in me!* She had a house; he needed a place to stay. She was working; he was not. He was thousands of dollars behind in child support and probation fees. In fact, he was arrested soon after he moved in with Peggy; he had missed several court dates and had several bench warrants out against him, so the police picked him up and locked him up.

Peggy bailed him out of jail, refinanced her home to help him pay off his debts, paid for an attorney to help with the child support fees and, being the "loving" person she was, paid most of the child support to clear Bart's warrants!

This all occurred within a three or four month time span. Bart still wasn't working. Why? Well, he needed to "finish up" a few hours toward his electrician apprenticeship, then pay to join the union. Guess what? Peggy so loved Bart that she helped him financially with this too!

Can you see how the Rescuer mentality comes into play here? Bart was in trouble: he needed money, a place to live and someone to take care of him, because he clearly couldn't take care of himself. Peggy was also in trouble: she desperately needed to be needed and to believe she was loved. He found out she was a willing giver and he was willing to keep taking as long as she was giving. It was a no-brainer for Bart. Peggy saw Bart as a man who needed to be saved and saw herself as the one person who could save him, so she "solved his problems" and, in return, he stuck around, leading her to believe she was loved. And, since he "loved her," she really should have been doing all she could to help the man who loved her. This relationship, which was actually parasitic and not symbiotic or fair in any way even though Peggy saw it as fair, would keep going until there was nothing Bart needed from Peggy anymore or until Peggy realized she was not actually getting anything *real* from him in return for her contributions. Or until something really big happened that helped Peggy to see things a bit more clearly…

A few months and many dollars into her relationship with Bart, Peggy discovered that Bart was addicted to heroin. Now Peggy was angry that Bart had lied to her after all she had done for him! She asked, "How could you love me and lie to me?" Peggy and Bart fought.

This fight is an example of the "exit points" that come up time and again in unhealthy, non-productive relationships. An exit point is when something happens (like a fight, a discovery, an arrest, etc.) in the relationship that is unacceptable to one or both people, providing an opportunity for one or both of them to face facts and end the relationship. In Peggy's case, this wasn't the first exit point that had cropped up for her to take advantage of and it certainly wasn't going to be the last. Often, even when we can clearly see the opportunity to move on, we continue to hope things will get better or we hang on to the idea of the "time and money" already invested and we let an exit point pass without taking any action. This never leads to a better relationship. Sometimes we acknowledge an exit point by requiring some kind of work in the relationship as a condition for not ending the relationship. This only works if there are clear rules and boundaries set, they are set in earnest and agreed to by both parties and they are followed!

In this case, Bart must have felt the sting of Cupid's arrow, because he convinced Peggy he was truly sorry for the lying and wanted to get help for his addiction. He didn't want to lose his provider! As you may have guessed, instead of taking full advantage of this exit point by ending the relationship, Peggy bought Bart's story and "felt the love" once again. I wish I could tell you this was the beginning of a turnaround for Peggy (and Bart), that they talked about the issues and were finally on their way to a positive, healthy relationship. But there were no clear rules and boundaries set by these two people (or even one of them) who were not being honest with themselves or each other *and* there was another problem: Bart had no health insurance to pay for help for the addiction.

Instead of running quickly in the other direction, Peggy dove in even further. Bart and Peggy married so he could be covered under Peggy's health plan. He went to counseling for his addiction; she sought help to learn how to be a better wife of an addict. It was at this point in Peggy's life that I met her.

Despite all of Peggy's giving, Bart did not make any changes. He continued using heroin and lying to her and he never found work. She eventually went from "bliss" to "boil." She felt used and manipulated, but she would not let go of the marriage. Why? Here again is the same rationale that I have heard over and over: "After all this work, I don't want some other woman he gets involved with to benefit from all the time and effort I've put into him."

How did Bart go from being the man of Peggy's dreams, the "one who saved her from loneliness," her "knight in shining armor" to being the "bastard I gave my life and life savings to and now I'm supposed to let him go in order to live happily ever after with someone else?"

It happened because Peggy had no Calm and Sense. When Peggy was a child, her father both abused her and paid her no attention. Knowing that, it would stand to reason that Peggy desperately wanted a man to love her, but she did not love herself enough to know that love does not depend on martyring yourself or refinancing your home to gain it. Peggy found a false sense of control over Bart's "love" for her by giving and "saving" him to the extreme. She thought, *If I sacrifice this for him, he will have to love me and never leave me.* Or, *I will do whatever it takes to keep him and his love.*

Love is the last thing that Bart and Peggy had for each other. She gave; he took. He told her he loved her; she believed it. Peggy heard what she wanted to hear, but her insecurity told her she had to *earn* love, which, of course, did not and can never happen.

I tried to convey to Peggy that she had a lot of work to do to gain Calm and Sense. She had to focus on changing *herself*, not her partner. She had to learn to love herself. Peggy was still married to Bart during our last session, unable to end the marriage after all she had "put into it." She still didn't want to "let someone else benefit from her hard work" with Bart, unrealistically hoping that Bart would somehow change and *really love her* eventually. But, as I stated earlier, we cannot ever enter a love relationship with the expectation of changing anyone. That never ends well and it makes no Calm and Sense.

Six months after my last session with Peggy, I received an e-mail from her. In it, she told me she was divorcing Bart as she had found the new "man of her dreams"—a realtor she met while he was showing her a home.

Chapter 21

We All Need a Purpose

What do you want from me? What am I supposed to do? Where do I fit in? What is my *purpose*?

"What is my purpose in life?" is a question we all struggle with at some time or another. We often question "what am I doing here" universally, vocationally, spiritually, romantically...the list is as long as there are an individual's needs.

I love Saint Bernard dogs. Anyone who knows me also knows I support and tolerate their slobber, hair, big kisses and sacrificing personal space for this wonderful breed of dog. To me, they are placid, majestic, proud, dignified, regal, loyal, loving, kindhearted, sensitive and intelligent creatures. They are also mischievous, destructive, obnoxious and have no clue as to why their massive size is intimidating to some or a problem when they want to sit on your lap.

I use Saint Bernard dogs as a reference on the subject of purpose for a very real and important reason. Given all their wonderful and not so wonderful traits, they are a breed of dog known as "working dogs." Working dogs need jobs to do. They are not fulfilled to "just be" all the time. To feel complete, they need to know what their role, job or purpose is. So do we, as human beings, with our good and not so good sides. What is life, work, friendships, relationships or love without a "job" or a purpose?

None of us would have a job or a paid occupation if there wasn't a problem to solve. Every job exists to solve a certain problem. A house painter solves the problem of a house needing a new look. A police officer solves the problem of people breaking laws. A fast-food cashier solves the problem of people who are hungry and need to buy some food. There is no job in the world that doesn't involve solving someone's or something's problems.

I have found as a therapist that relationships are a most significant factor that contributes to depression and people seeking help. Identifying and fulfilling our purpose or purposes in our personal relationships is critical to being able to feel good about ourselves and, therefore, feel good about our relationships. And when we feel good about both those things, our partners feel good about them too.

What is your purpose in your relationship? Do you know? What problems do you help your "customer" (e.g., spouse/partner/significant other) solve? Do you reassure the person that you have his or her best interests in mind? Do you generate trust and reliance? Do you hear your partner in his or her time of need even if that person is not speaking? Do you assure the other person that your outside activities or relationships do not condemn or criticize the partner in any way? Do you provide emotional support and understanding? Do you take care of certain chores so that your partner can take care of others without being overburdened? Have you ever thought of these things as purposeful to your loved one?

What is your job in your relationship? Love is not always easy. It requires, at times, self-sacrifice, intuition of your partner's needs, putting your partner's needs ahead of yours and a genuine desire to work your job to keep your partner comfortable, self-assured and supported at all times, no matter what.

These jobs define our purposes in relationships and it is our own responsibility to figure out (by asking, listening and paying attention) and take care of the specifics of what our loved ones need. True love is like a well-oiled machine that runs smoothly, because we are always making the effort to fulfill our purposes and meet each other's needs.

When Saint Bernard dogs know what their "job" is, they also know their purpose. So do we need to know our purposes when it comes to relationships. We ask ourselves, "In my relationship with this person, what 'jobs' do I do that no one else does for this person? What does he or she need from me in this relationship? What are the things about me that have led this person to choose me as his or her partner?" In answering these questions, either on our own or by asking our partners, we discover our purposes in the relationships. And in doing this, we ensure that we can fulfill those purposes—not only for the other person's betterment, but equally for our own senses of satisfaction and fulfillment.

We really only have one job in a relationship: to be as supportive and loving as we can to our partners. However, there are many components, or smaller jobs, that make up that one big job. As with any other aspect of our lives, focusing on only one part of the whole leads to our neglecting the others.

Our relationship "jobs" are as important as our occupations, yet we seem to give much more time, effort and attention to our occupations. Our relationship "jobs" are also much more important than season tickets, book club, bake sale, vacuuming, the golf game, etc.

Think about your time and effort. What do you do? What problems do you help solve? What does your partner need you to do? Do you know? Calm and Sense demands that we find out. How? Ask, observe, feel and think. If that doesn't work, you may not be ready for a relationship yet.

As with jobs, purpose isn't limited to one thing. We have many purposes in our relationships. Sometimes a purpose has a limited timeframe (like building an addition on the house so that there is room for your growing family); sometimes it goes on indefinitely (like making sure your spouse feels that you are there for him or her no matter what). Because we have many purposes and only a limited number of hours in each day, it's very easy to fall into focusing all our time on a single purpose, like raising children or working to keep things financially stable. When we focus on a single purpose—especially one that has a limited timeframe—and disregard all the others, we lose touch with the relationship itself. Then, when that single purpose has been fulfilled and its goal has been reached, we find ourselves lost and feeling purposeless, because we've lost our connection with all of our other purposes and, more importantly, with our partners.

Calm and Sense reminds us that after we identify our purposes, we must keep them *all* in mind and make sure that while we are putting our energy into fulfilling one, we are not ignoring all the others.

An example of what happens when we don't identify our purposes in our relationships occurs when we focus too much on one purpose and neglect the others—what happens when a relationship or marriage goes without attention, care or true purpose.

Joan and Neil were a couple who came to see me for about two years. When I first met them, he was fifty-five and she was forty-nine. Neil worked as a supervisor at a construction company; Joan was a teacher. This was Neil's first marriage; it was Joan's second. Joan had two children from her previous marriage. At the time I met them, her daughter was a senior in high school and her son was in his first year of college.

Joan and Neil's "presenting problem" (the term therapists use for the specific reason people have come in for counseling) was Neil's tendency to "blow up" when he got angry. Neil and Joan's background information tells more about their relationship before they came to me. Neil was, generally, a very laid back, mellow guy. Meeting him, you would never suspect that he ever got upset, let alone downright angry. Joan was a perfectionist whose children were her number one priority in life. She and Neil had been married for more than ten years and Neil truly was the children's "dad," since their biological father was generally nonexistent in their lives. Neil and Joan worked together on the children's success in sports, school and other activities for most of their childhood and adolescent years. Joan was more their academic mentor, Neil, the sports authority. This combination worked quite well as Joan, being a teacher, was better equipped to help them succeed in school and Neil, a sports buff, was a natural when it came to coaching them. The children excelled in track, soccer and softball.

As the children got older and spent less time playing sports, Neil and Joan began to notice problems in their relationship with each other. Still focused on the children, Neil and Joan just kept moving forward. Eventually, Joan's son went away to college and her daughter was almost finished with high school; both were becoming independent. Where Joan and Neil had worked so well as the "dynamic duo" of childrearing for so long, now Neil began to sense that he was not needed by the children as much as he had been earlier. As the children's educations were an ongoing endeavor, Joan was still supplying constant academic support. However, as time went on, the children became less involved in sports and were growing more and more self-sufficient. They required less "coaching" and support from Neil.

Neil felt like he didn't fit within the dynamics of the family anymore. Whenever he attempted to contribute something to the family that did not involve sports, his efforts were met with resistance from Joan and the children, leaving him feeling upset. Unable to find something he could do to rejoin the family dynamic, Neil felt more and more unhappy. Neil could not communicate his feelings to his family, because he was not aware of what he was actually feeling. Since he couldn't specifically identify what he felt beyond just plain feeling "awful," he withdrew into his own world and did not speak much to anyone anymore. What Neil was feeling and couldn't identify was hurt.

Joan became concerned over Neil's "attitude" (his moodiness and his silence) and the tension it brought to the family dynamics. Joan did not understand what had happened to Neil or why he had become so cranky and closed off. Neil did not understand why his family seemed to be treating him as an outsider. Not only had he lost his role in the family, but also things were becoming stressful and he couldn't fix what was wrong. He didn't know what was causing his family to distance themselves from him.

Why were things spiraling downward like this? Neil was feeling hurt, because he felt he'd lost his role in and his value to his family. He wanted and needed reassurance, comfort and understanding from Joan. Not really able to specifically identify what was bothering him, Neil did not communicate his feelings or needs to Joan. Since Joan did not react to Neil's "secret" feelings and needs, Neil felt even worse and upped the ante by getting angry. It was at this point that Joan finally noticed something was wrong, because now Neil was *behaving* differently (something she could see) instead of just *feeling* badly (something she couldn't see). She identified the problem to be Neil's *anger* and not what Neil needed her to see was the problem. Because Joan could not read Neil's mind, she fretted over the "big picture" (the impact his angry behavior was having on the entire family) instead of what Neil wanted her to focus on (his underlying feelings).

At this point, Neil was completely frustrated that his (still unidentified) feelings and needs for support and understanding were not being addressed by Joan and Joan was seeing an increasingly angry Neil, but she had no clues or information as to why his personality had changed so drastically. Now, in a more desperate attempt to find some purpose in the family again and to feel better about himself, Neil took on the job of "supervising" the household chores. He began to expect more from the family members in their chores and behaviors. He insisted on things being done a certain way—his way. As a result, Joan and the children felt that nothing they did was good enough for him. Because of Neil's new behavior, the family began to ignore him even more. The downward spiral continued.

Calm and Sense tells us—and it is important to recognize—that *hurt* is the seed of *anger*. We normally do not get angry until we have first felt hurt in some way. This is why Neil began to communicate his misunderstood feelings through anger. And without Neil being able to identify his feelings and share them with his family, Joan and the children could not understand what had happened to Neil and why he had suddenly become so angry.

Neil and Joan's situation is an example of how the guessing game in relationships not only never solves problems, but also makes problems more difficult by adding assumptions and unrealistic expectations between partners. It is also a great example of how we sometimes need a little help to clarify what is truly occurring beneath the surface of misunderstanding. The solution to this problem, and for Neil and Joan, is more communication, patience and understanding.

Joan had not seen that Neil was feeling hurt and only noticed something was wrong when Neil began to show anger. Neil had been feeling badly for a while and wanted Joan to understand and acknowledge his hurt and help him feel better, but he never communicated his feelings or his needs to her. He felt frustrated and even a bit let down: *Why can't she see what's wrong with me?* When Joan did not receive and react soon enough to his unspoken message, Neil subconsciously felt compelled to make the message more apparent, which is when the anger and controlling behavior began. The truth was that Neil was angry because the family was not paying attention to his needs. But he had never communicated those feelings or needs to his family, partially because he did not know exactly what he was feeling. Even though he definitely sensed a difference in the dynamics of the home, he could not identify that he was feeling as if he had lost his purpose and that he felt left out.

Seeing only Neil's anger, Joan did not understand what was bothering Neil so deeply. Instead of trying to communicate her confusion and concern about Neil's behavior to him, she believed, "He needs to go to therapy and get to the root cause of this anger stuff, because it's making the family very upset!"

This is the point at which they came to me. Once the true issue (that of Neil's diminishing feeling of being "useful" to the family) was brought out in therapy, the couple could better understand how the shift in Neil's demeanor came about. They discovered his real fear was that he had no other way to give to the family beyond helping the children with their sports endeavors, because sports was "all he knew." This was an irrational fear. Neil could contribute plenty more to the marital relationship as well as to the family, but because he had focused so intently on his sports role for so long, he was having a difficult time identifying how and what else he could contribute. The relationship, which had once flourished with teamwork and valued contributions from both Joan and Neil, was now missing a purpose for Neil.

Unfortunately, in many relationships partners often don't get "fed" as they move along. Neil and Joan and I discussed how their entire marriage—and all of their joint energy—was focused on the care of their children. All their activities were somehow connected to what the children were doing or what they needed, be it sporting events, school activities or their social calendars. Joan and Neil did not find time for their relationship with each other and, as the children got older, Neil felt useless, powerless, left out of the family and like he had no close relationship with his wife. This threw off his emotional equilibrium, resulting in his inability to identify his true feelings, which triggered a lack of understanding and, finally, anger.

Lots of couples find themselves in similar situations when their children grow up and move out: with a loss of connection to each other. I have seen many such couples in my office. With their children taking on more independence and adult roles, the partners seem to look at each other and ask, "Who are you?" or "What do we do now?" Calm and Sense tells us that relationships require constant care and "watering," much like a plant, to avoid the loss of intimacy and connectedness. They require each person to continue to learn about the other partner as life changes and they grow together.

So many people in relationships and marriages get *too* caught up in things like careers, raising children or other outside activities, leaving too little time for their partners and their relationships. As a direct result, the relationships suffer, starving for nourishment.

You might be thinking, *First you said that healthy relationships need each of us to do things without each other and now you're saying we shouldn't do that? Well, which is it?*

Each partner needs to "have a life" outside of the relationship. We are individuals before we are couples! But in order to keep our relationships healthy and happy, we need to attend to them by prioritizing our partners' needs *before* our outside activity needs. This makes very simple Calm and Sense. When we *don't* prioritize our time this way, our partners may begin to feel neglected, undervalued and, like Neil, unneeded and without purpose. When we begin to feel this way in a relationship, many negative consequences occur as we struggle to gain more attention and find meaning, purpose and usefulness in the relationship again. When those efforts don't work, our emotions and sense of security become threatened; panic sets in. This causes us to react in nonproductive or harmful ways—in ways that are not Calm and do not make Sense. Remember: *You* choose how you respond to the call for Calm (see chapter 4).

In instances of "relationship neglect" in couples, the worst case scenarios occur when the neglect has gone on for years and the individuals no longer feel romantic or sexual feelings toward each other. The marriage or relationship turns into a business arrangement or begins to feel "like we are roommates," as I have heard it described time and time again in my practice or, worse yet, "like brother and sister." In order for the relationship to survive, Calm and Sense says that in addition to feeling comfortable with the purposes partners serve in each other's lives, they must also stay in touch with each other emotionally, socially, personally and intimately *throughout the relationship*—not only when it's convenient, when they remember they're supposed to or when they aren't busy doing something else. There is no "autopilot" when it comes to love and romance. Constant attention, vigilance and consideration are necessary ingredients of healthy love.

Chapter 22

Having a Healthy Romantic Relationship

Calm and Sense defines what a healthy romantic relationship *is* and what it is *not*. Here are some important words and phrases that paint a clear picture of what a healthy romantic relationship is like:

- It *is* life enhancing; it is *not* the solution to our unhappiness.
- It *is* a gift and a privilege; it is *not* a right.
- It *is* supportive; it is *not* demeaning.
- It *is* encouraging of personal and individual growth; it is *not* restrictive or controlling.
- It *is* comforting; it is *not* anxiety producing.
- It *is* naturally developing and drawn toward successes; it is *not* dependent on "things" (e.g., houses, children, money, more children) to make love grow.
- It *is* pleasantly surprising; it is *not* secretive or elusive.
- It *is* hard work at times; it is *not* "supposed to be" any certain way.
- It *is* understanding; it is *not* blaming.
- It *is* safe; it is *not* insecure.
- It *is* trusting; it is *not* suspicious.
- It *is* honest; it is *not* deceptive.
- It *is* considerate; it is *not* selfish.
- It *is* unconditionally accepting; it is *not* judgmental.
- It *is* welcomed; it is *not* mandatory.

This is a list of the characteristics and guidelines for creating and maintaining a healthy, happy, consistent, stable and long-lasting relationship filled with romance, laughter, comfort, achievement, trust and warmth. The items on this list also clearly point out the areas of relationships that many people struggle with or experience extreme difficulties in managing when their relationships are missing other key elements of Calm and Sense. When two people who live lives of Calm and Sense get together, they are already well on their way to achieving this kind of relationship.

We have already discussed why two people who desire a wonderful life together must have established their own individual senses of security, social and emotional maturity, self-worth and self-love *prior* to the relationship's beginning and that they cannot seek (and will never find) these things from a relationship or another person. These qualities absolutely must be accomplished on a "solo" mission. Once *you* are energized with Calm and Sense, a partner, "soul mate," significant other, husband, wife, girlfriend, boyfriend, what have you, becomes a *complement* to your sense of well-being—not the cause or provider!

When we are no longer fearful of being in a relationship with ourselves, we do not fear that the relationships with our partners may end. It is that feeling of security and self-assuredness that fuels our love and appreciation of our partners—not the other way around. This makes perfect Calm and Sense.

When we have Calm and Sense before entering a relationship, we already have a sense of feeling *safe*. SAFE, in Calm and Sense thinking, is **S**ecure **A**nd **F**eeling **E**mpowered. A relationship should *double* that sense of safety between two people, not threaten or be the cause of insecurity where one partner forever fears "losing" the other! With Calm and Sense, if our partners want to go, who are we to stop them? We love them, we respect them and we honor their needs. If they need to go, we respect that. That doesn't mean we can't feel sad or even grieve for a while. Likewise, if *we* need to get out of the relationship, we go! Relationships based on Calm and Sense, however, have much greater chances of success. Remember, we "settle down"; we do not "settle."

Feeling safe is a basic human need (see chapter 5 for more on our need for safety). And while it's true that we need to bring our own sense of safety into our relationships, relationships themselves *do* require the component of safety to sustain them. We need to feel a sense of security with each other and not fear judgment, ridicule or belittlement from our partners. If a person is engaging in that type of behavior with his or her loved ones, that person is not using Calm and Sense. And if one partner is tolerating such actions from another, he or she is not using Calm and Sense. Demeaning, insulting or derogatory behaviors have no place where there is *true love*. We can all have a "bad day" and say things we regret every now and then, but I have worked with couples who have had bad *decades*. Calm and Sense demands that we draw the line. Kindness and consideration are the stones we use to build our castles of love. If you are treating yourself with kindness and consideration, how could you allow your loved one to not be as well? How could you treat him or her with any less than you treat yourself?

Another major factor required in a loving, romantic relationship (as well as *any* relationship, for that matter) is honesty. Calm and Sense defines HONEST as Heartfelt Openness, Not Elusive Sneaky Tactics. We do no one any favors by deceiving them. Be it concealing an affair we are having, not telling our loved ones they may need to shed a few pounds (for their good health), setting up a secret bank account, hiding alcohol or drug use or other hidden agendas, it's just not good for the relationship!

When a couple does not address real concerns openly and fearlessly in their relationship, they begin engaging in things like the "guessing game," the "silent treatment" standoff or the "you should know what I want" charade. Calm and Sense reminds us that our partners are not clairvoyant and we should not expect them to be! They cannot read our minds to figure out what is bothering us. Yet time and again I see people expecting mindreading proficiency from their partners. What is so hard about expressing our needs to our loved ones?

Picture a couple, perhaps driving in a car. One partner is silent and staring forward with an angry gaze. The other asks, "What's wrong?" "Nothing," is the response. We probably all know *something* is wrong and the angry partner wants attention or wants his or her partner to *know* he or she is angry, but refuses to speak up! This "dialogue" (which is really not dialogue at all) may go on and on, getting nowhere and provoking bitterness between the partners. The partner who is asking the questions *knows* that he or she must have done something wrong in order to be getting this treatment and wants to "fix" the problem or defend him or herself; the other partner is not giving the first partner that opportunity, keeping the information to him or herself and "punishing" the partner.

Calm and Sense tells us that what we all really want is to resolve our problems and to have our partners understand and support our needs, thereby strengthening our relationships. Playing those games (like the guessing game, the silent treatment game, etc.) will *never* get us what we want. The only way to resolve problems and to grow together in our relationships is to communicate openly and directly.

Note that the word *silent* consists of the letters in the word *listen*. To succeed in love, we must be able to *listen*! That means hearing without acting upon the urge to speak in defense before our partners have finished stating their cases or concerns. Most of us are so busy thinking about or preparing our defenses for the argument that we are not hearing what our loved ones are trying to say. To truly be able to resolve the issue, both partners must give each other the opportunity to fully express their thoughts and feelings. Both partners must express these thoughts and feelings in respectful and clear ways and both must listen to each other and allow themselves to hear what the other is saying without being dismissive or belittling. Sometimes it's difficult to hear from your partner that something you've done or said has hurt them, but becoming defensive, argumentative or both does not solve the problem either. This technique takes practice, but it is very effective and will help you understand your partner's needs much more thoroughly, not just for this particular problem, but in general as well.

This technique also supports having honesty in our relationships. We owe it to each other, when in a relationship, to allow each other to speak our minds, voice our concerns and not take offense if our partners are not being offensive!

Here is the Calm and Sense definition of LISTEN: Let It Settle, Then Evaluate News/Needs. Even when an immediate answer is not necessary, we seem to want to fix or defend *now*! That is not using Calm and Sense. When we are secure, we can *listen* to our partners' concerns, criticisms or needs. Then we can evaluate them, think about what was said and return to discuss the issue calmly and rationally. It is absolutely acceptable not to have an answer or response immediately. It may seem a bit awkward not to have something to say right back—especially if you are used to having "gut reaction arguments"—but sometimes taking a bit of time to really think about the issue is necessary. It is okay to say, "I need some time to think about this." The key here, though, is that you *must* return to your partner with your feedback within a reasonable amount of time. This technique is also very helpful in controlling anger and the tendency to blurt out things you may later regret.

We must feel safe in our relationships and not be afraid to speak openly and honestly with our partners. We must accept that we are responsible for speaking to what is or may be troubling us. We must also dispel the belief that our partners are mentalists. We must be willing to hear what our partners are saying whether we like what they say or not. We must take our time to listen silently before we respond and then respond in ways that embrace Calm and make Sense.

In addition to the need to feel safe, there is no way around the necessity of feeling truly appreciated in a relationship! Appreciation is the motivation and driving force of any successful union of two people. Without it, how or why would we continue to engage in the relationship? But how do you know or come to believe you are being appreciated? The latter is a very difficult question for most of the couples with whom I work—and possibly for many other people. It is just as hard to answer as "How do you know he or she loves you?" The answers to both usually are "Because s/he tells me s/he does." Calm and Sense says this is the most incorrect response to both questions. Calm and Sense knows, as do many of us, that "actions speak louder than words." We also know that "seeing is believing." We form the words and give them the opportunity to be aired. Some people are experts at saying what they think others want to hear. Some people have no problem saying, "I'm sorry, baby; I love you" even when they have no feelings of remorse or love. Words, when it comes to showing love or appreciation, are just words. That is not to say that every time anyone says anything it's not heartfelt. Many people do speak their hearts, but it's the actions they take that assure us that their words are genuine. It's the *showing* that truly tells us what our partners feel. The aspect of appreciation is another key component of having Calm and Sense in relationships.

While I have managed and directed several programs and agencies over the course of my career, I have had the pleasure of training and supervising staff in a number of capacities. I learned quickly that a director or manager is only as good as his or her staff. And, to maintain a happy, satisfied staff, motivated to do the best job they can, a manager must instill a sense of appreciation in his or her people.

What if I went to work every day, sat in my office and never paid any attention to what my employees were doing? What if I just assumed they were happy and believed they should feel honored to be working for such a wonderful, intelligent, super boss like me? I don't need to show or tell them anything. Of course they know I appreciate their work, right? They should work hard and be happy they have a job at all!

What if I invited an employee in to see me only when he or she had done something wrong? Certainly I have to address mistakes with my people, because it's my program and if something goes wrong because of a mistake made by one of my employees, well, then *my* reputation and integrity are on the line.

Ebenezer Scrooge in Charles Dickens' *A Christmas Carol* is the epitome of the unappreciative boss. He is also a man filled with self-loathing, the false belief that money is everything and a severe lack of Calm and Sense. He loves no one and no one loves him.

On the other hand, his employee Bob Cratchit is a man who radiates Calm and Sense. He does not allow Scrooge to infiltrate his sense of well-being, security or self-esteem. He *knows* he is a good person and deserving of self-love and he gives and receives an abundance of love from his family. He doesn't pout or ponder over "what ifs," nor does he gravitate toward self-pity or fantasy thinking over his situation. He loves himself, loves and is loved by others, makes the best of what he has and takes care of himself and his family. He even takes care of mean old Scrooge by working the best he can for the miserly old guy.

Cratchit has Emotional and Social Maturity as well. He never blames anyone for how "horrible" he has it. In fact, he is the type of guy whom many of us would want to be around, because he radiates self-determination, kindness, calmness and sincerity. Cratchit is impoverished, has a handicapped son near death and has a horrible job with a miserable, unappreciative boss! Kind of makes you wonder how he does it and how he continues to move forward in a positive way. How does he maintain Calm and Sense? That's easy. He does it by believing he deserves it, taking responsibility for everything in his life and moving forward realistically—not expecting someone or something to come along and take care of him or make him happy.

Toward the end of the story, Scrooge realizes that he is going to die a lonely, rich man, with no one who truly cares for him. Scrooge also learns that Cratchit's son Tiny Tim will die if Scrooge doesn't help Cratchit by giving him a raise in pay. In the end, Scrooge, himself, finds this too much to bear. Then he, too, embraces the teachings of Calm and Sense and begins to appreciate and be appreciated by others.

At work and especially in relationships, we must *sense* appreciation! Hearing people tell us we are appreciated is part of how we gain that sense. We all need an "attaboy/girl" once in a while. A pat on the back for a job well done never hurts either. But the substance of appreciation is in *showing* it in our actions. Scrooge brings a huge turkey and gifts as well as a pay raise to Bob Cratchit and his family. Now *that* is showing appreciation.

Tokens of appreciation are also essential ways to thank people for doing what they do and also for being who they are. I took my employees bowling once in a while and had everyone to lunch at various times, "just because." I also spent time with them individually, just to chat or to catch up on how they were doing. I truly cared about them as people—not just on the job, but also as people who have lives and feelings and interests outside of the office. This is showing appreciation by expression of genuine care and *this* expression of appreciation is the strongest method of showing it!

Showing appreciation in a work environment is critical to maintaining a happy, productive business. Shouldn't these types of behaviors be paramount in our closest relationships as well? Of course! Unfortunately, many of us take for granted that our loved ones know we appreciate them. We often tell ourselves, "I bring in the money, I wash the clothes, I pay the bills, I take care of the kids, etc." Calm and Sense questions, "Yeah and...?" These are only necessary tasks to keep life moving; they are *not* forms of showing appreciation. These assumptions and actions do not make appreciation. In fact, "assuming" is *never* a good practice.

Being playful with our partners can also show appreciation. Joking around, lightening up and being silly once in a while shows others that we are happy. It also shows them we are comfortable letting go of ourselves, being "the fool" or making fun of ourselves for the sake of enjoyment when we are around them, because their company creates an atmosphere of safety and security, comfort and openness.

I have heard many times from my clients, "He only tells me when I've done something wrong!" and "She never notices the good stuff I do!" Just like in the workplace I spoke of earlier, if this is the type of partner (or boss) you are, how can you possibly expect your partner (or employee) to want to do things for you? Your partner is not motivated, because it comes across that no matter what he or she does "right," you notice only the "wrong."

Parents should take particular note of this tendency in their interactions with their children as well. Your children need to know what good they do too. It makes them feel good and it builds confidence and self-esteem. It also makes your job of correcting the "not so good" much more effective. The specific things you choose to show your appreciation are up to you.

Also, recall the giddiness of Scrooge on Christmas morning. He seems to be "drunk" with the spirit of Christmas and dances, laughs, sings and truly feels elation. Take some of that spirit into your marriage, relationship, work, friendships—all of your personal relationships. When others see us as content, sometimes stepping out of ourselves, confident and caring, they will feel a great sense of appreciation, because the message we are sending to them, through our behaviors, is that we are comfortable enough with them to let our guard down.

It is also wonderful once in a while to present your loved one with a token of love—a phone call just to say hello, an offer to prepare a meal (if you normally don't), a greeting card, a balloon, breakfast in bed, a massage, etc. The impacts of such expressions are strongest when they are *unexpected*, so do some surprising things and don't be afraid to be silly here and there. The results of such actions will reap bounties of appreciation and years of happiness.

An article in *The Week* states that "arguments in relationships are caused by two basic issues" that have little to do with the actual content (i.e., money, garbage, toothpaste, etc.) of the arguments. Those two issues, according to the research done by Baylor University psychologists, are "one person feeling that he or she is being 'unfairly controlled' or 'feeling neglected'" by a spouse, mate or partner.

Researchers gave 3,539 married couples a questionnaire. The measurement and analysis of the words the couples used to describe the feelings they experienced in arguments with their spouses determined that the "tension that sparked the arguments almost always involved deeper issues relating to whether the partners felt understood or valued" by the other.

The author of the study, Keith Sanford, said, "If a husband realizes that his wife's anger over his coming home late is really about her feeling disregarded, he could fashion an apology that includes demonstration and expressions of appreciation."[1]

Now *that's* using Calm and Sense!

Chapter 23

Trust Me: I Love You Just the Way You Are

I have touched briefly on the element of true love: the emotion that propels us to encourage our partners to be who they are and not who we want them to be, much the same as Calm and Sense requires us to be who we are. If you have fallen in love with someone, you have fallen in love with that person and his or her personality. All the traits, characteristics, passions, goals, visions and hopes that person has belong to him or her and it is no one's right to try to alter them. This is especially true for *you* if you are pledging your "love" for the person. For better or for worse, what you see is what you get!

Why, then, do some people treat their "loved ones" like a high school science project, attempting to change the people for whom they have vowed love in the first place? Wanting to and trying to change your partner is not how Calm and Sense works in a relationship and it is a certain way to send the message to your partner that you don't find him or her "good enough" for you! If you find yourself wanting to change things about your partner or think that once your partner makes some change he or she will be perfect for you, your Calm and Sense is not working properly.

The real reason most people try to change who their partners are is rooted in their own personal insecurities. There may be things in which one partner is involved—such as social groups, hobbies, family functions or activities—that take some time away from the relationship and cause the other partner to feel threatened in some way. Or the style in which one partner dresses or carries him- or herself causes the other partner to think "someone is going to take him or her away from me!" We need to ask ourselves, What is trust anyway?

Calm and Sense says TRUST is True, Real Understanding Securing Two (people). Without it, any relationship is destined to self-destruct. Our own insecurities are probably the largest contributors to our having a lack of trust in others. There are people who directly violate our trust in them through their behavior or obvious defiant actions against us. Those behaviors and actions are usually quite clear. They include things like outright lying or intentionally withholding information, stealing and cheating. They are things that you can experience and identify or describe; they are actual things that have happened. People who treat us like that are not the people with whom we should be getting intimately involved. This type of lack of trust is *not* the lack of trust I am speaking of here. The lack of trust to which I am referring, the kind that eats away at a relationship and causes it to self-destruct, is a "gut feeling" or a false belief that tells us we cannot trust our partners. It comes from within us and not from anything our partners did or said.

The trust of Calm and Sense is the firm belief that our partners always have our best interests at heart and support our thoughts, feelings, goals, ideas and intentions—no matter what! We know that our lovers "have our backs" and we have theirs. He knows that if she's dressed up, looking hot and sexy for a "girl's night out," that she has dressed that way because it makes *her* feel good about *herself* and not because she's looking to pick up a guy somewhere. She knows that if he tells her he has to work late every night for the next two weeks to make sure this account does not get lost then that is exactly where he will be and what he is doing. The relationship depends on it for financial security and she does not think he's making it up to sneak around behind her back!

In a relationship that embraces Calm and makes Sense, there is mutual true love and real trust. Most of us have moments of weakness and get a little paranoid once in a while and, frankly, sometimes life does hand us some pretty strange looking situations. When something happens that initially causes some concern, this true love and real trust allows non-accusatory questions to be asked and non-defensive answers to be given. For example, Bob has had a bad day at work. His boss has come down pretty hard on him and has made him feel undervalued and disrespected. He's coming home a bit early today, because staying in the office for the last hour just didn't seem like the best thing for him to do. He drives down his street on his way home from work and sees a strange car pulling out of his driveway with a good-looking young man behind the wheel. He knows his wife, Kathi, is home alone.

Without true love and real trust in a relationship, the scenario might continue like this: Bob speeds into the driveway, slams on the brakes, turns off the car, slams the door jumping out of the car and runs to the house. Heart pounding, barely even noticing that he can hardly breathe, he throws the front door open and shouts, "Who the hell was that?" He rushes in, frantically searching for Kathi and looking carefully at everything, inspecting for signs of something inappropriate, things out of place or things that don't belong there. He fully expects Kathi to appear disheveled and looking like she's hiding something. "Where are you? What have you been doing?" he screams as she comes hesitatingly out of the kitchen. "What the hell is your problem?" she wails as she watches him grab her cell phone off the table in the entryway and start paging through her caller ID list. "Who the hell was that?" he repeats, louder this time and with spit flying from his lips. "What are you talking about?" she screams back at him, her blood pressure and contempt rising quickly. "You are always accusing me of something and you're not so perfect yourself!" she continues. He responds, "Answer me or I'm leaving!" She says, "Go right ahead! Don't forget to slam the door again on your way out!"

In a relationship where both parties truly love and trust each other, here is how the scenario plays out: Truly trusting Kathi, Bob goes inside the house and says (*without* his heart pounding and his mind wondering if he really wants to hear the answer), "Hi, honey, I came home early, because my boss was giving me a hard time and I was starting to feel bad about myself. I needed to get out of there and wanted to get home and spend some time with you before you went to the bake sale at the school. When I was coming up the street, I saw a car I didn't recognize coming out of our driveway. Who was that? Is everything okay?" Kathi can answer (without feeling defensive or offended by the question, because she knows Bob trusts her), "It was Mary's son. He was returning my cake pan, because Mary is running late and couldn't do it herself. She knew I needed it for tonight."

Trust is also what gives us the ability and freedom to show every side of our emotions to our partners and not feel embarrassed or shameful in the process! Trust allows us to express what we're thinking and feeling without fear that it will be held against us or thrown back in our faces. We trust our lovers to take care of our emotional needs and not ridicule them or dismiss them as irrelevant concerns or "whining." Trust comforts, consoles, contributes, supports, believes, understands and reassures us. The trust of another, especially a loved one, is perhaps the greatest gift we have to offer. It must be earned, protected, nurtured, reaffirmed and treated with as much care as the very lives we live. Without it, we are not only deceiving the world, we are also deceiving ourselves.

Trust also makes us truly valuable in a relationship. When we are trustworthy, we are indispensable to others. When we understand and accept that our relationships and partners are counting on us to be trustworthy, we take that responsibility with pride and due diligence. Our very character and integrity rests upon it and it shows others we are confident, reliable and worthy of their trust in return.

Our partners also trust us to make them look as good as we can. Be it with their friends, family, coworkers or even strangers, they count on us to never say or do things to embarrass or belittle them, even in jest, around other people or in private.

These elements of trust are what stabilize a relationship and cause us to "fall in love" with our partners over and over again through the years. When we never cease to amaze our lovers by our actions and intentions (in the best possible ways) and they do the same for us, love remains alive and healthy. We become closer and closer in trust, friendship and, of course, love.

When you love your partner for all of who he or she is, just as he or she is and you show it through your respect for and trust in him or her, you make it even easier for your partner to love you just the way you are in return. This makes Calm and Sense!

Chapter 24

Some Tips for Women

Through my many years of helping couples work through their relationship difficulties, I have found that there are certain similarities and issues that arise with some regularity and can cause much more discord than necessary unless you know how to manage them. Calm and Sense calls them Core Couple Complaints. Some are specific to women (complaints women frequently have about their men in relationships), some to men (complaints men frequently have about their women in relationships) and all are important for both men and women to understand in order to have a better grasp on what may be behind some common relationship problem areas. I would like to share them with you in this chapter and the next, along with tips and methods to eliminate them from your relationship. By following these tips, you may save yourself months of therapy, save your marriage or relationship and save your sanity!

Once there was a little boy. He liked to play with lizards, spiders, snakes and mud. He climbed trees, threw rocks in the river and dreamed of being a baseball player, rock star or fireman. He played with trucks and liked to take apart radios and engines and try to put them back together again. Sometimes he could, sometimes he couldn't; but he always loved the challenge.

As he got a little older, he learned how to fish, ride an ATV and build a tree house where he could hang out alone or with friends. He and his buddies shared stories about ghosts, cars, sports and video games. They did a lot of sharing but never stuff consisting of emotion or feelings. In their minds, that stuff was for "sissies."

Perhaps his dad was a rough and tumble guy who never expressed how he felt to anyone, so the little boy never really felt a need to do so either. Maybe he heard his mother say, "Boys will be boys," further assuring him that his feelings were not really something that needed to be discussed openly or frequently. He was happy to be with his friends, lighting firecrackers, skateboarding, bicycling, chasing fireflies or digging holes in the yard.

If his mom took "too good" care of him, he learned to throw his dirty clothes on the floor, leave dishes in the sink and not put down the toilet seat or flush after using the toilet. She did all that for him. In this case, the boy learned that "I can do whatever I want. My mom will take care of the rest!"

As the boy matured, something very curious and strange happened. He started to notice girls. His world was changing quickly, as were most of his old interests. This "girl thing" had him in a tizzy and his natural curiosity shifted from bugs to breasts practically overnight!

The boy began to dress differently and pay more careful attention to how he was coming across as a person. This feeling of wanting to be accepted was a huge part of adolescence, but looking and being "cool" was paramount! The boy was somewhat at a loss, though. Even though he may have learned how to dismantle a lawnmower and put it back together, catch a fish and ride a skateboard and flip it over in the air three times (and land on all four wheels every time with ease), he was absolutely lost when it came to understanding what girls were like, what they wanted or how to communicate effectively with them!

The boy's natural curiosity and his raging hormones, nevertheless, kept him steadfast in his pursuit of the opposite sex. Having seen a good bit of television and watched a lot of movies, he may have picked up some idea of what girls wanted or needed—but that's not reality! Sure it looks easy on a screen, but it doesn't come that easy when it's "live and in person."

Perhaps the boy learned something from his parents' interactions. However, in adolescence, no child truly understands those adult dynamics yet and certainly cannot see themselves acting "like Dad" in trying to be cool and accepted by the girls! What's a boy to do?

Without a "script" or specific rules to follow, the boy will engage in a lot of hit-or-miss behaviors, relying on advice from peers and incorporating his own interpretation of messages learned from the media (song lyrics and music videos, television shows, movies, etc.). For better or for worse, dating begins and so does relationship drama—complete with unfamiliar feelings of jealousy, lust, insecurity, "love," caring, hurt and elation. This confusing diversity of feelings is introduced to the mind and heart of the boy as he learns by trial and error what works and doesn't work for him in relationships with girls. For the boy who is experiencing so many of these new and powerful feelings at the same time, great conflict can begin, causing him to retreat, at times, to "being a boy" again in order to find balance in his life and feel better prepared to deal with the new stresses and emotions of "love."

If the boy matures physically, socially and emotionally as he grows into adulthood, even the man with Calm and Sense will always have some of that "boy" still in him. While he may have come a long way in his experience with and understanding of women (or his partner, in particular), he will still have an occasional need to go play in the dirt, "spend time in the tree house" with the boys or go fishing by himself. His soul requires it since it brought such comfort and joy to him at a time when the world was simpler and his mom took care of everything.

For women, it is important to understand this innate need men have to occasionally "be boys" and to encourage it, instead of feeling threatened, hurt or insulted by it. That is not to say or suggest that a man should not be responsible for himself in a relationship or that he should have total freedom to go to the local bar six nights a week for "male bonding." These behaviors are indicative of emotional avoidance, fear of intimacy, a lack of true maturity or alcohol dependency, not Calm and Sense! However, a fishing trip every month or so, a camping trip with "the guys" once a year, stopping in at "the lodge" on Wednesdays or time alone building a model airplane are quite appropriate and necessary for men to "rebalance" themselves so they can be more functional and responsive to their relationship with their partners.

"Why doesn't he want to spend each and every moment with me?" is a question I hear frequently in couple's therapy. The answer is that a man's need to be alone should not be taken as a threat to a woman's security. If a woman allows him the time he needs (within reason), he will be all the more responsive to her! Quality versus quantity applies here.

Here is another secret for women: Men like to pursue and they love women who lean a little to the mysterious side! Women should dip into their feminine "spell" bags and conjure up some healthy ways to be more "unavailable" sometimes in the most positive of ways. Most men want what they can't have or can't get all the time. So, if a woman is not always right where he thinks she will be, all the better. I am *not* advocating lying about whereabouts, withholding information or being unreliable and undependable. However, instead of sitting home waiting for his call or waiting for him to come home, a woman should go out and do something for herself. This gives her the opportunity to get involved with people and activities outside the relationship, allows him to have some "boy time" and ultimately makes the couple's time together more interesting, exciting and fresh.

It is a positive thing for both partners to have social, self-development and self-betterment needs outside of the relationship, not a threat. If we smother our partners by either needing them to provide for *all* of our needs or by insisting that we provide for *all* of their needs, they suffocate. On the other hand, if we allow each other to develop outside of the relationship, the relationship will also develop more beneficially.

Men are much like dogs in that they are pack creatures at heart. They need time to be with "the pack," howl at the moon, shake the silliness out of themselves and talk "man talk." It is for this very reason that fraternal organizations are so popular in this country. They provide a place for men to be men and feel brotherhood, camaraderie and a place of belonging.

Some women may be wondering, *Why can't our relationship provide that place of belonging?* The relationship *does* provide him a place of belonging, but it is a very different kind of belonging. A man's need for connection with other men is long ingrained in him and in culture (as is a woman's need to be connected with other women). Not all men feel drawn to joining male-only organizations to satisfy that need. Some men may join a bowling league or a band or they may have a group of friends that gets together to play darts once a week at the local bar. Perhaps they will join a men's Bible study group. The list goes on and on, but what's important to understand is that sometimes men need to be around other men to feel like men and that is okay, as long as they keep their comradeship within reason and it doesn't deplete too much time from their relationships.

If a woman does not understand or encourage her partner's need to have "alone" or "man" time or if she denies him the ability to "retreat to boyhood" once in awhile (which all men do require to maintain Calm and Sense), he will end up feeling restless or "trapped." That can result in behaviors that are *not* healthy for the relationship.

Perhaps the most troubling situation that a woman will encounter in her relationships with men is in comprehending why her man does not understand what she wants and needs from him. For men, it can be very difficult to truly know and understand what women need most or when it is needed most.

Perhaps you already know that, in general, men and women think and experience things very differently. Calm and Sense agrees. Men are more often "right brain thinkers" (the right side of the brain is the part most responsible for logic) whereas women are more often "left brain" thinkers (the left side of the brain is the part that is more emotionally based). As a result, men are often more "on the surface," "let's just solve the problem" kinds of people and women see things from a more emotional, detail-oriented point of view. This isn't to say that women aren't or can't be logical or that men are unemotional. It just means that for the most part, men and women think a bit differently and it's important to recognize that—especially when it comes to building a healthy relationship.

The good news is that where logic and emotion meet harmoniously, Calm and Sense will be found. Here's an example of how the two different ways of thinking and experiencing can clash and cause stress in a relationship:

On their first Thanksgiving together at their new home, both Joyce's and Charlie's families are coming for dinner. Joyce has been preparing for this meal for weeks. She has researched dozens of recipes, gone to many specialty stores for specific ingredients and even rearranged the living room and dining room furniture just a bit to make this a perfect Thanksgiving holiday.

The house is in impeccable order, the table is set beautifully and the guests are expected to arrive in a little while. Everything is ready and Joyce is almost finished cooking the turkey, all the side dishes and desserts when she realizes that she forgot nutmeg. She panics a little and then calls to Charlie to say she has to run to the store for the nutmeg. He offers to go for her, but she insists that it is a *certain* kind of nutmeg she needs and "you won't know where to find it." She asks him to keep an eye on the turkey and "take it out in ten minutes." Charlie offers again to go to the store for Joyce, but she insists she'll be right back and asks him just to "*Please* take the turkey out in ten minutes." Charlie agrees and Joyce goes to the store.

The phone rings. It's Charlie's mom calling from her cell phone to say they are lost finding the couple's new house. Charlie, the logical problem-solver he is, is very willing and able to give her the *exact route* to get to the house. The cell phone signal is weak, so Charlie's mom needs him to repeat himself several times as she writes down every word he says.

Joyce is at the supermarket and cannot find the right nutmeg she needs for the perfect dinner! Now she has to go to another store, which is ten minutes away from the first store. It's taking her a bit longer than she'd expected and she's anxious to get back, but she trusts her husband will take the turkey out on time. After all, he said he would and it's a very simple task.

At home, Charlie hangs up the phone and notices that his team has taken a lead over the opposing team. He decides he must have a look to see how that happened! The phone rings again. His parents are still lost and "must have written something down wrong on the directions." Charlie tries to clarify the directions again. "Touchdown!" he hears from the television. He runs back to see the happenings of the game.

Meanwhile, on the road, Joyce arrives at the next store. It's closed. "Damn!" She'll have to try the small food market which is open and settle for a different brand of nutmeg.

As she finally pulls her car into the driveway at her home, Charlie hears the sound of the motor and remembers: "Oh, nuts! The turkey!" He dashes to the kitchen to take it out of the oven, hoping all will be well (and Joyce none the wiser), but the ten minutes she told him to let it cook have turned to fifty and now the perfect turkey is overdone and burnt.

Joyce rushes into the house. The guests will be arriving any minute now and she wants to get everything in order…but she smells the burned turkey. "What happened?" she calls out.

Charlie quickly admits that it's his fault and explains his mother called for directions so he got distracted and completely forgot about the turkey. He apologizes profusely and immediately says, "I'll run to the supermarket right now and get a precooked turkey. Dinner will be fine!"

"Fine?" Joyce cries out. "All I asked you to do was take the turkey out in ten minutes and you forgot. I can't believe you did this to me!"

Charlie responds, "I didn't do anything *to* you. I really just forgot. What's the big deal? I'll go get another turkey. Nobody will know the difference! I told you I should have gone to the store to begin with."

Now Joyce is raging! Her long thought out, meticulously made plans for the perfect dinner have been ruined, because her husband didn't care enough about what she was preparing and how important this dinner was. *All I asked him to do was take the turkey out of the oven in ten minutes!* Joyce fumes to herself. Charlie thinks, *All I have to do to fix this is go to the store and buy a new turkey.*

What Charlie fails to understand here is that it is *not* "just about the turkey" for Joyce. It is about the day as a whole, the plans put into it, the atmosphere she was creating, the memories she was going to establish and the importance of the one thing she trusted her husband to do while she made that "one last preparation" to have "everything I needed for the perfect day."

Imagine you are Joyce. At this point, you cannot understand how or why your husband does not understand how important that one request was to you or how he could just say, "Let me go buy another turkey."

Your husband, on the other hand, truly believes that just going out to buy another turkey is the perfect solution. He wants to fix the problem quickly and logically and may see your behavior as irrational and unreasonable. Neither of you is wrong, because, again, where logic and emotions meet, Calm and Sense exists.

Had both parties been better informed of each other's individual emotional needs and aware of their differing ways of looking at things, perhaps the husband would have been a little more "on guard" and attentive to the importance of the turkey and what the day symbolized and truly meant to his wife. That *may* have helped prevent the "burnt bird," but perhaps not. As well, if the turkey was destined to be burned, as accidentally as it was, it may have helped for the husband to respond to the disaster with more of an understanding of what it meant to his wife. "Oh, honey! I can't believe I did that. I am so sorry! I know how much effort and care you put into making everything so perfect for today and I blew it. What can I do to help you now?"

The wife might still be furious and extremely disappointed by what happened (which is fine and almost expected), but the acknowledgment from her husband of her feelings, her hard work and the meaning of the incident to her would carry more weight and show her more of a connection with him than just his immediate response to attempt a "quick fix" and dismissal of how and what she was feeling at that moment.

Calm and Sense tells us that recognizing that men and women experience things from different perspectives (right brain versus left brain, for example) and then often operate from those different places can help us to be more understanding and supportive of each other when these differences come into conflict.

With that in mind, the next tip is: Women need to help their partners understand their needs more clearly. Men need help in this area. What works for men in troublesome situations, especially in relationships, is usually a far cry from what women really need at those times! Men need to know more of women's feelings and how they see and envision events in their own lives to better respond to the needs women have.

This takes two willing parties, though, and a mutual agreement that these types of discussions are not meant to determine who is right or who is wrong. There is no right or wrong when it comes to feelings! The purpose of these discussions between partners is to attain clarification and information. In the example of Joyce and Charlie, having not had this kind of discussion prior to the turkey disaster, Charlie would have done well to have responded to Joyce's frustration by saying, "Honey, I obviously really screwed up by burning the turkey! What do I not get here? What can I do to help you?" After all, if we really want to help others, we have to find out what *they* need and not just do what *we* think they need. If the discussion had taken place prior to the discovery of the missing nutmeg, Charlie would have been able to understand (and therefore be more mindful about acting on) the importance of getting the turkey out of the oven on time. If, for some reason, he still wasn't able to get the turkey out on time, he would also have known how to handle the situation in a way that was helpful to Joyce when the disaster was discovered.

If a woman feels like her man never understands her or if he seems never really to care, educate his logic with a dose of emotion. The woman should let him know what she's thinking, what she's feeling and what she needs.

This brings us to another vital element of Calm and Sense logic for a happier relationship: Your partner is not a mind reader!

Charlie burned the turkey, but cannot understand the enormity of how this has affected his wife—because she's never shared her perspective on this kind of thing with him. When men see a problem, men want to fix it. Women do not usually operate that logically or simply. Women, especially when they are entertaining guests in their homes, are very aware of presentation, preparation and their guests' perceptions of the events. Men do not normally operate with such attention to detail. Without the knowledge of what's important to each other, it's almost impossible to "do right" by each other in these kinds of situations.

This is true in other areas of intimate or romantic relationships as well. Sometimes men just don't think something they did or did not do was "such a big deal," but their women see it as far more than that, what Calm and Sense calls an Initiating Event. Initiating Events are those events where logic and emotion cross paths, but rather than acknowledge each other's presence and attempt to see who has the "right of way," they crash. For example, the burnt turkey. The logic of the event was to solve the immediate and obvious problem of an inedible dinner. The emotion of the event was to acknowledge that there was much more to it than just a burnt turkey. If Charlie kept pushing the "let's just replace the turkey" point and Joyce kept pushing the "you're not getting how this entire day is now ruined" point, the guests would arrive to find the extended family's first joint Thanksgiving dinner a very unpleasant event. If Charlie was able to acknowledge Joyce's entire effort, from decor to nutmeg, and Joyce was able to accept his appreciation and recognition of her feelings and allow him to solve the problem by replacing the turkey, the family's dinner could end up being a positively memorable one. And let's not forget the benefit to the relationship of having positively navigated through a "crisis" together.

Calm and Sense places the responsibility of correcting Initiating Events on *both* parties! It is a mutual obligation of both people involved to understand where the other is coming from and to understand it clearly enough to be able to avoid as many future "collisions" as possible. Men must understand how their actions may potentially affect their women and the women's "whole picture," as much as women must understand that their men are acting out of caring, supportive, "logical" components most of the time and *are* truly trying to help but simply are missing the emotional piece of the women's anguish. Men need help in seeing and understanding the whole picture when it comes to what upsets as well as overjoys women.

Problems arise when women expect that their men "should know me well enough" or when they feel things like, "I shouldn't have to tell him all the time how much this upsets me!" This would stand true if women have already tried to teach their men how to understand them and their men don't pay attention. From my experience as a therapist, however,

I too often see that these types of thoughts and feelings come from Initiating Events and *not* from women who have been in relationships for suitable amounts of time where their needs were openly discussed *before* trouble came up! There is a huge difference in the way couples handle and react to Initiating Events between those who have had the discussion and those who haven't.

In a therapeutic setting, the discussion of each other's needs takes place during the session, so each party learns more about where the other is coming from without the emotions of anger, hurt or frustration looming between them. What Calm and Sense suggests, then, is to have these discussions before Initiating Events arrive. And they *will* arrive! In this way, partners are both more prepared to react differently—with more understanding and with Calm and Sense—and not let the event snowball into a worse situation than it needs to be.

The key is to get to know each other when things between you are good. Ask questions, be honest and tell each other exactly what you need from each other in times of trouble. That is generally what happens in a therapy session where Calm and Sense is being used. The good news is you can do this at home, on the beach, on your deck, in the car, wherever you want. You truly don't need a therapist to mediate the discussion, unless you are so at odds with each other that civil conversation is impossible.

The simple question, "What do you need me to do right now?" can reap large rewards and understanding from each partner when tension or turmoil is present—but only if the question is answered! The question *must* be answered, even if the response is "I don't know right now." In that case, take some time to think about it. Then when you *do* know, tell your partner. "I don't know right now" is not an excuse to get you out of your part of the bargain; it's an honest statement that must be backed up with thought and follow-up conversation within a reasonable amount of time.

Silent treatments and huffing, puffing behavior do not bring you rest or resolve when you are upset; neither do they inform your partner of anything he or she can do to be helpful or supportive! As an answer to "What do you need me to do right now?" the silent treatment says, "I want you to read my mind and know exactly what I want." That is a double-edged sword with no positive edge. Your partner is damned if s/he does (and takes a guess that is wrong) and damned if s/he doesn't know (and does nothing). Your partner asks, "Honey, what's wrong?" You say, "Nothing." Your partner says, "I can tell by your look that something is wrong" and may also then ask, "What did I do?" You say either, "Nothing" again or, "You know what you did!" What is this guessing game all about?

Men want to fix, fix, fix! Women, in this situation, want their men to understand them completely but often are not willing or able to be forthcoming and honest about their immediate needs during these times. Calm and Sense tells us that these behaviors are seated in insecurity and a lack of self-worth. Why self-worth? Because many of us are simply not comfortable telling others what we need. We may think that to do so is selfish or childish. We may feel that we are unworthy or we mistakenly believe that relationships should include our partners' full understanding of our every need all the time. The truth is the opposite. Expecting a partner, boss, friend, relative or anyone to "know what I need" and to be able to "read my mind" is acting with emotional and social immaturity.

The good news is you can use Calm and Sense to fix these behaviors!

Chapter 25

And Some Tips for Men

I hope the men have not skipped the previous chapter and read what Calm and Sense has offered women to help better understand men and their needs. Now I offer tips for the men. With a bit of application and practice, using these suggestions will improve relationships greatly.

Women do not think of and experience sex the same way men do. Men need to understand this fully in order to find great satisfaction in their intimate relationships.

According to evolutionary theory, before there were things like marriage or monogamy, the sex drive of men was (necessarily) extremely high in order to ensure the survival of the species. The role of prehistoric man was to copulate anywhere, everywhere and with whomever he could. Women, then, were considered the bearers of the children. The intention and need was "the more the merrier!" Human beings had to copulate to populate. As time went on and society continued to advance, men and women learned that some form of order and institutions were necessary to organize all the people who were then on the earth. Along those lines, marriage and monogamy eventually evolved so that families could remain together and so that genes were shared "not so close to home" anymore.

Men, in addition to evolutionarily retaining facial hair, upper body strength and a drive to be "the provider," still have a lot of that prehistoric sex drive in their twenty-first century lives. That is not to say that women do not have sex drives or that they don't enjoy having sex. Calm and Sense says that men need to understand that women operate much differently from men when it comes to sex.

For many men, the old "wham, bam, thank you ma'am" constitutes "good sex" much of the time. That's it! Women (and Calm and Sense) say: Recognize that the drive to have sex and the need to achieve that goal or fulfill that urge are vastly different from the human need for physical intimacy.

I came up with a proverb years ago when I began working with couples. It goes like this: If you want to make love to your woman on Sunday, start *showing* her love on Monday. The reason for this is that the sexual encounter for most women is usually much more than the act itself.

Men must also remember that their wives or girlfriends are (most likely) not porn stars and that porn stars are actors. Expecting a partner to behave like the women in porn films or magazines is fantasy thinking and although women are known to enjoy getting sexually adventurous from time to time, do not expect that always to be the norm. Remember that men's and women's perceptions of sex are usually very different. It is logic versus emotion. Mae West, the movie star, said, "Sex is emotion in motion."

Calm and Sense says that if a man is showing his partner that she matters and is appreciated and that man leads with confidence, courage, fairness and emotional strength, the chances of his sex life being better and more adventurous are certainly going to increase!

Next we will discuss some Calm and Sense tips which will help men show the women in their lives how much they love them and will draw partners closer together, making the act of love more beneficial, beautiful and mutually enjoyable.

Women are usually attracted to men who are in control. A man who is "in control" is a man who can lead but is also comfortable following and who shows confidence and strength in his actions and belief in his abilities. Most women do not feel safe or "turned on" by men who doubt themselves, are timid around their partners or others or are indecisive or lacking in confidence and determination. Men need to show women that they are natural born leaders, not Neanderthals (there is a huge difference). Most women do not want to be put in charge of or be held responsible for planning everything a couple does together. "Mr. Nice Guys," who are overly agreeable, forever accommodating and never have or communicate an original idea, don't seem to the majority of women to be "real men."

If a man finds himself saying things like, "I don't care where we go tonight" or "Whatever you want to do is fine with me", Calm and Sense has two words of advice for him: Stop it!

Be more assertive, start *planning* and *leading* when it comes to relationships. I hear this complaint in couple's therapy all the time and it is most avoidable. Women want their partners to plan, plan and plan! A man should make arrangements, for example, for dinner at a place of *his* choice (respecting any food preference his wife or girlfriend has) then call his partner and tell her, "Hey, listen, I want you to put on your favorite dress and get yourself ready by six o'clock tonight. I'm taking you to a luxury restaurant for dinner and then we're going to a nightclub for some drinks and dancing. See you at six." Men just don't do enough of this type of arrangement and many women tell me they want it. Men need to lead, radiate confidence and pay attention to their partners.

Some women like to share the responsibility for making plans. If a man's partner likes to do this, then what she needs from him is the opportunity to participate as well.

When was the last time you paid attention to your partner's new hairstyle, clothes or shoes? Do you compliment her when she looks good? Do you notice small changes she makes to her appearance? If not, begin to make these compliments. Women put great time and effort into how they look and their partners ought to pay more attention to them. Men have to mean it when they let their partners know they've noticed and they appreciate it. A woman can smell a phony compliment a mile away, so don't fake it; but when she looks good, great or smoking hot, tell her!

Remember, as I commented earlier: The fastest way to a woman's heart is through humor. More than looks, more than money, more than *anything*, studies show again and again the first thing that attracts a woman to a man is his ability to make her laugh. Here's Calm and Sense's definition of HUMOR: Have Unlimited Mental Orgasms Regularly. Laughing feels so good and it's good for your health too! Find a way to lighten up and be funny. Take life less seriously, do whatever it is you need to do to find a healthy sense of humor and use it. If you can make your partner laugh once a day, your partner will find one more reason to love you every day.

Recently I attended the funeral of a good friend's wife. My friend Harry is eighty-eight years old and was married to his wife for sixty-seven years. Although I knew Harry well, I was not as well acquainted with his wife, Romaine. However, as time passed I wanted to talk to Harry about his marriage. After all those years, I figured he must have priceless "secrets" to having a happy marriage that I could share with my clients.

Harry, being the kind man that he is, agreed to sit down with me. With my pad and pen in hand, I listened carefully as Harry told me his "secret" to a long and healthy marriage. Harry's gem of wisdom is this simple statement: "We survived on love and laughter." I thought, *How beautifully simple*. What perfect Calm and Sense! Love and laughter. *Not* worry, money, problems or things, but love and laughter. "Laugh more, worry less." This advice keeps finding its way into Calm and Sense living. Embrace it!

Another tip that men need to embrace is this: Be attentive to a partner's friends and family. When a woman can be proud of how her partner handles himself around her friends and family, she responds by heaping bounties of appreciation and respect on him. Ask yourself: Do you "disappear" when your partner's family comes around? Do you stay in front of the television when your partner's friends come over? Do you avoid those social situations when your partner needs you to be there for her?

A man who can make positive impressions *for* his partner and show her that he is there for her demonstrates the leadership and confidence she so desires from him. Women like when other women notice how their partners treat them. All of us want attention, so when we demonstrate confidence and humor with our partners' friends and family and show others how much our partners mean to us, that's well-appreciated attention for any woman. Are you proud of your partner? Show it in your actions! Make your partner proud of you too.

These are general guidelines for any couple. However, though they may appear to be simplistic, do not be fooled! They are powerful behaviors that, when used regularly, genuinely and consistently will generate and maintain much harmony, love, mutual appreciation and respect from a partner and, in turn, keep the relationship well nourished with Calm and Sense.

Part Four

Some Calm and Sense Tips

"Happiness depends, as Nature shows,
less on exterior things than most suppose."

William Cowper
English poet and hymnodist

In this book we have taken a momentous journey together. I have endeavored to share with you the foundations of the Calm and Sense method to living and stories and examples to which I hope you have been able to relate and have found inspiring. Congratulations!

Now I would like to share several brief examples of Calm and Sense techniques, which you can also begin using along with the tips, strategies and techniques you have already learned. I am sharing these with you to help you put Calm and Sense into some of your "everyday" situations and relationships so you can move away from worry, benefit further from less stress and less anxiety and be more able to enjoy every day of your life.

Chapter 26

Family Matters

In my field of practice, we often (partially) joke, "If it's not one thing, it's your mother." I think it was actor/comedian Robin Williams who made that particular concept part of pop culture. It has some validity for many people. Are your parents pushing you forward or pulling you back? Many people suffer a great amount of stress and conflict when it comes to their parents. These conflicts and struggles present themselves more powerfully as we become adults and build lives and families of our own.

Sometimes parents have a very difficult time letting go of their children and continue to act as if their adult children are still really young; they constantly monitor what their adult children do, giving unsolicited advice or criticism about how their sons and daughters live their lives. Many of us have experienced this to varying degrees and in one form or another. When it happens to you, do you truly despise it but put up with the treatment, because some part of you believes you are obligated to out of respect for your mom or dad? Do you feel powerless over it, because your relationship with your parent(s) has always been this way?

Let's look at the other side. Parents, are your adult children having a hard time growing up on their own, depending too much on you to do things they should be able to do themselves? Do they constantly need your reassurance, assistance or support while you try to gently get them to be independent?

The discord between generations can come from either situation: parents hanging on too long or children hanging on too long. If there is discord being felt, it's important to determine who is holding on tighter. Ideally, nature helps children "grow up" and healthy parents help children "grow away." From the moment of conception, our mothers are our life-givers, but when and how we grow up and grow away determines our new (and always evolving) relationships with our parents and adult children as they (or we) start to live independently.

When entering (and sometimes even years into) serious relationships or marriages, many people (men more so than women) seem to have a difficult time balancing their roles and responsibilities as adult children (son or daughter) *and* partners (husband, wife, boyfriend, girlfriend). A parent may still be expecting to be an adult child's primary interest, while a partner expects the same. Logic (and stressful experience, for some of us) tells us that it cannot be both, yet many of us continue to struggle and experience a tremendous amount of stress and relationship turmoil over this particular issue. To make it possible for everyone involved to continue to have healthy and positive relationships with their families of origin *and* of choice, Calm and Sense tells us that healthy boundaries must be established between adult children and their parents. Setting boundaries is not a one-time activity, though. As time passes and circumstances change, boundaries should be reassessed and clarified to match the current situation. This is especially important when adult children are raising families of their own.

Issues tend to arise when either the parents want more from the adult child than they should rightfully expect (like spending *every* holiday together, as if the in-laws don't exist) or the adult child feels some sense of obligation or duty to continue caring for the parent(s) beyond what is appropriate (like taking a portion of the down payment for a joint home and using it to replace the windows in Mom and Dad's house). In order to be fair, boundaries should reflect a reasonable distance in emotions and duties such that the adult child can create and live his or her new life and thrive in his or her new role(s), free from any guilt or undue obligation toward the parents, while the parents are not totally excluded from the events of the adult child.

As roles change from family of origin to new family, make changes! Choosing spouse over parent can be a difficult thing to do and can leave you feeling guilty, powerless and defeated, believing you are "damned if you do and damned if you don't." However, as life moves on, sometimes decisions such as these must be made. Open, honest and upfront communication can go a long way to help make the process smoother and less painful. Talk to your spouse about any concerns you have regarding distribution of time (or money) *before* it becomes a major source of friction! This is also important to do as parents get older. For many of us, our parents require more care as their abilities become more limited. In addition to talking about it, it may be helpful to plan out what different situations might look like and make the necessary preparations.

Calm and Sense says setting healthy boundaries and limitations with our parents as we grow older allows us to do what we can and to feel good about doing it, rather than feeling we have no other choice but to do what we feel obligated to do. Setting healthy boundaries not only helps us find balance and improve relationships with our parents, but also allows us to have healthier and less stressful relationships with our partners.

Chapter 27

You Can Pick Your Friends

Let's talk about the importance of having and being a friend. Friends are the people we *choose* to include in our lives and who can choose to include or not include us in their lives. Many of us have heard Wayne W. Dyer's quip, "Friends are God's way of apologizing to us for our families."

Ralph Waldo Emerson said, "The only way to have a friend is to be one." Calm and Sense agrees and offers some vital tips that will make you a *great* friend rather than *just* a friend. As we discussed in chapter 22, listening is perhaps the most distinguishing factor in a great friend! The ability to listen, *really listen*, supersedes any other trait necessary to make a person a great friend.

Have you ever had something happen to you, perhaps something very painful or disturbing and you went to a friend to tell him or her all about it, because you just wanted to share it or perhaps you needed to vent and have your feelings validated? Maybe you needed to hear words like, "That must have been awful!" or "I can't believe you had to go through that!" Most times, when we share stressful or painful experiences with a trusted friend, that's really all we are looking for.

Consider this scenario: Your father was rushed to the hospital in the midst of a massive heart attack and had to have an emergency triple bypass. The surgery is done, but your father still may not live. You are worried and scared, because his life is in the balance and if he dies your life will never be the same.

You call your friend to tell him what happened and you explain the entire course of events. Your emotion is evident in your tone and in your words and it's clear that this is something quite life-altering for you. When you finish talking, your friend responds by saying, "I know how that is! We took my mother to the emergency room last year, because we thought she was having a heart attack, but thank God, she wasn't. She just had bad heartburn." Does that response help you in your grief and panic? Does it provide you validation of your feelings and demonstrate true concern for what you have gone through and are going through? Not even close. It would probably leave you thinking, *Did you really just compare your mother's heartburn to my father's potentially unsuccessful emergency triple bypass surgery? Did you not hear (or feel) a word I said? Did you not hear anything I said after the words* "emergency room" *made you think of yourself?*

Here's another example with which you may be familiar. You call your friend after having a horrible week both at work and at home. You say something like, "I am so sick and tired of commuting two hours a day to work for that idiot of a boss I have. She doesn't appreciate me! Every time I do something right, she always finds something wrong. Then I come home and the kids are screaming and making a mess. I can't take it anymore! I'm seriously thinking of buying a houseboat to live on and leaving all this crap behind!" Your friend responds only by saying, "Yeah, me too."

Calm and Sense says that if you want to be a great friend, do not become a "me too" or an "outdo" person. "Me too" people are not listening; they do not allow you to express yourself or to feel like anything you have communicated has been heard at all! "Me too" people are busy thinking about themselves, not about you, their "friend" and the importance of what you are trying to say. These types of responses to others' feelings are underdeveloped, self-serving and demonstrate a lack of empathy and ability to be a great friend with a true ability to listen.

"Outdo" people are those who, no matter what you have to say or are trying to communicate, always "up your story" with one of their own. "I had such an awesome weekend! We went power sailing and fishing and I caught a huge bluefish that almost pulled me into the water! Then we took the boat and docked at this great little restaurant where the food was incredible!" An "outdo" person says, "Yeah, I was at a U2 concert in Australia, flew there in my private jet, met Bono, got a record contract and then came home and hit the lottery for two hundred thirty-two million dollars!" Of course, that's an extreme example of "outdo" people's methods, but you get the idea and probably know people who just have to outdo whatever it is you have done.

Both of these types of "friends" (and I use that term loosely here) quickly lose friendships, because there is no true dialogue, exchange, identification or appreciation of what *you* are saying to *them*! They are self-centered and not acting as friends at all. Friendship is about mutual support, not about competition or about seeing what you can get from another person when you need it without being willing and available to give the same in return.

Friendship is essential to Calm and Sense, because it provides us with a means of having someone there for us when we need someone, allows us to be there for that person when he or she needs us (which is good for us too, as it makes us feel valuable and needed), opens up opportunities to enjoy social events and activities without restrictions and ensures us that our "friendship" exists merely because we like or love each other. There are no strings attached; no dues to be paid. Calm and Sense says to cherish your friendships like you cherish yourself and listen to your friends as you would have them listen to you!

Friendship also helps us understand who we are, because it serves as a mirror of our actions and soul. True friends will not pretend we are okay if they see something we are doing as hurtful to ourselves and they will help us clearly see the good we have in us as well.

An anonymous poet described friendship eloquently when he wrote, "A friend is someone who knows the song in your heart and can sing it back to you when you have forgotten the words." Calm and Sense agrees and adds that true friends are those whose love and reassurance help us to retain a positive belief in ourselves in times of difficulty or self-doubt.

Chapter 28

Career and Finances

Many people stress and worry about money and about paying their bills. We know that money is not the source of true happiness or Calm and Sense, but we also understand that if *worry* paid the bills, most of us would be millionaires by now! Worry and stress over these matters cause only more of the same and don't change our bank account balances by even one cent. What falling into a state of worry and stress *does* do for us is to make us fearful, indecisive, immobile and unable to act.

Look at where you are today. Consider your job and your debt. How did you get there? Debt means you have achieved something and you are surviving! Are you paying a mortgage and a car payment? Great! You have a home and a means of transportation. You also have to feed and clothe yourself and perhaps your family. Are you doing that too? Awesome! College tuition? Congratulations! You have a son or daughter who made it to college. This is wonderful.

Now you may be thinking, *Yes, that is great, but I am strapped! And then there's my sister who married some rich guy and has no stress when it comes to money! She doesn't have a worry in the world* (at least by your perception).

Calm and Sense tells us that if we need to make some changes and buckle down a bit to better manage our money, the freedom to make those changes comes from the ability to cease comparing ourselves to others of whom we may be envious and take responsibility now!

Take a good look at just how much effort and energy you have actually invested in getting ahead versus the amount of effort and energy you have invested in blaming others or life itself for "bad luck" or your inability to get ahead. Do a reality check to identify what you have and haven't done, then make your action plan to get back on track financially! Easier said than done? No. Calm and Sense says all you need to do is simply reverse the debt process. You spent time and effort creating what you owe. Now turn it around and make the challenge of paying it down your priority. Recognize too that no matter whether you accrued your debt over time or it came all at once, it's going to take some time and effort to reduce it.

There are a number of ways to reduce your debt. One of the most reliable is to find creative ways to save money, like by cutting out and using coupons, waiting to buy things until they are on sale and eliminating extraneous things like pedicures or the landscaper for a while. When you start acting on your debt and stop wasting valuable time worrying about it, you will be amazed at how quickly you see results! And when you earn money and start paying off your bills, you begin to feel better and you also gain a great sense of pride in doing it.

How about your job? Are you happy where you are or do you hold resentments there? Do you see other people getting ahead while you feel you are stuck? You don't have to love what you do, but you can do what you love! That means outside of work too. Calm and Sense agrees with the adage, "Work to live, don't live to work."

Perhaps you are feeling bored or underappreciated at work. This happens to a lot of people, but most of us are not aware of the actual need that underlies these feelings. Our basic need to feel challenged and for change every once in a while often shows up as feelings of boredom or being underappreciated. What can you do if you are feeling underappreciated or bored? Perhaps you have an idea of how to do what you do better. If so, why not present this idea to your supervisor or personnel department? The goal is to be in touch with the real issues feeding your worry or stress at work and make any changes that you can. Communicate your concerns to the right people and make yourself stand out.

Maybe it's a total career change you need. That's fine too! Make the challenge of determining what you want to do for a living your goal, then start figuring out how to get there. Calm and Sense tells us when we feel uncomfortable, unsettled, bored or frustrated, we need to begin a new chapter in life. Listen to the call for change and answer it.

No one is stopping you from moving forward or getting ahead. Make it happen by using your Calm and Sense!

Chapter 29

In Closing

We live in a world today that has us falsely believing that a solution to depression and unhappiness should be a pill or a click of the "mouse" or otherwise instantly cured; that happiness and satisfaction should be instantly accessible if we only had the "secret" to it all. As technology and communications continue to advance, we as people seem to be falling backward, losing the ability to connect with others on a personal level as human beings. E-mail, text messages and voice mail have replaced letters and cards, phone calls and visits. There exists an air of desperate detachment from one another, from learning how to feel good about life and who we are, from appreciating that there are stepping stones before the milestones of life that we must cross in order to truly appreciate our abilities and resourcefulness. We need to accept that sometimes we make mistakes along the way.

Calm and Sense proclaims that there is no such miracle pill, click or secret to happiness and satisfaction. Calm and Sense also tells us that the reality of living a satisfying life relies on loving and appreciating ourselves and others. It also reinforces the basic need for time-tested wisdom, patience, humor and community with others that truly brings Calm into our lives and helps us make true Sense of who we are and why we are here.

A major reason depression is on the rise is because many people surrender their power of well-being and happiness with life to the actions of others, situations or circumstances instead of harnessing their own strength to choose to see themselves and the world around them. In doing so they erroneously tell themselves over and over again "I can't." Calm and Sense says, "You can!" To have Calm and Sense, you must learn and love who you are as an individual, the uniqueness of yourself and your life.

Have you assessed and observed the elements and people in your life as well as yourself? Are you associated with and surrounded by others who show you support, care, love and concern? Do you seek these characteristics in those around you? Do you steadfastly believe you deserve nothing less than these things from others and do you openly give them to yourself and others as well? Are you able to laugh away or shake your head and let go of insulting people? Can you truly laugh at yourself in the midst of a mistake and learn from it rather than dwell on it? Have you stopped searching for that proverbial "pot of gold" and realized that your time is now? Perhaps most importantly, can you wake up in the morning and go to sleep at night firmly believing that you have you and no one could be more fortunate than you because of that fact? If so, you have embraced and learned the true elements of Calm and Sense living and the secret to defeating depression. Congratulations!

Hopefully you will now believe and accept the essence of Calm and Sense living which lies in truly believing in who you are and what you can do, not what you cannot. When we become stuck in negative thinking about ourselves, what we do not have, what everyone else does have, how life is not fair, how we can "never change," why our spouses are unappreciative, our bills are so high, our houses are so small, our jobs are so bad, etc., we are far from utilizing any of our Calm and Sense and ultimately become more and more depressed. Then we isolate, ruminate, grow irate and become desperate. We look in all the wrong places for what we believe we "need" to make everything better in our lives, blaming everyone and everything under the sun for our misery instead of stopping and realizing that this blame game only makes us more and more depressed, frustrated and unsatisfied. These bad feelings are an indication that what we are doing is not working and we need to employ our Calm and Sense to turn things around, take responsibility, take risks, find our Identity Fortifiers, fear less, laugh more and ultimately start rewiring the faulty circuits in our thinking that do not serve us any good purpose.

Remember, defeating depression is not always easy. However, there is a source of power and enlightenment when one has that moment, that breeze of understanding and feeling of utter relief when one connects to the basic principle of understanding that no one has caused us to be depressed. No job, relationship or other outside event brought this feeling of desperation upon us. This is the moment when you say, "Wait a minute! I am not helpless, doomed, unlucky, unloved, unneeded or never going to feel better!" This is also when your engine turns over and starts the gears in your mind turning again and you eagerly begin to take responsibility for your life and make changes and improvements. Your social, emotional and personal (SEP) portfolio starts to show growth and movement like it never has before. The depression is lifted and the economy of your life escalates! If your life's economy is healthy and full of value and strength, your Calm and Sense is thriving.

Choices and power. I have spoken of these extensively throughout these chapters. We are not only what we eat, but also what we think and feel. Most, if not all, people who are depressed, unhappy or unsatisfied in life are choosing to be to some degree. Also, most, if not all, depressed people are relinquishing their power to forces, people or situations outside of their control in hopes of "being happy." Why do people do this?

Among the reasons we've discussed are the media's persistent influence on what and who we "should" be, our parents' voices in our minds "reminding" us over and over again that we "didn't score high enough," our bosses nagging at us about how little we do. However, to defeat depression, Calm and Sense living demands that we stop giving so much of our ability or power to be happy and satisfied to others. This sacrifice of power and choice only results in disappointment and resentment, because it is not a reality. The reality of defeating depression lies within each of us. We hold the answers to our own happiness. We decide what satisfies us. We are the voices of true reason in our own minds and we must not allow ourselves to believe that *if* this happens, *then* I will be happy.

Calm and Sense assures us that *if* you truly believe that you can defeat depression and love yourself, take total responsibility for your self-care, seek positive emotional nutrition in all you do, repel negativity from others and want only what is in your best interest while being determined to find it yourself, *then* happiness and satisfaction will come to you in abundance. Others will see Calm and Sense radiating from all you do and will be inspired by you as you continue to inspire yourself!

The tools and techniques presented in the book are true. They have delivered countless people from lives of discomfort, despair and depression. It must be acknowledged again that depression is a very real, very common and very stifling illness. There are those suffering with this illness who require intensive medical care and treatment. However, there are also many, many others who are silently struggling with situations in their lives that lead them to believe they are not happy, unsatisfied and therefore depressed. Indeed, they are.

The good news for these individuals is that defeating depression is possible with the use of Calm and Sense. I previously noted that psychiatrists' offices are constantly busy; it can take months to get an appointment. Pharmaceutical companies continuously "invent" new and improved antidepressant medications. Does this make any Calm and Sense? If one is depressed today, should one be expected to wait months to see a doctor? Similarly, how many times will it take pharmaceutical companies to invent, create or get "right" a solution to defeating depression? Depression is big business, however, nowhere near as big as your need to enjoy your life today!

With Calm and Sense, we can see and appreciate that there are "stepping stones" before the "milestones" we reach, the joy and excitement in moving on to the next level after having succeeded at last in something, the lesson learned when things didn't go the way we'd expected they would and the good in each of our relationships. We can see and appreciate "life's miracles" in a child's curiosity, a beautiful desert storm, the touch of a loved one, a lick from a dog or cat, the flight of an eagle, the chorus of a symphony, stories from our elders, the laughter and humor of our own mistakes or the peace of a campfire. When we truly accept that we are doing the best we can in all we do and know that every moment of life counts, we will find blessings and appreciate being human during times of true communication, sharing of feelings, belief in ourselves and freedom from worry and stress!

Social and Emotional Maturity are the rewards of seeking wisdom instead of things, money or even intelligence. Author Ben Irwin said, "Most of us spend our lives as if we had another one in the bank." Calm and Sense tells us we do not. We have what we have here and now. Calm and Sense believes that this life is not a dress rehearsal; it is showtime and every moment of it is precious and nonrefundable. Only *we* can make it better. The choice is ours if we choose to make it: happiness or depression. It is up to you! Remember, deciding not to choose is also a choice. Not taking action is choosing to remain where you are. This is why the search for wisdom in all we do is so very important. With it, we gain understanding and acceptance for who we are and what we have. If you take to heart the information, strategies and tips you have read in this book, I believe you have chosen happiness, satisfaction and Calm and Sense!

I believe in you. Your life is going to change today, now, this instant! You are free from your past, let it float from you. Celebrate! Your depression will melt away in the warmth of loving yourself and making positive changes around you. You are done waiting for happiness to find *you*, because you will find *it*. Satisfaction with life is your responsibility and only you have the power to satisfy it, so make no mistake about it! You owe yourself the opportunity to challenge, explore, initiate, change and live the life for which you have "wished" for so long. Fear not, for fear inhibits; envy not, for jealousy steals valuable time and emotions from you. Laugh more, worry less, listen to the call for Calm and answer it. Use your Sense in all you do and think, especially of yourself, and defeat depression from the inside out.

Calm and Sense says to start where you are now, stay focused, get to know yourself intimately and thoroughly and move forward! The past has served its purpose and time has kept you safe thus far. Build bridges, keep promises, listen to your heart as well as to others', plant seeds along your way, learn from any mistakes you make, stop punishing yourself, be a friend to yourself and others, love yourself and enjoy loving others. And always, always use your Calm and Sense!

Appendix

Calm and Sense Acronyms

ALONE: A Little Oneness Needed Every day (chapter 19)

COURAGE: Ceasing Our Unfounded Resistances And Gaining Endurance (chapter 17)

FAIL: Find Another Important Lesson (chapter 18)

FEAR: Feeling Embarrassment And Risk (chapter 16)

HONEST: Heartfelt Openness, Not Elusive Sneaky Tactics (chapter 22)

HUMOR: Have Unlimited Mental Orgasms Regularly (chapter 25)

INSECURE: Identify Needs So Emotions Can Understand Rational Explanation (chapter 19)

INSECURITY: Intense Need, Sensing Everything Can Unravel, Reacting Irrationally Toward Yourself (and others) (chapter 19)

LISTEN: Let It Settle, Then Evaluate News/Needs (chapter 22)

PANIC: Pain And Nervousness In Control (chapter 19)

SAFE: Secure And Feeling Empowered (chapter 22)

SECURITY: Seeing Everything Clearly Utilizing Realistic Intentions Toward Yourself (and others) (chapter 19)

TRUST: True, Real Understanding Securing Two (people) (chapter 23)

WAITING: Willing All Initiative To Identify No Gain (chapter 18)

WORRY: WithOut Real Reason Yet (chapter 16)

Acknowledgments

First and foremost, I have to share with you my feelings about getting to this section of *Defeating Depression*, the acknowledgments page! To be here means that the creation of this book is complete except for the "thank yous" to the important, key role players who have helped me get from the start to now. It is a bittersweet feeling to see the creation stage of *Defeating Depression* come to an end. I imagine it is similar to the feeling parents get when a child begins his or her first day of school. You have prepared your "baby" as best as you can. You fed him well and experienced his first word, steps, laughs and tears. You have connected with each other in such a way that now it is difficult to imagine watching him "fly on his own" as he walks out the door.

I have so much enjoyed "raising" my "baby," *Defeating Depression*, that it saddens me in many ways to "send it off," yet I know that was the whole intention of its creation to begin with and doing so makes me very, very proud! In its journeys, I am hopeful that my "baby" meets many, many people and makes them equally as happy or touches them in some certain way that their lives will forever be better, brighter, more fulfilling and beneficial!

While driving home today, I thought about how I could possibly or adequately thank my team of "Identity Fortifiers" (you have learned more about Identity Fortifiers in the book) and a song came to mind. It was written by Arlo Guthrie and it has become a staple tune that helps some celebrate the Thanksgiving holiday. The song is called "Alice's Restaurant" and the story it relates is reportedly true. It is funny as well as long; let me summarize the idea.

Arlo was spending Thanksgiving with some friends at their friend Alice's restaurant. Alice had a pile of garbage she needed disposed. Arlo volunteered to get rid of it and did so—or so he thought. However, police officer "Obie" found some documents in the trash that led back to Arlo and Arlo was arrested for littering.

Arlo met some very interesting people at police headquarters but eventually paid the fine and had a "Thanksgiving dinner that couldn't be beat." End of story? Not yet.

Later, Arlo was informed of a draft notice and had to report to the draft board for a physical and mental evaluation. He met many more funny and interesting people there. When the draft officer asked Arlo if he had "ever been arrested," Arlo said he had, for "littering." That wasn't enough to get him out of the draft board office. So what did Arlo do? He started singing! "You can get anything you want at Alice's Restaurant." He did this to convince the draft officer he was "nuts" and unfit to join the Army.

Now you might be wondering what in the world I'm talking about. Arlo realized that if he, alone, sang that song to the draft officer, the officer would think he was "crazy" and let him go. Then Arlo brainstormed that if a *group* of people started singing "Alice's Restaurant" all at the same time, maybe, just maybe, the draft officer would think it was a "movement" and the war might come to an end. The more people singing the song, the stronger the case to stop the war. Power in unity! *This* is my point.

My team of supporters in developing *Defeating Depression* from the cradle to publication has provided the power, fuel, inspiration, understanding and direction I needed to create the Calm and Sense "movement"! As we all "sang together in unison," the power of *Defeating Depression* grew stronger and stronger. It is my hope that all who read this book will also join in its "movement" in defeating depression.

So, in the spirit of Thanksgiving, I only have thanks to give to these wonderful, loving and supportive people and wish to acknowledge them fully and wholeheartedly here.

First of all, my lovely, lovely wife, Cori. Had you not carved out the "writing time" for me, kept our three dogs content, kept the neighbors quiet, kept the faucets from leaking and printed out no fewer then seventy thousand pages of drafts, this book would never have had a chance. You are everything to me and I love you so very dearly with all of my heart! You are also my very best friend and show me that Calm and Sense *is* real in relationships.

My loving sister, Barbara Ann Battenhausen. It was you who convinced me so many years (and degrees) ago to attend college. For that I will be forever grateful, but also your continued belief in my writing over the years, your support in countless ways and your ceaseless assistance in so many matters are precious to me! It was you who introduced me and *Defeating Depression* to its dedicated, talented and gifted editor, Ruth H. Cohen.

Ruth, you have been a God-send to this project in so many ways. I will forever remember our first experience working together as a "team" and look forward to more of the same! You entered this project at a very crucial time, picked up the pieces, glued them back together, polished the words, motivated me with your sincere belief and enthusiasm in *Defeating Depression*, added style, clarity and a much-needed "woman's touch" and did a wonderful job as a "surrogate mom" for this "child." I know you are as proud of the result as I am!

I cannot forget to graciously thank my spiritual advisor, Diane Holub. Diane, you were the spark that got me to stop just thinking and talking about this book and actually start writing it! You foresaw wonderful things coming from this book and told me, "People need to hear what you have to say." Those words have rung loud and clear in my mind every single day since you spoke them and they have motivated me over and over again enough to give up weekends, trips and many other things to get the job done. I needed that and I am forever thankful for it!

John Kelly, my colleague and mentor, must also be acknowledged. John, you are the person who pulled me out of the deepest, darkest bowels of "occupation frustration" and gave me the chance to begin my work as a private clinician. This move actually allowed me to work *with* real people, rather than with their charts—which is an unfortunate reality in many mental health care facilities and was never a good fit for me. You put me in the therapist's seat, allowed me autonomy with my craft and supported me every step of the way—both professionally and personally. If not for you, I would not have had the opportunity to grow, learn and progress.

I must also thank my parents, Mary and Charles Battenhausen. Although they are not physically here anymore, their spirits never leave me. I know how proud they would be to see this book come to fruition and I know they are watching and with me now. They taught me that whatever situation life throws your way, it could "always be worse." Their words and phrases remind me frequently of how to use Calm and Sense and how never to let "things, people or situations" get me down. I love and miss them both every day.

Last, but in no way least, I must thank each and every client, couple or family I have had the honor to help throughout my career. You all have taught me just about everything I need to know in helping others and have proven over and over again that you can defeat depression when you use Calm and Sense. Thank you all for allowing me into your lives and trusting me with your well-being!

Editor's Note

There are many, many "self-help" books on the market. I've read quite a few of them. Some have had great value to me in my life's journey; some haven't. This one came to me at a youth recreation league soccer practice. Until I began to read the manuscript, I had no idea just how incredible this book really is! This one is a "keeper."

You will, I hope, find this book so helpful and exciting that you will want to share the information in it with the people you care about—but don't loan them your copy, because you will keep referring to it time and time again! This book *will* change your life, no matter who you are or what your life looks like. In each chapter is information that can and will help you feel better about yourself and your life immediately. For those of you who are happy and feel fulfilled, you too will find gems of advice within these pages that will add quality to your life and your relationships.

You will find it easy to understand the information and to incorporate the concepts presented here into your life *immediately*.

I've spent most of my adult life working in the human services field in a variety of positions (EMT, firefighter, women's self-defense instructor, personal safety educator/writer/lecturer, rape crisis support provider, to name a few) and doing graduate work in the fields of psycholinguistics and drug and alcohol counseling. I've had the opportunity to spend time with people who are experiencing crises in their lives, listening to their stories of pain and frustration and providing emergent and acute care. Over and over, and for many different reasons, people have told me they can't seem to move past some issues, are unhappy with some aspects of their lives and feel depressed and resigned to lives of unhappiness. No matter who the person was or what the specific issue was at the time—relationship, career, parenting, health, etc.—there was a common theme of feeling "stuck" and this was causing that person to experience stress, anxiety and some degree of depression.

During our counseling relationship, I tried to give advice or suggestions that were helpful. I always wished, though, that there was a book to which I could refer people that would help them even more. Something that would help them get "unstuck." Something they could use "right now" to start feeling better.

It was a fortunate coincidence that Leo and I met. Life flowing the way it does led to my working with Leo on this book. As soon as I read his draft, I knew that *this was the book*—the one that would provide the solution for which so many people are looking. *This is it*! Within these pages is a simple, realistic approach to helping solve the life problems with which so many people are struggling!

While editing this book, I found myself using Calm and Sense to improve the way I was handling one troublesome situation or another in my own life. Calm and Sense guided me toward putting particular parenting issues into a clearer perspective, helping me to be a more effective and confident parent; Calm and Sense helped me understand how I was allowing my past to keep me from moving forward so that I now no longer allow my past to dictate my present or the direction of my future; Calm and Sense gave me insight into the components of romantic relationships, adding much value to the wonderful relationship I already have. Calm and Sense also helped to give me a clear picture as to why relationships in the past did not work! Since beginning work on this book, I continually find myself sharing bits of Calm and Sense with people in my life who are experiencing frustration with one thing or another. I'm thrilled, now, to be able to tell them they can get the entire book and have all the information right at their fingertips. And now you do too!

I'm sure you'll find, as I have, that reading this book is like sitting comfortably on the couch and talking with a trusted friend who loves and respects you unconditionally—one who truly understands where you're coming from and who wants you to be happy. It is easy to read and you'll find yourself putting the concepts into practice in your own life immediately. There is something in this book for everyone. Calm and Sense living is a sure and simple way to help you defeat depression and begin living the life that you want for yourself *today*.

I would like to thank Leo for the incredible opportunity to work on this wonderful book and for his faith in my work. Leo, it was truly a pleasure working with you. From you I have learned so much about creating and maintaining my own happiness and success; I have learned how to more fully embrace the simple, life-enhancing principles of Calm and Sense. For that I am grateful and my life is forever changed for the better! I know this book and your work will continue to touch many people in profound ways, helping them to live the lives they envision for themselves.

I also want to thank my amazing partner, Mark, for his constant love, support and encouragement. It is truly a beautiful thing to have a relationship that is based in Calm and Sense, openness, honesty and trust. Darling, you are a wonderful human being and I admire you tremendously. You are my true love, my best friend and I love you "all ways." Alec and Trevor, I thank you from the bottom of my heart for welcoming me into your lives and for truly letting me in. Each in your own way, you have given me more support on this project than you probably know. Your friendship means so very much to me and I love you both. Most of all, I must thank my own beautiful children for encouraging me by showing their excitement about my work (even when it kept me from being able to play); for loving me with their silent but frequent "sneak-up-quietly-on-mommy-so-as-not-to-distract-her-when-she's-working" kisses and hugs; and for always reminding me that no one is perfect and that's *exactly* how it should be. I love you, Jonah and Jordan, with all my heart.

Ruth H. Cohen

Endnotes

Introduction

[1] Gail Saltz, "Am I just sad—or truly depressed?" *Today, MSNBC,* March 2004, http://today.msnbc.msn.com/id/4489902#.

[2] World Health Organization, "The World Health Report 2001: Mental Health: New Understanding, New Hope," World Health Organization, 2001, http://www.who.int/whr/2001/en/whr01_en.pdf.

[3] Satellite Corporation, "Facts and Statistics," Depression Perception, 2009, http://www.depressionperception.com/depression/depression_facts_and_statistics.asp.

[4] Bob Murray and Alicia Fortinberry, "Depression Facts and Stats," Uplift Program, January 15, 2005, http://www.upliftprogram.com/depression_stats.html#3.

[5] Saltz, "Am I just sad—or truly depressed?"

[6] "10-year Retrospective Study Shows Progress in American Attitudes About Depression and Other Mental Health Issues," Mental Health America, June 2007, http://www.nmha.org/index.cfm?objectid=FD502854-1372-4D20-C89C30F0DEE68035.

Part Two: How to Live a Life of Calm
Chapter 7: You Are Not a Slave to Your Past

[1] Anthony Flacco and Jerry Clark, *The Road Out of Hell* (New York: Union Square Press, 2009).

[2] "John Forbes Nash, Jr." Wikipedia, http://en.wikipedia.org/wiki/John_Forbes_Nash,_Jr.

Chapter 15: Surviving

[1] A.H. Maslow, "A Theory of Human Motivation," *Psychological Review* 50, no. 4 (1943): 370-96.

Chapter 16: Worry and Fear

[1] Kathleen McGowan, "Taming Your Worries," *Psychology Today*, August 2005, http://www.psychologytoday.com/articles/200509/taming-your-worries.

[2] Anne Driscoll, "Learning to Worry," *People* 50, no. 15 (October 26, 1998) http://www.people.com/people/archive/article/0,,20126602,00.html.

[3] ASHA International, "Startling Statistics About Mental Illness," ASHA International, 2007, http://www.myasha.org/node/12.

[4] National Institute of Mental Health, "New NIMH Video Describes Depression, Importance of Treatment," National Institute of Mental Health, June 2, 2009, http://www.nimh.nih.gov/science-news/2009/new-nimh-video-describes-depression-importance-of-treatment.shtml.

Chapter 17: Finding Courage

[1] World Health Organization, "The World Health Report 2001."

Part Three: Calm and Sense in Love and Relationships

Chapter 22: Having a Healthy Romantic Relationship

[1] "What couples are really arguing about," *The Week* 1, no. 472 (July 5, 2010).

NOTES

NOTES